D1071729

THE ART OF BEOWULF

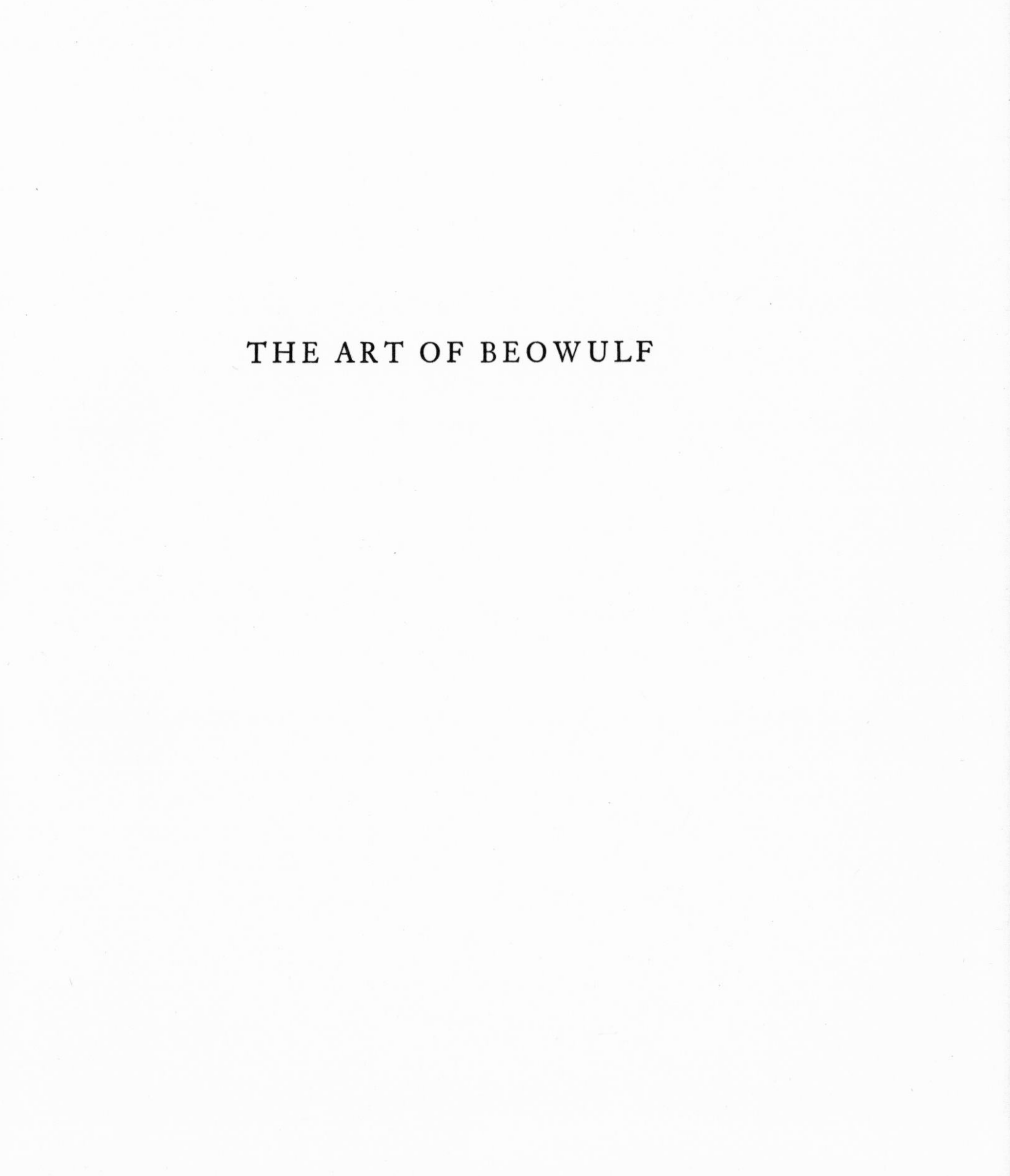

THE ART OF BEOWULF

by

Arthur Gilchrist Brodeur

UNIVERSITY OF CALIFORNIA PRESS
BERKELEY AND LOS ANGELES
1960

University of California Press
Berkeley and Los Angeles, California

Cambridge University Press
London, England

Second Printing, 1960

Library of Congress Catalogue Card No. 58-12828

Designed by Ward Ritchie
Printed in the United States of America

TO

ALVA R. DAVIS

DISTINGUISHED SCHOLAR

GREAT ADMINISTRATOR

AND

GENEROUS FRIEND

PREFACE

During the twenty years that have passed since the publication of J. R. R. Tolkien's famous lecture, "Beowulf, the Monsters and the Critics," interest in Beowulf *as a work of art has increased gratifyingly, and many fine papers have made distinguished contributions to our understanding of the poem as poetry and as heroic narrative. It is scarcely too much to say that Tolkien has given a new and significant direction to literary scholarship. Much more, however, remains to be done: we have still no systematic and sensitive appraisal of the poem later than Walter Morris Hart's* Ballad and Epic, *no thorough examination of the poet's gifts and powers, of the effects for which he strove and the means he used to achieve them. More than enough remains to occupy a generation of scholars.*

It is my hope that this book may serve as a kind of prolegomenon to such study. It makes no claim to completeness or finality; it contributes only the convictions and impressions which have been borne in upon me in the course of forty years of study of the poem. It may seem all too incomplete: it will be noticed, for example, that I have *said little of the poet's use of understatement, and that my study of his style is largely restricted to the single figure of variation. This was deliberate: in the matter of litotes I have nothing substantial to add to the excellent study, "Understatement in Old English Poetry," published in 1937 (*PMLA, *LII, pp. 915–934) by Dr. Frederick Bracher; and a complete analysis of the style of* Beowulf *would have required a volume in itself. Other omissions will be obvious, and will inevitably, in the course of time, be supplied by critics better qualified to deal with matters which I have not considered.*

I have tried to supply sufficient evidence to support my conviction that Beowulf *is the work of a great artist, a work carefully planned and organized, excellent in form and structure, and composed with a sense of style unique in the poet's age. It will appear that I regard the work as composed in writing, and the author as trained in the art of the scop and educated as a clerk. In him the best of pagan antiquity and of the Christian culture of his time had fused; and we have in his work an achievement unequaled in English poetry before Chaucer.*

In common with all other living students of the poem, I am most deeply indebted to the unsurpassed learning and wisdom of Professor Klaeber. My obligation to him will be obvious to every reader; when I am compelled to express disagreement with him I do so humbly. I also acknowledge my very considerable debt to Walter Morris Hart, to W. W. Lawrence, and to the late R. W. Chambers. I owe more to my own great teacher, George Lyman Kittredge, than I can express. I am deeply obliged to my most generous and learned friend, Professor Kemp Malone, for his constant and unfailing kindness. I am grateful to Dr. Caroline Brady for the help she gave me in fixing my views on the nature of the kenning. My colleague Professor Benjamin H. Lehman has my deep and abiding gratitude for encouragement and help without which I should have hesitated to undertake this work. I wish also to record my appreciation of the kindness of the staff of the University of California Library.

The third chapter of this book, now carefully revised and expanded, first appeared in PMLA*; the fourth chapter was published in part in the* Journal of English and Germanic Philology. *I offer these journals* *my warmest thanks for permission to use these materials, with such changes and additions as time and circumstance have made desirable. Some few pages of the sixth chapter first appeared as part of a paper entitled "Design and Motive in the Finn Episode," published by the University of California Press; and some pages of Appendix A have been somewhat altered from appropriate portions of my paper "The Meaning of Snorri's Categories," also published by the University of California Press. I deeply appreciate the courtesy of the Press in permitting me to present this material in revised form.*

A. G. B.

CONTENTS

I

THE DICTION OF BEOWULF

Fr. Klaeber, in the sixth section of the Introduction to his superb edition, has described with admirable clarity and judgment the salient features of the poetic language of *Beowulf*.[1] The quality of its diction and style as compared with those of other Old English poems has been appraised by W. W. Lawrence in these words: "Anglo-Saxon verse was, of course, as much confined by 'measures and rules' as that of Dryden or of Pope, and it was deeply rooted in the traditions of professional singers, the main features of whose craft were shared by the poets of the other peoples of Germanic stock.... Clearly, so far from being in any way primitive, it was over-elaborate, on its way to decadence. Variation and repetition were too freely and mechanically employed; set epic phraseology too often took the place of inspiration. The art of the singer was coming to resemble that of a worker in mosaic, placing in new combinations pieces ready to his hand....

[1] *Beowulf and the Fight at Finnsburg,* edited, with Introduction, Bibliography, Notes, Glossary, and Appendices, by Fr. Klaeber (third edition, with supplements; Boston: Heath, 1950; hereafter cited as Klaeber's edition, or Edition), pp. lviii–lxxi.

Beowulf, the finest extant example of this poetry, shows less exaggeration in rhetorical artifices, but enough to bear witness to their dangers . . . it is . . . extremely conventional, the product of an *ars poetica* of settled principles and careful development." Its author was "a gifted poet," and his work was one of "beauty and artistry."[2]

To describe a poem as the finest example of its kind, and the work of a gifted poet, is to imply that its author made whatever his age accepted as the media of poetic expression serve his ends as they did not serve those of other poets who used the same media. There were other poets contemporary with Homer; Gower and Chaucer composed for the same age. But Homer and Chaucer are unique and incomparable. Similarly, no other poet in Anglo-Saxon England composed poetry comparable with *Beowulf.* Since much of the poetry composed within the conventions which dominated England before the Norman Conquest has survived, it should be possible to compare the achievement of the poet of *Beowulf* with the best that has come to us from other hands, and to arrive at a firm judgment of relative values.

The author of *Beowulf* composed in the vernacular for a public accustomed to, and expecting, conformity to the disciplines and the conventions with which they were familiar. His work was necessarily a product, and an expression, of the age and culture which gave it birth. His mastery of the conventional modes of poetic utterance and of traditional measures "shows him," as Lawrence says, "to have been trained in the full technique of the professional poet."[3] Yet he lived at a time when certain new things were happening in poetry: for the first time in England, men were composing religious poems, of which at least one, *Genesis,* broke the bounds of the short Germanic narrative lay, and undertook to cast a long story in poetic form. And secondly, the pressures of long narrative had compelled poets to make extensive use of the run-over line, in place of the end-stopped line characteristic of the older nonreligious poetry. In his own long heroic poem, the author of *Beowulf* uses the run-over line with remarkable ease and flexibility; and similarly he adapts to his own occasions the

[2] *Beowulf and Epic Tradition* (Harvard University Press, 1928), pp. 3–4, vii, viii–ix.
[3] *Ibid.,* p. 281.

conventions which he had inherited from Germanic antiquity. Once he elected to compose in the vernacular, he was bound to work within those conventions. What concerns us is the quality of his work as poetry: the degree of his power to infuse with dignity, eloquence, and beauty the conventions which he accepted, or to transcend their reach without violating their essential limits.

Quite recently Francis P. Magoun, Jr., has published the partial results of his researches in the formulaic language of Old English narrative poetry, inclusive of *Beowulf*.[4] He has rendered a real service by directing our attention to the pervasiveness of formula in all such poetry, going far beyond observation of the larger and more obvious formulaic patterns, and making us aware how deep the formulaic manner lies in the expression of Old English poetic thought. Yet I think he presses his case too far, and makes certain questionable assumptions. Acknowledging indebtedness to Parry's work on the formulaic character of Homeric poetry,[5] and on the basis of his own analyses, Magoun concludes that the language of Old English narrative poetry is totally formulaic; that the poets whose work has survived had inherited from generations of scops formulaic patterns adequate to the expression of any idea, so that novelty or individuality in the choice of phrase had become unnecessary. He assumes that a lettered poet would be incapable of composing in this formulaic manner, derived as it was from the cumulative contribution of unlettered court poets. Accordingly he regards the author of *Beowulf* as an unlettered singer, in spite of the rather considerable body of evidence that our poet was familiar not only with the Old Testament, but also with some patristic writing, and probably with the *Aeneid*.

Magoun is troubled by the case of Cynewulf, since Cynewulf, who composed in the same formulaic manner as the author of *Beowulf*, is known to have been an educated man. He avoids this difficulty by arguing that Cynewulf must have *composed* his works orally,

[4] The references in this chapter are to Magoun's paper, "Oral-Formulaic Character of Anglo-Saxon Narrative Poetry," *Speculum*, XXVIII (1953), pp. 446–467, especially to pp. 446, 453–454, 464.

[5] Milman Parry, "Studies in the Epic Technique of Oral Verse-Making, I: Homer and Homeric Style," *Harvard Studies in Classical Philology*, XLI (1930), pp. 73–147; "II: The Homeric Language of Oral Poetry," *ibid.*, XLIII (1932), pp. 1–50.

as an unlettered singer would have done; and then, at some later time, reduced them to writing by dictating, either to another or to himself. Now it is of course not the ability to write, and so to compose in writing, which could inhibit the man of letters from composing in the manner of the unlettered scop; it is the exercise of the ability to *read,* which, after much practice, has given him an intellectual background, a way of looking at men and at life, and a sense of style essentially different from those of the analphabetic court poet of earlier times, or of his own. Furthermore, if Cynewulf could have "dictated" his own poetry to himself, so could the author of *Beowulf:* in that case we could not call him an unlettered singer, and should not be troubled by his indebtedness to Gregory or Augustine on the one hand, or to Vergil on the other.

I think Magoun is wrong in his belief that a literate author could not have composed in the traditional, formulaic manner. It is clear that Cynewulf *did* so compose, and it is equally clear that he had not been trained as a scop. The language of *Beowulf,* at almost all points, indicates that its author had been trained as a professional scop; and it is most unlikely that a man so trained should ever lose the ability to express himself in the conventional modes of traditional poetry under the influence of a Christian education. The author of *Brunanburh* was obviously an educated man; and no poem in Old English is more nearly "totally formulaic."

But the language of *Beowulf* is, in my opinion, not totally formulaic, nor comparable in its load of formula with most other Old English narrative poems. I agree with Lawrence that "it appears altogether probable that *Beowulf* was composed pen in hand, or written from the poet's dictation."[6] The structure and the style of the poem, no less than its incomparably rich and sensitive diction, attest that the poet was a man of cultivated taste as well as an accomplished scop. He possessed a highly developed sense of form, which shows itself in his language as well as in the structure of his work. The traditional scop, unlettered as he was, was a trained and sophisticated artist: within the brief limits of lay and poetic eulogy he was a finished craftsman. The poet of *Beowulf* was enabled, by his experi-

[6] Lawrence, *op. cit.,* p. 10.

ence with non-English sacred and profane learning, and compelled by the greater scope and range of his work, to exceed the limitations of the modes and forms which he had inherited from Germanic antiquity.

It is only on the unprovable, but probable, assumption of his literacy that one can explain the difference between his poetry and that of any other Anglo-Saxon. There are other good poems, good in various ways: *Andreas* is an excellent work, with notable passages; *Exodus* is vivid and colorful; *Judith,* technically not without blemish, has a fierce eloquence and a savage power; there are moments of marked beauty in *Elene*. All of these seem to be the work of lettered men; but they are the works of men in whom learning had awakened no inner Renaissance: none of them attains the dignity, the beauty, the nobility of thought of *Beowulf;* none exhibits its conscious mastery of form. Since these qualities must be communicated in words, phrases, and sentences, they affect the choice and the arrangement of those means of expression. *Beowulf* has, as we shall see, a marked individuality, a unique grandeur, of diction and of style.

I do not mean to impute to Magoun more than he means to say. On the basis of the formulas and "formulaic systems" which he has discovered in his analyses of passages from Old English narrative poems, including *Beowulf,* he finds that approximately seventy per cent of the verses examined recur in identical or in very similar phrasing elsewhere in Old English poetry; and he concludes that, if the surviving corpus were "twice as big and if, above all, we had other songs of any extent dealing with anything like the same thematic material, there well might be almost nothing in the language here used that could not be demonstrated as traditional."[7] He does not assert that the actual words—the individual simplices and compounds—of *Beowulf* are completely an inherited vocabulary; he rather lays emphasis upon phrases and verses. Nevertheless the expression "almost nothing in the language here used" suggests that he regards the vocabulary of any Old English narrative poem as an inherited vocabulary, containing little or nothing original. He spe-

[7] Magoun, *op. cit.,* pp. 449–450, 452.

cifically mentions those poetic appellations usually called 'kennings' as "traditional and formulaic."[8]

If this be his meaning, I cannot agree. I find more justice in Klaeber's statement that ". . . the abundance of compounds used [in *Beowulf*] testifies to the creative possibilities of the alliterative style. A good many terms are nowhere recorded outside of *Beowulf*, and not a few of these may be confidently set down as of the poet's own coinage. . . . Fully one third of the entire vocabulary, or some 1070 words, are compounds, so that in point of numbers, the *Beowulf* stands practically in the front rank of Old English poems. . . . The good judgment and taste of the author are shown in his finely discriminating way of handling the inherited devices of rhetoric. . . . Clearly, the author has mastered the art of varying his style in response to the demands of the occasion."[9]

It is true enough that "the Beowulfian stylistic apparatus (taken in its widest sense) was to a great extent traditional, deeply rooted in time-honored Germanic, more particularly West Germanic, practice."[10] But a sufficiently detailed study of the language of the poem, while it confirms this, reveals as well a large element of originality in the poet's diction. That diction goes far beyond the inherited stock of words and formulas. Certain words which do not form compounds in other extant poems are more or less richly used in the formation of compounds in *Beowulf;* other words which form many compounds in other poems form, in *Beowulf,* compounds not elsewhere recorded. The poet does things with words and phrases which were not done by other poets: the dominant mood of a particular passage, or its dramatic character and function, operate significantly in the poet's choice and combination of words. In both diction and manner the conventional element is indeed strong; it is the element which we may safely presume to be original that determines the quality of the diction and style of *Beowulf*. In this chapter I shall examine the diction; in the next, I shall discuss variation, the most important element of style.

[8] *Ibid.,* p. 452.
[9] Edition, pp. lxiii–lxiv, lxviii.
[10] *Ibid.,* p. lxvi.

In the language of Old English poetry the substantive is pre-eminent; it is the major element of the poetic vocabulary. In the 3,182 lines of *Beowulf* I count 903 distinct substantive compounds, 518 of which occur in no other extant text. And 578 substantive compounds occur only once each in the poem. These figures alone suggest both a high degree of originality and a very wide range in the diction of the work.

Second in importance to the noun is the adjective; and the adjective compounds are impressive. I count 86 compound adjectives both elements of which are adjectives (*brunfag, gromhydig*), or in which the first element is an adverb (*feorrancund*); 36 of these are peculiar to *Beowulf*. Adjectives the first element of which is a noun and the second an adjective (*lagucræftig, morgenceald, wlitebeorht*) number 164; 86 of these are found only in *Beowulf*. In 36 adjective compounds the first member is an adjective and the second, when used as simplex, a noun (*blodigtoð, blondenfeax, bolgenmod, brunecg, collenferhð, fæstræd, fætedhleor, famigheals, gearofolm, scirham, wollentear, wreoþenhilt,* etc.); 15 of these are peculiar to *Beowulf*. The total number of compound adjectives unknown except in *Beowulf* (counting those the first elements of which are nouns, adjectives, adverbs, pronouns, or prepositions, but excluding those formed with *ge-* or *un-*) is approximately 150.

In addition to its extraordinary wealth of compounds, *Beowulf* contains about 675 distinct substantive simplices, and a great many uncompounded adjectives. The overwhelming majority of these simple nouns and adjectives may be found in other poems, and many of them in prose. Many of the substantival simplices are restricted to poetic use, or occur only rarely in prose; most of the adjective simplices, on the other hand, are literal, and are freely used in prose; they do not belong to the special language of poetry.

The number of distinct verbs in the poem is very large, probably about one thousand. I have made no careful count of them, because most of them are used in prose as readily as in poetry. A large proportion of the verbs in *Beowulf* are mere compounds of common verbs with *æt-, bi-, for-, ge-,* etc.; their simplices were certainly part of the vocabulary of speech. Only a few belong to the diction of poetry, and the sources of artistic effect seldom reside in them, although these may be found in a good many striking combinations of verbs admirably chosen to express the impact of an action upon its object, or the action especially appropriate to the subject. In such cases the effect lies in the harmony of the verb with other elements of the clause.

The richest and most meaningful content-words in the poetic vocabulary are the substantival and adjectival compounds; they not only express concepts, often very forcefully or imaginatively; they often contain or imply partial description of concepts as well. Moreover, they play a very important part in the rhetorical devices of variation, enumeration, and progression. From these compounds, more than from other parts of speech, we must form our estimate of the language of *Beowulf*.

Since *Beowulf* is longer than any other Old English poem, we should expect its vocabulary to be larger. But it is not much longer than *Genesis;* and *Juliana* and *Elene* are, in respect of length, fairly comparable with *Beowulf*. So, in other respects than length, is *Andreas,* which is of considerable interest to the student of *Beowulf*. But in view of the fact that most poems are much shorter than the epic, it has seemed proper for my present purpose to treat together, as if they constituted single works, groups of poems united by a common theme or constituting a special treatment of related matter. The individual Psalms or Riddles are short; to secure a safer basis for analysis I have treated the *Psalms* as a single poem, and I have done likewise with the *Riddles* and the Boethian *Metra.*

In view of Magoun's conviction that, except in minor particulars, one cannot speak of the 'style' of any Old English narrative poem, or trace influence from one poem to another through similarities of word, phrase, or line,[11] it is interesting that *Genesis, Exodus,* and *Andreas* resemble *Beowulf* more closely than do other poems in their types of compounds, and to a considerable degree in the individual compounds used. There are, however, some striking resemblances between Beowulfian compounds and many that appear in *Elene,* in

[11] Magoun, *op. cit.,* pp. 460–461.

Guðlac,—even in the *Psalms* and the *Riddles.* These resemblances between compounds appearing in works otherwise so dissimilar may be accounted for on the ground that the words in question do represent a common traditional vocabulary, to which at least a large proportion of the compounds peculiar to *Beowulf* did not belong. We must not be too hasty in drawing such conclusions; after all, we have no other long narrative poem heroic in theme to compare with *Beowulf.*

One phenomenon is certainly significant, if not altogether easy to evaluate: in the majority of instances, the substantive compounds formed on any single base-word are not so distributed in the extant poems as to indicate that they were the common property of poets. A great many of them occur in only one poem each; many more in but two. This is true, for example, of the compounds of *-faru, -dream, -egesa,* and *-bearn.* Of the *-candel* compounds, three (*dæg-, heofon-, weder-*) occur frequently in various poems; five occur each in only a single poem.

Some base-words form compounds which must be regarded as the common property of poets, since they all occur in more than one poem, some in several poems. Among these are the compounds in *-wær, -hreoða, -legu, -sefa,* and *-rinc.* I should think that only those compounds which occur more than once, and in more poems than one, could safely be regarded as belonging to a common, traditional poetic stock. Indeed, many of those found in but two poems may have been derived by one poet from another.

If we consider the compounds in *Beowulf* from the point of view of their base-words, we find that 115 base-words form each a larger number of distinct compounds in *Beowulf* than in the whole body of Old English poetry outside the epic; and 143 base-words form more compounds in the *totality* of other poems than they form in *Beowulf* alone. This, like the disproportionately large number of compounds peculiar to *Beowulf,* suggests that its author was himself responsible for the creation of many of his compounds. Forty-four base-words form exactly the same number of compounds in *Beowulf* as in all other poems combined; 148 form more compounds peculiar to *Beowulf* than to any other single poem; 109 form more compounds peculiar to *Beowulf* than the total number of their compounds occurring only once each outside *Beowulf;* 53 form the same number of compounds peculiar to *Beowulf* and peculiar to any other single poem.

Still more surprising is the number of distinct base-words no compounds of which appear anywhere except in *Beowulf,* namely, 52. These represent an astonishingly wide range of concepts: 56 base-words form a much larger number of compounds in the total corpus of other poems than in *Beowulf* alone; but a very large proportion of these consist of abstract nouns: e.g., *-cræft, -cwalu, -gewinn, -lac, -hæmed, -lufu, -nyd, -plega, -rædenn, -searo, -sorg, -þrym.* In these, even when the limiting word compounded with them imparts to them a somewhat more specific meaning, the compound often remains rather general in sense. No single word which, as a simplex, denotes any weapon forms a significantly larger proportion of compounds in all other poems than in *Beowulf* alone.

As against these, among the base-words forming compounds altogether peculiar to *Beowulf* we find such specific terms for arms and armor as *-grima, -hilt, -iren, -spreot, -steng, -sweord;* no compounds of these appear in any other poem. *-Syrce* forms five compounds peculiar to *Beowulf;* only one, *hilde-,* occurs elsewhere. Compounds in *-getawa* and *-pad* are restricted to *Beowulf.* Four words for the common concepts 'wound,' 'slaughter,' 'death in battle,' namely, *-bite, -feall, -fyll, -scear,* form no compounds recorded in any other poem than *Beowulf.*

Among terms denoting 'retainers,' 'officials of a royal household,' compounds of *-æðeling, -drincend, -gesella, -scenc* are peculiar to *Beowulf;* whereas *-bearn, -berend,* and *-mæg* each form more compounds in other poems than in *Beowulf.* Broadly speaking, the author of *Beowulf* is more inclined than most poets to the use of specific and vivid words: most of the compounds which designate objects, persons, or actions in sharp, specific terms occur more frequently and in greater variety in *Beowulf* than elsewhere.

This is in part the consequence of the nature of the material and the theme of *Beowulf;* in respect of both it is closer than most other Old English poems to the traditional poetry of the pagan past, to the heroic lays and the poems composed by scops in honor of princes—poems which deal with concrete actions, in which specific instruments, notably weapons and armor, played an important part. We should therefore expect the language of *Beowulf* to be more conventional, more traditional, than that of the Christian religious poems; and fundamentally it is. It makes heavy use of epic formulas; its vocabulary reflects the life of the court, the mead-hall, the battlefield, and the sea. Nevertheless it differs from heroic lay and encomium in its greater length, in its variety of scene, in the frequency and spaciousness of dialogue and monologue, and in its almost dramatic emphasis upon the emotions of its personages. In all these points it requires a greatly expanded vocabulary, a sharper precision in its terms, than we find in the heroic or martial poems that have been preserved, or in the religious poetry. A great many of its compounds, and perhaps all of its simplices, must derive from the traditional stock accumulated through generations of singing by scops; but whatever that stock may have been, it could not have been adequate to the composition of a poem as rich and as thoughtful as *Beowulf*. The diction of our epic differs from that of other Old English poems both quantitatively and qualitatively.

Old English is a compounding language: like the other Germanic languages, it depends heavily upon compounding for the expression of the more specific or complex concepts. Moreover, in many compounds the base-word is capable of either literal or figurative meaning, or of a variety of meanings. The first, or limiting, element in compounds usually affects more or less materially the sense of the compound. Therefore we can find, among compounds made with the same base-word, a wide range of meanings on different poetic levels. *Gleobeam* is a much more poetic word than *ficbeam:* in the latter, both elements are perfectly literal, and the whole simply designates a specific variety of tree; whereas in the former the base-word is an instance of metonymy, and the limiting word designates not a variety of wood, but the appealing use to which the wooden object is put—a use the contemplation of which has a distinctly pleasant association for the listener. But *deađbeam* (*Genesis* 638), even though its second element is literal, is on a higher imaginative level; this 'tree of death' is the tree from which Eve plucked the fatal apple. *Sigebeam,* the Cross (*Dream of the Rood, Elene*), represents the highest use which poets found for *-beam:* it denotes that sacred wood on which victory over eternal death was won, and through which the 'tree of death' forever lost its power. But this is a specifically Christian concept, which has found expression in a nontraditional compound; Germanic poetic tradition is represented, on the one hand, by *gleobeam,* and on the other by the kenning *garbeam* (*Exodus*), which means 'warrior.' A warrior is a 'spear-tree,' presumably, because he stands armed, unshakable in battle, as a tree stands in the forest.

Compounds of *-wylm* have a similarly wide range, from the literal *brimwylm, sæwylm, streamwylm,* through the very slightly figurative *brynewylm,* denoting the 'surging of flame' from the dragon's mouth, to the purely figurative *breostwylm* (*Beowulf*), *cearwylm* (*Beowulf, Elene*), and *sarwylm* (*Guðlac*). In these *-wylm* compounds, the first or limiting elements are suggested naturally by the sense of the base-word, and in the figurative as well as in the literal compounds the relation of the first member to the second is a valid one. *Brynewylm* is conceived by a simple association of the surging of fire with the welling billows of the sea. *Cearwylm* is a step farther removed from the literal, but the step is an easy one. In *breostwylm* the entire image resident in *cearwylm* is contained in the base-word alone, and the element *breost-* expresses the seat of emotion. But what shall we say of the kenning *heafodwylm* for 'tears' (*Elene* 1132)? Here is a figure which springs not from the poetic imagination, but from the over-ingenious brain. Its base-word grossly exaggerates the physical phenomenon in the poet's mind, and there is too wide a separation of meaning between its two members, too much strain between the concept and the word chosen to express it.

The *-fæt* compounds likewise illustrate the rich variety of meanings of which a base-word may be capable in combination with different limiting elements. Of the five in *Beowulf,* four are quite literal (*drync-, maðþum-, sinc-, wundor-*), and denote cups or vessels for human use; of these four, only *sinc-* appears elsewhere in poetry (*Waldere*). *Maðþum-, sinc-,* and *wundor-* add to the basic concept the quality of high value or of beauty, but neither element is figurative. The fifth, *banfæt,* also used by the poet of *Phoenix,* means 'body'; the body is envisaged as a 'vessel' containing the bones. If the term seems artificial to the modern mind, there are many other compounds which reveal a far greater degree of strain between literal sense and poetic association. There is no such strain in those *-fæt* compounds which are metaphors for 'sun' and 'moon,' and which arise out of association of these great natural lights with a lamp—the common term for which is *leohtfæt.* We find this word applied to sun and moon in *Psalms* 135, 7: *he leohtfatu leodum micel geworhte.* But *lyftfæt* for 'moon' (*Riddles* 30, 3) combines with the base-word a limiting noun which destroys the metaphor: what is a 'vessel of the air'? *Wægfatu* for 'clouds' (*Riddles* 4, 37) is a similarly meaningless extravagance. But the most extraordinary instance is one found in poetry and in a prose passage strongly influenced by poetic models:

> ðær gelicade þa . . . . . .
> in þam hordfate halgan gæste
> beorht on br . . . . . . scan,
> se wæs ordfruma ealles leohtes[12]

And in *Blickling Homilies* 105, 15: *se Halga Gast wunode on þam æþelan innoþe and on ðam gecorenan hordfæte.* This is a clear instance of the influence of the Church upon the diction of religious poets: in nonreligious poetry, *hordfæt* would have been used of a precious vessel of the sort called *maðþumfæt* in *Beowulf,* not of the Virgin's womb. As we shall see, the compounds in *Beowulf* rarely, if ever, embody such strained thought: its poet avoids even the more artificial kennings of traditional Germanic use. For all his astonishing wealth of poetic compounds, his diction is remarkably restrained.

The substantive appellations used by Old English poets to express concepts may be classified according to content, into literal and figurative; or, in terms of structure, into simplices on the one hand and compounds and combinations on the other. Classification by structure affords the firmer basis: the figurative quality of a particular word or word-group tended to fade with time and use; and we are often

[12] Grein's *Bibliothek der angelsächsischen Poesie,* ed. Wülker, II, 2 (1894), p. 281.

unable to determine how much, if any, of metaphor or metonymy a poet and his hearers felt in a given appellation. Structurally, then, we observe, first, simple uncompounded nouns; and secondly, compound nouns or nouns qualified by a modifying or limiting noun in the genitive case. Thus a poet might express the concept 'sea' by one of the simplices *sæ, brim, geofon,* etc.; by the compound *yðgewinn,* or by the combination *yða gewinn.*

Among the simplices for almost any concept we may distinguish purely or primarily poetic words, and those which are as freely used in prose as in poetry and belong to the vocabulary of speech. Inevitably the language of poetry must draw more or less heavily upon that of speech. The purely poetic simplices very often—but by no means always—contain (or once contained, before their meaning faded) a metonymy or a metaphor: most frequently they designate the referent in terms of one of its aspects or functions, of its material, or of one of its essential qualities. Thus a ship may be called *flota,* a warrior *freca,* a shield *lind,* a spear *æsc:* the ship is designated in terms of its principal function, the shield and spear in terms of their materials, the warrior in terms of his ferocity in battle. Some simplices, however, are archaic words which had fallen out of speech-use but survived as part of the more conservative diction of poetry; these are usually literal. *Heoru* and *mece* are archaic words for 'sword,' *guð* and *hild* for 'battle.' According to the need of the moment, a poet might use either a literal or a figurative simplex for any concept: a ship may be called *scip* or *bat,* or it may be designated by the more figurative *flota* or *ceol.*

Compounds, too, may be literal or figurative: a ship may be called *sæbat;* or it may be termed *wegflota,* which preserves the metonymy in the simplex *flota* and associates with it the medium in which the ship floats. Similarly a sword may be called, quite literally, *guðsweord,* or—in a striking metaphor—*hildeleoma.*

Poets seem to have felt no distinction between the poetic compounds and the combinations of basic noun with limiting genitive. The two types are indeed logically identical: *yðgewinn* and *yða gewinn* mean precisely the same thing. The first element of a compound limits or characterizes the meaning of the second, or basic, element; just as the genitive in a combinatory appellation limits or characterizes the meaning of the basic noun combined with it. The limiting word most frequently expresses the area, the medium, or the object of the action or function denoted by the base-word. In *hildeleoma,* the sword is conceived as a flame which flashes in battle; in *beaga brytta,* a prince is thought of as one who breaks gold rings in order to give precious gifts to his followers.

The poet had wide latitude for substitution in these compounds and combinations: he could substitute for either member an exact or an approximate synonym. Thus the concept 'sword' may be expressed by the compounds *guðbill, guðsweord, wigbill, hildebill, hildemece;* or the poet might use any of the simplices for 'sword': *bill, sweord, mece, heoru.* Words sufficiently archaic to have lost something of their original sense, or to have acquired wider connotations, might be used rather loosely as first or limiting elements in compounds. *Heoru* originally meant 'sword'; but *heorowearh* means 'savage outcast'; *heorodreor,* literally 'sword-gore,' means no more than blood shed from mortal wounds; yet, when the poet says that Hygelac died of 'sword-drinks' (*heorodryncum swealt*), the first element of the compound is literal, and the metaphor—almost a personification—resides in the basic noun.

It is clear, then, that the various appellations available to poets for the expression of a given concept may differ considerably in rhetorical elevation or in imaginative content. *Mece* is as literal as *sweord;* but its restriction to poetic use gives it greater value. Once—perhaps twice—the poet of *Beowulf* calls a sword *brand:* the usual meaning of this word is 'fire-brand,' 'torch'; in the sense of 'sword' it appears only in *Beowulf* and rarely in prose. This metaphorical use reflects a poetic conception of the sword as giving off light of itself. Similarly, Norse tradition represents Valhalla as lighted by the flashing of swords; and in the Old English *Finnesburh* we are told that "the gleam of swords arose, as if all Finn's stronghold were on fire." The author of *Beowulf* embodies the same figure in two compounds for 'sword,' *hildeleoma, beadoleoma,* neither of which is found in any other work.

The more poetic compounds are commonly instances of metonymy (*hilderond* for 'shield,' *mægenwudu* for 'spear'), or are metaphors (*hildeleoma* for 'sword,' *herenet* for 'corselet'). In many compounds the base-word, as simplex, is not poetical in itself, but in the compound is elevated by the limiting word, which conveys a pleasant or otherwise special function of the referent. A bench, for example, is a common thing, with no poetical connotations; but a mead-bench is a seat in a royal hall, where the dispensing of good drink symbolizes the warm relationship between lord and retainer. *Wæd* means simply 'clothing,' 'garment'; but *hildewæd* means 'corselet.' *Weard,* as simplex, means anything from a porter to a guardian; *heofonrices Weard* is God, and *eðelweard* is one of the most elevated terms which could be applied to a king.

The multiplicity of simplices, compounds, and combinations available to express almost any specific concept was most useful in meeting the requirements of alliteration, and freedom of choice among them allowed a good deal of metrical latitude. But it is unlikely that this wealth of exact and approximate synonyms, this reservoir of appellational potential, arose solely out of the need to satisfy these mechanical exigencies. On a small scale, this appellational variety appears in the runic inscription of Eggjum in Norway, the alliterative pattern and metrical structure of which are too loose to impose formal demands, but in which the elevation and the secrecy of the thought required mysterious and elevated language. I think that the poetic compounds and combinations owe their origin for the most part to the urge felt by generations of poets to create a poetic language adequate to express elevated thought and feeling and heroic action. Richard Meyer long ago observed that poetry so traditional in form and heroic in theme must both concern itself with an ideal and represent this ideal as typical.[13] The tendency toward idealization affected the poetic vocabulary, and influenced it toward typical rather than toward individual or representational expression. In the heroic lays and eulogies which Germanic court poets were called upon to compose, the situations were typical; the themes commonly illustrate the ideal relation between warrior and lord, or those conflicts of duty or of interest which might

[13] Richard M. Meyer, *Die altgermanische Poesie nach ihren formelhaften Elementen beschrieben* (Berlin, 1889), pp. 17–18, 32, 40, 69–70, 108.

confront an honorable warrior. The resolutions inevitably tended to become stereotyped. This poetry exemplified and maintained the warrior's code, and expressed an ideal of conduct conditioned by the nature of the Germanic social order. Accordingly the concepts with which poets dealt found expression, for the most part, in terms which named or described them typically, and which, directly or by connotation and suggestion, stressed those qualities of person or thing which seemed right, good, pleasant, or characteristic to that society for which the poetry was composed. In matters of scene and setting—in the creation of appellations for 'sea' and 'fire,' for example, the words most favored were those which labeled the referent by its observed salient characteristics. The pressures of metre and of alliteration did of course exercise an influence upon the poet's choice of appellation, and even stimulated the creation of other appellations. Some terms for persons and things no doubt owed their existence to tabu or to magic, since in early Germanic times verse served an apprenticeship to incantation: such terms as *forðweg* for 'death' and *beadurun* for 'a provoking speech' may be cases in point. But not many such appellations seem to have survived in Old English poetry.

There is no doubt that the accumulation of many appellations which with time received conventional sanction produced a vocabulary out of which an inferior poet could produce a composition mechanically acceptable. *Brunanburh* is an example; it is rich in its traditional language and poor in thought. But heavy as the hand of convention may have been, it must have rested lightly upon the gifted poet; and the pressure of his feeling and his thought upon such a poet must often have been strong enough to leave its mark upon the poetic vocabulary. So it is with *Beowulf,* the language of which echoes back to us in later poems.

Speaking specifically of *Beowulf,* Klaeber observes: "Generously and withal judiciously the author employs those picturesque circumlocutory words and phrases known as 'kennings,' which, emphasizing a certain quality of a person or thing, are used in place of the plain, abstract designation, e.g. *helmberend, wundenstefna, ȳðlida, lyftfloga, hǣðstapa, hronrād; bēaga brytta, goldwine gumena, homera lāf, ȳða gewealc,* or such as involve metaphorical language, like *rodores candel, heofenes gim, bānhūs, beadolēoma.*"[14]

Klaeber's rather loose definition of the kenning comes fairly close to Meissner's: a simple kenning is "ein zweigliedriger Ersatz für ein Substantivum der gewöhnlichen Rede."[15] Under this broad definition any substantive compound, or combination of base-noun with limiting genitive, which is used in place of the literal prose term for a person or thing is a kenning; and we should have to lump together utterly disparate and imaginatively unequal appellations under the label 'kenning.' As Andreas Heusler pointed out in his review of Meissner, "Worauf es ankommt ist doch, die stilfiguren seelisch zu erfassen, also das seelisch ungleichwertige zu unterscheiden."[16] I prefer to follow Heusler in restricting the term kenning to those periphrastic appellations in the base-word of which a person or thing is identified with something which it actually is *not,* except in a very special and artificial sense: in a specially conceived relation which the poet imagines between it and the sense of the limiting element. The skaldic instance *hlíðar þang,* 'tang of the hillside,' for 'grass,' is a case in point. Grass is not tang; it is called tang because it grows on the hillside as tang grows in the sea.

Old English kennings are simpler and more transparent than the Norse: *hildenædre,* 'battle-adder,' is a kenning for 'arrow' or 'javelin' (*Elene, Judith*); *garbeam* (*Exodus*), 'spear-tree,' is a kenning for 'warrior.' In these, as in the skaldic kennings, the base-word identifies the referent with something which it is not, except in a special relation to the concept expressed in the limiting word: an arrow is thought of as stinging those struck by it, as an adder stings. In all kennings there is a tension between the concept and the base-word; the limiting word partly resolves the tension.

My adherence to Heusler's more restricted definition of the kenning, and my use of the term *kent heiti* for those more direct periphrases which identify the referent with something that it *is* (e.g.,

[14] Edition, p. lxiii.

[15] Rudolf Meissner, *Die Kenningar der Skalden* (Bonn und Leipzig, 1921), p. 2, 17.

[16] See *Anzeiger für deutsches Altertum und deutsche Litteratur,* XLI (Berlin, 1922), pp. 127–134; for the sentence quoted, p. 130.

'wave-traverser' for 'ship,' 'heath-stepper' for 'stag,' 'breaker of rings' for 'king'), are defended in Appendix A, which discusses the various types of circumlocutory compounds and combinations in Old English poetry.

It is one of the characteristic traits of Old English poetic style that all types of appellational circumlocutions are most often used in variations: the variation, rather than the individual appellation, is the prime consideration; the poetic simplex or periphrasis is the material out of which the variation is made. They are also freely used in the rhetorical devices of enumeration and progression, which are sometimes difficult to distinguish from variations.

One is apt to think of the several members of a variation as synonyms. Synonyms often do serve as terms of particular variations; but most commonly the elements of variation are not actually synonyms: they have the same referent, but they designate it in more or less different terms, the entire sequence of which serves as a kind of total characterization of the referent. The cumulative application of consecutive appellations to the expression of a single concept is, in fact, the essence of substantival variation. We cannot sunder the two things, and regard one as a peculiarity of diction, the other as an element of style. A single, isolated kenning or *kent heiti* can be considered as an element of diction, an item in a glossary; but the moment two or more combine to express more than one aspect or attribute of the same referent, they become part of a poetic texture; and each enriches the other.

Often enough we find sequences of appellations for the same person or thing in a narrative passage, without variation; and here again the individual terms used are occasionally synonyms, but more commonly are not. In the sequence applied to Beowulf in lines 1492–1512 (*Weder-Geata leod, hilderinc, guðrinc, hringa þengel, eorl*), *hilderinc* and *guðrinc* are exact synonyms; the other terms are not synonyms of these or of one another: they characterize their common referent in very different terms. This fondness for the accumulation of various designations for a single referent seems to reflect a deep interest, on the part of poet and audience alike, in the contemplation of all the functions, qualities, and values of a person or thing: a desire to savor all its typical aspects.

Their interest, indeed, seems quite generally to have been centered upon the *typical* aspects; those qualities peculiar to the individual, the visible features which lend themselves to representational description, are either suppressed or minimized. Characterization in *Beowulf*—the only Old English poem to achieve genuine characterization—is managed through the representation of the actions of the personages and their interrelations with others, and through what is said, not about their qualities, but about their thoughts and motives, by the poet or by the other acting persons. Physical depiction is not so contrived that persons or things assume definite shape and color; they are described typically: what is said of one fine sword or corselet (the golden hilt of the sword with which Beowulf kills Grendel's dam is a very special case) applies with equal truth to all good swords and corselets. Poet and listener knew what such things looked like; no individualizing descriptions were needed. What mattered was the essential qualities of persons and things—which are their typical qualities. This holds good even of so superlative a thing as the hall Heorot: we are told that it was large, wide-gabled, bright with gold; the joys experienced in it are repeatedly stressed. Yet it is only an idealization of the typical Germanic royal residence. Beowulf's helmet is represented as 'white' (i.e., shining), set with splendid chains, wondrously adorned, crested with boar-images, impenetrable to weapons: this again is merely an idealization of a typical helmet. Interest centered upon the *values* of persons and objects; upon substance rather than accident. For this kind of representation the substantival and adjectival vocabulary inherited from age-long poetic practice, and expanded by such special taste and power as the poet was able to exercise within conventional patterns, was admirably suited.

But a poet of exceptional taste and power would inevitably break through the conventional patterns upon occasion. Here and there in Old English poetry we find visual images delicate or sharp, pure metaphors clothed not in traditional appellations—kenning or *kent heiti*—which reflect the poet's own sense of beauty. There is a fine example in *Phoenix* 248b–250a:

> . . . . . . þonne forst ond snaw
> mid ofermægne eorþan þeccað
> wintergewædum . . .

This is the only instance of the compound *wintergewæde* in Old English. It is neither kenning nor *ḳent heiti*, for it has no referent: the construction shows that the poet conceived frost and snow as the agents which cover the earth with winter garments.

Now it is one of the special glories of *Beowulf* that it, far more than other Old English poems, abounds in such spontaneous, perceptive images, in the projection of which the compound or appellative combination plays a vivid part but is not itself a mere periphrastic substitution or synonym for a direct term. Thus, in *Beowulf* 1208, *yða full* is an image of the sea; but it does not merely denote 'sea' as do the *ḳend heiti yða geswing, yðgewinn.* It projects an image of the sea contained in the circular horizon, as water is contained in a cup. There is an image yet more vivid in lines 1605b–1610a:

> . . . . . . Ða þæt sweord ongan
> æfter heaþoswate hildegicelum,
> wigbill wanian; þæt wæs wundra sum,
> þæt hit eal gemealt ise gelicost,
> ðonne forstes bend Fæder onlæteð,
> onwindeð wælrapas . . .

'When the Father loosens the bonds of frost, unwinds the water-ropes . . .' *Forstes bend, wælrapas* do more than express a concept: they embody ideas elevated and projected as images, in the evocation of which the verbs play an essential part. These are fine metaphors. The unique compound *hildegicel* also must be distinguished from the mere periphrastic substitution. It has no specific referent: 'the sword began . . . to diminish *in battle-icicles.*' The poet imagined the blade as melting in the she-troll's hot blood as icicles melt in the sun. This is an implied simile, projecting before the mind's eye the aspect of metal melting into the fingered shapes of melting ice. Curiously enough, *hildegicel,* though it is not a kenning, was evoked by an imagination working in a manner resembling the processes of thought behind the skaldic kenning *diguljökull,* 'ice of the crucible,' for the concept 'silver.' As silver melts in the crucible, so ice melts in the sun. In *hildegicel* the thought is similar, but it is not concealed and strained as in the skaldic kenning; it is visualized and communicated in a clear and lovely image. The first element of the compound directly links the image of steel dissolving like icicles with the warlike function of the sword itself.

Such images are frequent in *Beowulf,* although most of them are expressed in the form of *kend heiti* with specific referents: the sea is 'court of the winds' (*windgeard*); Grendel's dam is 'she-wolf of the deep' (*grundwyrgen*); the steely, talon-like hand of Grendel is vividly expressed in the compound *handsporu.* The compounds in which all the images cited above are clothed occur nowhere else in any extant text, and appear to have been coined for the occasion.

The adjectives in *Beowulf,* for the most part, describe persons and things as typically as the substantives express them. A ship is 'broad-bosomed' (*sidfæðmed*)—that is, capacious, as a good ship ought to be. It is 'new-tarred,' as a ship should be for a voyage. There is beauty in the epithet 'foamy-necked,' applied to Beowulf's ship; but the term is equally applicable to any ship breasting a high sea. A princely estate is 'productive' (*welig*); armor is shining and hard; gold is glittering. The hero is 'good,' 'fierce,' 'valiant of spirit,' and in the end is praised as 'kind, liberal, eager for praise'; but all these are qualities of any great hero; it is not through epithets that Beowulf's character is disclosed. Of his appearance we are told only that he is stately, large-framed, and 'unique' in appearance.

Nevertheless the poet often uses adjectives with marked freshness and vividness. When the ship which is to bear the body of Scyld into the unknown is called 'icy and eager to set forth' (*isig ond utfus*), the first adjective indicates both the appearance of the ship and the time of year—a season most appropriate for the departure of the great king to his mysterious haven; the second has the vividness of personification. The dawn of day is heralded in the words: "The black raven, blithe-hearted, announced the joy of heaven." The first adjective is purely typical; the second suggests the effect of the fine day upon men through its effect upon the least sympathetic of all birds—a bird usually conceived in poetry as 'blithe-hearted' only as eater of the corpses of the slain. Again, Beowulf's mortal wound is called *wæl-bleat;* the first element indicates its fatal character, the second directly appeals to the sympathy of the audience.

The poet of *Beowulf* chose and combined his nouns and adjectives, with singular skill, to achieve specific effects. An excellent example is supplied by the passage in which the poet comments upon the armor worn by Beowulf and his men on their way to Heorot (lines 321–328a):

> . . . . Guðbyrne scan
> heard, hondlocen, hringiren scir
> song in searwum, þa hie to sele furðum
> in hyra gryregeatwum gangan cwomon.
> Setton sæmeþe side scyldas,
> rondas regnhearde wið þæs recedes weall;
> bugon þa to bence,— byrnan hringdon,
> guðsearo gumena . . .

The first word for 'corselet,' *guðbyrne,* is purely literal, the direct name for the referent. *Hringiren,* formally and in content a periphrastic synonym, is a metonymy: its base-noun labels the referent in terms of its material, and its limiting noun reminds the listener of the manner of the corselet's construction through the linking of rings. *Gryregeatwum* stresses the terror inspired in an enemy by the sight of men wearing such armor. In the last three verses the simplex *byrnan* is varied by *guðsearo,* which suggests both the function of the corselet as war-garment and, in its base-word, the skill with which it was fashioned: *searo,* like Middle English and Old French *engine, engin,* signified either a cunning contrivance or the ingenuity required for its making.

Now if we look at the adjectives which modify these nouns, we find the simplex *heard* used to characterize the primary quality of a corselet, its imperviousness; this word modifies the literal name for the thing. *Scir,* describing the referent in terms of its brightness, is applied to the substantive, *hringiren,* which pictures the corselet as an interwoven whole; the adjective compound *hondlocen* reinforces this characterization, stressing the manner in which the corselet was fashioned.

In the second part of this passage the poet deals with the shields of the Geats: they are *side scyldas,* 'broad shields'; both noun and adjective are literal simplices. In the following line the simplex *rondas* is a poetic term, a metonymy; the rimmed shields are described as *regnhearde.* This word, literally translated, means 'divinely hard'; but the first element had undoubtedly lost its original sense and had become merely a strong intensive.

Taking the passage as a whole, both substantives and adjectives denote typical things and their typical qualities; but they are admirably selected and combined. The simple adjectives emphasize the toughness and brightness of the corselet and the hardness and breadth of the shield; they describe the objects literally, emphasizing their essential quality and appearance. The compounds are more suggestive, more evocative, than the simplices. It is significant that the compound substantives *guðbyrne, hringiren, gryregeatwe* and the adjective compounds *hondlocen, sæmeþe, regnheard* occur only in *Beowulf;* the poet's choice of words is his own.

Among the combinations of adjective and substantive which are clearly formulaic is *wlitebeorhtne wang* (line 93), common to *Beowulf* and other poems. It occurs in the Song of Creation sung by Hrothgar's scop: the newly formed earth is called 'beauty-bright' not merely in its own fairness, but also in its freshness from God's hands. God, looking upon His work and seeing that it is good, is *sigehreðig,* exultant in the joyous victory of creation. The compound adjectives in *Beowulf*—even those obviously conventional and used by other poets—are never flatly used in the epic: they are so aptly applied, and so skillfully combined with other elements of the sentence, as to give the effect of suggesting more than they say, or of possessing unusual vitality. The 'blithe-hearted raven' heralding the day is a case in point.

Often the poet selects his adjectives not for their immediate effect alone, but for their ability to convey a mood, or for their overtones; as in the striking instance *morgenceald.* The Geats, soon to be attacked by a foe of overwhelming power, must raise many a spear 'cold at morning': the epithet not only denotes the chillness of the spear to the hands in the hour of dawn attack, but also conveys that sense of fatality which the word 'cold' connoted to English minds for centuries. The compound *wohbogen* (line 2827) is used in a similarly pregnant sense:

. . . . . . Beahhordum leng
wyrm wohbogen wealdan ne moste.

Beowulf has slain the dragon, and is dead himself: the lines suggest the greatness and valor of his exploit by picturing the dragon as it had lived, 'wickedly coiled' in savage readiness to defend its treasure.

One of the finest passages in *Beowulf* is the description of the landscape leading to and surrounding the Haunted Mere; and much of the power and terror of the description resides in the admirably chosen adjectives. Beowulf is first told of this region by Hrothgar: it is 'a *secret* land, wolf-slopes, *windy* headlands; a *frightening* fen-path, where the mountain stream dashes downward under the mists of the crags—flood under the earth.... Over the mere stand *frosty* groves; a wood *fast-rooted* shadows the water. There on any night one may see a *fearful* wonder, fire in the flood.' Then a concrete illustration of the terror of the place: 'Though the stag *strong of horns, pursued* by hounds, *put to flight* from afar, seek the forest, he will rather give up his life on the shore than go in there to hide himself—that is *no canny* place!' Later, as Danes and Geats advance through this grisly region toward the lair of the ogress, it is described once more, its salient features pictured as they exert their influence upon the spirits of the warriors; and now the poet adds new details of a singularly horrible nature: the bloodstained water of the mere, the evil creatures that swim in it; the discovery of the gory head of Æschere exposed on the cliff.

In this bipartite description the adjectives are not extravagant, nor even striking in themselves; they are mostly combined with nouns which designate the features of the landscape. But it is a terrifying landscape, and the mood of terror is admirably conveyed. A few nouns (*mor, wudu, gelăd*) are carried over from Hrothgar's account of the region to the narrative of its crossing by Danes and Geats; but there is almost no repetition of the adjectives used in Hrothgar's description. The moor is 'murky' (*myrce*); the rocky slopes are 'steep'; the paths narrow and mysterious (*nearwe, enge, uncuð*); the water of the mere is bloody and troubled (*dreorig ond gedrefed*). The only adjective at all unusual is *wynleas,* applied to the forest that overhangs the water. The water-monsters are 'strange' (*sellic*), cruel, and enraged; the one slain by Beowulf is 'wondrous' and 'grisly' (*wundorlic, gryrelic*). The nouns and adjectives are carefully selected, not so much to *portray* a particular landscape as to *suggest,* vividly and powerfully, the peril and horror to which the hero and his companions must expose themselves to reach the fearful lair of the troll. The description is symbolic rather than representational—symbolic of evil in its most appalling form.

Such symbolism is comparatively rare; but the poet often selects his adjectives for their power of suggestion. In reporting to Hygelac his fight with Grendel, Beowulf thus describes the monster's approach:

> '. . . . . .   Syððan heofones gim
> glad ofer grundas,   gæst yrre cwom,
> eatol, æfengrom,   user neosan,
> ðær we gesunde   sæl weardodon.' (2072b–75)

The three adjectives applied to Grendel convey the fury of the ogre's mood (*yrre*), his dreadful nature (*eatol*), and his character as nocturnal predator: he is 'terrible at evening' (*æfengrom*), when all the powers of evil are most dangerous. This epithet carries on the thought of the clause 'As soon as the gem of heaven had glided over the earth,' and looks forward to the horror to come; the word is found only in *Beowulf,* and illustrates the poet's fondness for adjectives the first element of which expresses the time when the quality expressed in the base-word is exercised: *morgenceald, morgenlong, nihtlong*. The epithet *gesunde* is grimly ironic: when Grendel enters the hall, the Geats are *as yet* unharmed; but the shocking murder of Hondscio follows in the next moment. Later in this same speech, Beowulf tells of the murder, and characterizes Grendel in two shudderingly appropriate and unique terms: *muðbona* and *bona blodigtoð,* which emphasize Grendel's inhuman ferocity.

Adjectives are sometimes used in striking progressions, as in the characterization of Grendel as *grim ond grædig,... reoc ond reþe.* The finest instance of this is the sequence of epithets in lines 2419b–20, immediately used to describe Beowulf's state of mind, but serving also to foreshadow his impending death:

. . . . . . Him wæs geomor sefa,
wæfre ond wælfus...

The first two of these adjectives are common enough; the third and strongest is peculiar to *Beowulf.* The three are grouped climactically: the hero's spirit was 'gloomy,' 'wavering,' 'ready for bloody death.' Through them the poet prepares the audience's minds for what is to come, and fixes the dominant tone.

The adjectives used to qualify the precious vessels and weapons in the dragon's hoard are chosen to invoke a mood of melancholy: *feormendlease, hyrstum behrorene, eald ond omig;* and they echo—I think deliberately—the terms used in the lament of the Last Survivor who had placed the treasure in the barrow:

'. . . . . . Nah, hwa sweord wege
oððe *fe(o)rmie* fæted wæge,
dryncfæt deore;...
Sceal se hearda helm (*hyr*)*sted* golde,
fætum befeallen; *feormynd swefað,*
...
ge swylce seo herepad, sio æt hilde gebad
ofer borda gebræc bite irena,
brosnað æfter beorne...' (2252b ff.; cf. 2761 ff.)

Although adjectives are ordinarily as typical as substantives, and like them commonly denote a single trait, quality, or thing, occasionally a compound adjective possesses a special and moving fitness; thus 'the morning light of another day' is 'clothed in radiance' (*sweglwered*); Beowulf's ship, speeding to its home port, is *lyftgeswenced;* the hero's death-wound is *wælbleat;* his men, as they view his body, are *wollenteare;* all these compounds are peculiar to *Beowulf,* as are nearly all those hitherto discussed.

It is of course possible that, if all the poetry composed in Anglo-Saxon times had been preserved, many of these adjectives and substantive compounds which now appear restricted to our epic would be matched elsewhere. But two facts must be reckoned with: first, the proportion of such compounds in *Beowulf* is very much higher than that in any other extant poem; and, secondly, the number and the richness of the compounds found in *Beowulf* and nowhere else is astonishingly large. It seems reasonable, therefore, to regard the many unique compounds in *Beowulf,* finely formed and aptly used, as formed on traditional patterns but not themselves part of a traditional vocabulary. And to say that they are formed on traditional patterns means only that the character of the language spoken by the poet and his hearers, and the traditional tendency toward poetic idealization, determined their character and form. Their elevation, and their harmony with the poet's thought and feeling, reflect that tendency, directed and controlled by the genius of a great poet.

The limitations imposed upon lesser poets by the traditional manner seem not to have hampered the author of *Beowulf.* I doubt that he consciously tried to free himself from them: we find in his work a great many formulas that appear in other poems. But he was able to treat them as more or less plastic: in using them he went his own way when it suited him. This will appear if we compare the rigidity of the *maðelode* formula in *Hildebrandslied* with its extreme freedom in *Beowulf.* And in his diction it appears very significant that the majority of substantive and adjective compounds—the richest content-words—in *Beowulf* occur in no other extant texts. This implies that he was the greatest master among all those poets who composed in Anglo-Saxon England, great enough to make the inherited modes serve his ends.

It does not detract from the originality of his language that a great many of the unique compounds in *Beowulf* are, individually, composed of elements one or both of which appear in other poems, either as simplices or as elements in *different* compounds. That is due to the character of Old English, which depended heavily upon compounding to express thought, in prose as well as in poetry.

It is, moreover, of some importance that we can find individualities of diction in other long poems—and in some short ones—as well as in *Beowulf*. Many compounds are peculiar to *Andreas,* many to *Elene;* the vocabulary of *Phoenix*—which has a direct Latin source—is unique in a number of respects. If we consider the distribution of the various compounds formed with any single word as first element, we find a surprising diversity. There are, for example, 26 substantive compounds in *Beowulf* formed with *guð-* as first element; only six of these 26 appear in any other poem. On the other hand, 23 *guð-*compounds scattered among other poems are not found in *Beowulf;* no more than three of these are peculiar to any single poem. If this kind of distribution should prove typical—and a glance at my Appendix B will reveal that it is typical—it would indicate, first, that the vocabulary of *Beowulf* has a singularly wide range; and, secondly, that the diction of almost any of the longer poems is more individual than one might expect.

These compounds in *Beowulf* which it shares with other poems were, at least in large part, the common stock of poetry, and the hearer experienced in them the pleasure of recognition. The very large number which appear to have been coined by our poet, being formed on familiar patterns, also conveyed this same kind of pleasure; but being new formations (though made of familiar elements), they both had the charm of freshness and lent themselves more aptly to contextual situations not present in other poems. They were conceived, that is, for use in specific contexts, and designed to fit them. The combination of such words in the sentence with other elements equally fresh and apt often evokes vivid and beautiful images in *Beowulf*—much more often than in other poems. In that passage which pictures the melting of the blade of the magic sword (lines 1605b ff.) the compound *wælrap* is unique; the metaphor *forstes bend,* taken with its immediate context, is so closely paralleled in *Exeter Gnomic Verses* 75–76 that we may think of it as formulaic:

. . . . . .   an sceal inbindan
forstes fetere   fela-meahtig God . . .

But in *Beowulf* the image is part of a comparison: *þæt hit eal gemealt ise gelicost, þonne forstes bend,* etc.; the explicit comparison reinforces the implied simile *ongan . . . hildegicelum . . . wanian;* and the formula-like clause itself is given additional vividness by the variational metaphor *onwindeð wælrapas,* in which the verb participates with the unique compound.

In two passages which, I think, are often misinterpreted, other sentence-elements combine with compounds to form fine metaphors. When Beowulf's men lean their spears against the wall of Heorot, the clump of spears standing together is called *æscholt ufan græg,* 'an ash-grove tipped with gray' (line 330a). Later, when Beowulf promises military aid to Hrothgar, his words are: '. . . so that I may . . . bring to thine aid a forest of spears' (*þæt ic . . . þe to geoce garholt bere*). *Garholt* is peculiar to *Beowulf; æscholt* occurs in *Maldon* also, but there has the literal sense of 'spear-shaft.'

Unhappily there exists no other long Old English poem on a traditional theme with the diction of which that of *Beowulf* might be compared. The other extant poems of considerable length are based on the Scriptures or the lives of saints, or are otherwise religious or edifying. Nevertheless, thanks to the considerable amount of military action or imagery in *Genesis* and *Exodus,* and to the propensity of religious poets to clothe the relationships of God to His faithful, or of Satan to his legions, in terms derived from the relations of an earthly king to his thanes, the language of religious poetry is, in the main, comparable with that of the epic.

Composing within the convention that had been fixed by the practice of earlier English poets, and in substantial ignorance of any culture but his own, the Anglo-Saxon religious poet, like the author of the *Heliand,* made the fullest possible use of the poetic vocabulary which he had inherited. Christian poetry, however, had to express many concepts unknown in pagan times; and there were three possible ways of meeting this requirement. In the first place, many of the appellations inherited from pre-Christian times could be used in new applications: *heahcyning* served equally well as a term for a powerful earthly ruler or for God; *ordfruma,* originally denoting a military leader, was used by Christian poets as an appellation for

Christ or God. In the second place, nouns inherited from the ancient stock might be preserved as base-words for new compounds, and supplied with limiting elements which adapted their meaning to the Christian concept to be expressed: thus, over against the ancient compound *bælfyr* we find *hellefyr* for the flames of hell. As against *garbeam* 'spear-shaft' we find *sigebeam* for the Cross. Finally, wholly new compounds might be struck off to express a concept, by prefixing to a base-word which had denoted a very different concept in earlier times a limiting word which would bring it closer to the meaning to be expressed. Thus *ærn,* which in nonreligious poetry generally means a hall, acquires, in the new compound *holmærn* (*Genesis*), the meaning 'Noah's ark.'

Although *Beowulf* was composed by a devout Christian, it is not a religious poem. The Christian concepts expressed in it are almost altogether restricted to God, heaven, hell, devil, and judgment; and the words which clothe these concepts are relatively few and simple. In the religious poems, on the other hand, the specifically Christian appellations are numerous and highly developed. Even the most pious sentiments placed in the mouths of Hrothgar and Beowulf are scarcely comparable with those uttered by Juliana, Elene, Andreas, or Guðlac. Difference in theme, and the lack of dogmatic or theological matter in *Beowulf,* reduce to a minimum the basis for comparison between its religious terms and those of the poems primarily religious in character. It must be borne in mind that the great expansion in the poetic vocabulary which took place to make possible the expression of Christian concepts in the religious poetry is effective evidence against a rigid, exclusive formalism in poetic diction. The vocabulary of poetry *could* be indefinitely extended; it was extended by the religious poets. There is, therefore, no reason to suppose that the heroic vocabulary could not also be extended, particularly in a work as long, as full, and as rich as *Beowulf*.

In Appendix B I have presented the results of a detailed study of the compounds formed in Old English poetry on 57 base-words, all of which form compounds in *Beowulf* and in other poems. If the reader will examine this study, it will be clear that a great many compounds were created by the authors of religious poems; and that many others, originally without any Christian denotation or connotation, were adopted from the traditional poetic vocabulary and used for—sometimes rather violently adapted to—the expression of Christian concepts. Thus there came into being a large corpus of compounds upon which religious poets could draw at will: many of the adapted compounds continued, in nonreligious poems, to be used in their original senses; the compounds actually coined for religious use were employed mainly in religious poetry, and sparingly if at all in works of a secular character. The consequence was that the diction of religious poetry became differentiated to a perceptible degree from that of nonreligious—and specifically of heroic or martial—poetry. There remains a very large body of words, simplices as well as compounds, available for use by all poets.

The fact that the poetic vocabulary could be so expanded and adapted to meet the needs of the new religious poetry affords sufficient evidence that the body of words and the patterns of poetic compounds had not been fixed once for all in the period of preliterate oral composition. Although no actual break occurred in the modes of poetic composition, nevertheless poets began, in the seventh century, to compose long narrative poems, which so far exceeded in scope and measure the shorter forms produced by the earlier scops as to present new problems of structure and of narrative manner. One consequence was, as we have seen, the free use, in long poems, of enjambement. It seems probable that the composition of heroic as well as of religious poetry in longer form compelled an expansion of the poetic vocabulary as well as a freeing of the line. Heroic poetry, making use of legendary themes inherited from pre-Christian antiquity, may well have demanded a less extensive expansion than that imposed upon the authors of the longer religious poems; nevertheless the facts which Appendix B exhibits with respect to the distribution of compounds show that very many new appellations were coined for the fuller expression of old and familiar concepts. The incomparable richness of *Beowulf* in its compounds, the great number of appellations peculiar to its vocabulary, and the occurrence of compounds in *Beowulf* made with base-words which form no compounds in other poems, afford clear evidence, first, that a general expansion in the poetic language did take place, and secondly, that the author of *Beowulf* was a prime mover in that expansion.

It is easy to underestimate the extent of the new, specifically Christian element in the vocabulary of religious poetry, which was quite large enough to justify us in finding significant differences between the style of *Beowulf* on the one hand and that of any of the religious poems on the other. The author of any poem concerned with traditional heroic themes would have little use for such compounds as *wuldorgæst, feorhgifa, freoðoscealc, heofonþrym, frumhrægl, ærendgæst, heahgæst;* and he would have abundant occasion to use compounds for concepts relating to the life of a Germanic court, with its paraphernalia of weapons and objects of luxury. The majority of base-words for compounds denoting 'royal hall,' to say nothing of the large majority of the actual compounds for that concept, appear very sparsely in the religious poetry, and abundantly in *Beowulf,* which is also incomparably rich in compounds denoting 'corselet,' 'earthly king,' 'sword,' 'spear,' helmet,' etc. If, in the larger elements of style, religious and heroic poetry tended to keep pace together, in diction considerable differences arose.

Among the compounds which Appendix B records for religious poems, those which appear to be adaptations of traditional terms are often used in a violent or far-fetched manner which is completely foreign to the practice of the poet of *Beowulf*. This is natural enough: in adapting a traditional compound to the expression of a completely nontraditional thought, some force must now and then be exerted. Eve's 'hostile onslaught' (*feondræs*) upon the fatal tree in the Garden (*Genesis*) is a case in point, as is the use of *goldhord* to denote Christ or the Cross. On the other hand, the religious poets occasionally struck off compounds more attractive to us than consonant with traditional Old English practice, such as *deaðwæge* (*þone bleatan drync deopan deaðweges*), a figure which the poet of *Guðlac* exploits twice within seven lines: Eve 'poured for her dear husband a bitter compulsive cup (*bittor bædeweg*), so that none of the sons of men thereafter might avert the wretched drink of the deep cup of death' (*Guðlac* 958–964). Such instances as this, and the (*hungres*) *blates beodgæstes* of *Andreas,* show that the authors of religious poems sometimes allowed themselves greater freedom in the coinage and use of new compounds than purely traditional practice would have sanctioned. The poet of *Beowulf* kept more closely to traditional patterns; but within those patterns he apparently felt free to coin new compounds and conceive fresh and vivid images.

The testimony of the specifically Christian elements in the vocabulary of the religious poems has considerable indirect value in determining the approximate date of *Beowulf*. Miss Whitelock has argued that the Christian element in the language of *Beowulf* is larger and more developed than we should expect in a poem composed as early as 725.[17] Now even the small sampling of the compounds which I have presented in Appendix B demonstrates that hardly a religious poem exists in which the essentially Christian elements in the vocabulary are not enormously richer than in *Beowulf,* more highly developed and elaborate. Even *Genesis A,* which is almost certainly earlier than *Beowulf,* has a much greater wealth of terms for religious concepts. The piety of the author of the epic does find expression, both directly and in the speeches of his personages; but the number of Christian concepts which he expresses is small, and their variety is not rich. The Christian element in his vocabulary does not greatly outrange that of Cædmon's Hymn; it is not comparable with that of *Daniel* or of *Exodus.* On the basis of his words for Christian concepts, his diction affords no evidence for a later date than 725.

It is surprising how many compounds appear with marked infrequency. Of the various compounds formed on a single base-word, a very great many are restricted to a single poem each, or at most are shared by two poems. This raises the question whether the majority of poets may not have permitted themselves a good deal of originality in the formation of compounds, and whether tradition may not have supplied merely the basic patterns on which compounds could be acceptably formed.

The lists of compounds in Appendix B also reveal that, in spite of the large number of finely imaginative metaphors in *Beowulf,* a great many of its compounds are literal, or embody simple figures;

[17] Dorothy Whitelock, "Anglo-Saxon Poetry and the Historian," *Transactions of the Royal Historical Society,* XXXI (London, 1949), pp. 83–84.

whereas very many of the compounds formed on the same base-words in other poems embody strained figures. Moreover, the compounds of *Beowulf,* taken by and large, tend to be more specific than those in the religious poems. Over all, then, the compounds in *Beowulf* are formed and used with more precision and restraint than those of most other poems. This is particularly true of the kennings. Kennings, as Heusler has defined them,[18] are fewer and less strained than in *Genesis, Exodus, Elene,* or *Andreas.* The most striking instances in *Beowulf* are peculiar to it: *hildeleoma, beadoleoma, guðwine* for 'sword'; *merehrægl* for 'sail.' Others are found in various poems either in identical form, or with the same base-word and a different first element: e.g., *woruldcandel, rodores candel, heofones gim* for 'sun'; etc. *Banhus, bancofa* for 'body' are clearly among the older traditional kennings, and are common to *Beowulf* and other poems. But we do not find in *Beowulf* such riddle-like and far-fetched kennings as *werbeam, garbeam* for 'warrior' (*Exodus*), nor such strained figures as *heafodwylm* for 'tears' (*Elene*) and *heafodgim* for 'eye' (*Andreas*). Of course the absence of far-fetched kennings of a specifically religious nature is explained by the heroic and traditional character of the theme and material of *Beowulf;* but its author also abstains from the more extravagant kennings for concepts essential to his theme. We do not find in *Beowulf* such kennings as *hildenædre* for 'missile weapon' (*Elene, Judith*); *sæhengest* (*Andreas*), *wæghengest* (*Guðlac, Elene*), *yðmearh* (*Crist, Whale*) for 'ship.' *Guðwine* and *merehrægl* are his closest approximations to the more extreme kennings; the language of the author of *Beowulf* is restrained and temperate in comparison with that of other poets.

Something should be said of the limiting words which form the first element of poetic compounds. I shall speak in general terms: specific lists are given in the second part of Appendix B.

Thirty-two limiting words which form compounds in *Beowulf* form none in any other extant poem, though compounds of many of them are found in prose. Thirty-five form each more compounds peculiar to *Beowulf* than compounds peculiar to any other poem, although many of them form more compounds in the *totality* of

[18] Heusler (see note 16, *supra*), pp. 129–131.

other poems than in *Beowulf* alone. The total number of limiting words which form no compounds except in *Beowulf* plus those which form more compounds in *Beowulf* than in any other single poem is sixty-seven. On the other hand, sixty form fewer compounds in *Beowulf* than in the *totality* of other poems. No other poem compares with *Beowulf* in the wealth of limiting words used in the formation of compounds. The compounds denoting war, battle, most weapons, sea, hall, and treasure show a marked excess in the epic over other poems.

The exceptional wealth of substantive compounds in the language of *Beowulf* appears impressive indeed when we regard it from the point of view of the limiting words, which are the distinguishing, the particularizing element in the formation of compounds. The obvious explanation for the abundance of its compounds is that this longest of Old English poems deals, more extensively than any other, with those concepts and ideas which, in the days of oral composition and communication of poetry, formed the favorite matter of poetry. But this is not the only reason for the richness of the language of *Beowulf,* as the next chapter will show. The diction of the poem was heavily influenced by the author's feeling for style and structure.

We distinguish, in Old English poetry, three more or less distinct strata of compounds: (1) those common to poetry and prose, and necessary to the communication of thought in either; (2) those restricted to poetry, though essentially literal; (3) those peculiar to poetry and figurative. Among the compounds of the first level in *Beowulf* are: *folcriht, fotlast, freondscipe, foreþanc, handgeweorc, lichoma, sciphere, wælstow.* Among those on the second (words literal, yet part of the special language of poetry) are: *þeodcyning, guðcræft, brimclif, eoforlic, wræcsið, merefara, medoful, guðhorn, swyrdgifu, bælwudu, wiflufu.* On the highest level, that of words restricted to poetry and figurative, and either inherited from earlier poetic practice or coined in harmony with the principles of that practice, stand such words as *medoærn, ecghete, mearcstapa, gifstol, yðlida, wægholm, sundwudu, gomenwudu, dædhata, cearwylm, sorhwylm, gryregeatwe, higeþrym, goldsele, cwealmcuma, feorhlast, gomenwaþ, medostig, handsporu, beadufolm, brimlad, swanrad, lindplega, laðbite, bencsweg, wæteregesa, hæðstapa,* and hundreds of others. In virtue of the special *kind* of its metaphoric content, the kenning stands by itself among the compounds and combinations on this third level; but in the *degree* of its metaphoric content it is so close to the more figurative examples of the *kent heiti,* the unstrained poetic metaphor, that it is sometimes difficult to distinguish between the one and the other. *Gryregeatwe* and *swanrad* stand on as high a poetic level as *hildeleoma* or *guðwine;* yet the first two are *kend heiti* and the last two are kennings.

The boundaries between one level and the next are not clearly delimited. There are words which in some contexts stand on one level and in other contexts on another; the same compound may be used now literally, now figuratively; or the same compound may, in different contexts, stand for different referents. In line 1143 *hilde-leoma* is a kenning for 'sword'; in 2583 its plural denotes the flames issuing from the dragon's throat. In 1369 *holtwudu* is a literal, tauto-logical compound meaning 'forest'; in 2340 it is a metonymy for a wooden shield. In 719 the plural *healðegnas* denotes the Geatish thanes who are actually guests in Hrothgar's hall; in 142 its singular is applied ironically to Grendel. The plural *renweardas,* in 770, is used of Beowulf and Grendel: literally of the hero, and ironically of Grendel. *Wælfyr,* in 1119, is the fire which consumes the warriors slain at Finnsburg; in 2582 it is the 'murderous fire' of the dragon's breath.

The abundance of compounds and simplices available for the ex-pression of significant concepts was of course most useful to poets for the satisfaction of alliterative and metrical demands. But, as I have suggested, these mechanical pressures alone cannot account for the entire word-hoard of Old English poetry; a great many of them must have been struck off, from time to time, by individual poets; and in the large the poetic vocabulary arises out of the need for a language capable of expressing the thought and feeling of poets. Giving all due weight to the accumulated effect of generations of composition, we must still recognize the need of the individual poet to communicate, and his power to satisfy that need. Oral composition and communication do not, invariably and remorselessly, constrict the poetic vocabulary and suppress individuality; we need look no farther for the truth of this than to the poetry of the Norse skalds. Although, in Scandinavia, the earlier skaldic poetry was orally composed and transmitted, and the period of oral composition lasted longer than in England, the hallmark of the individual poet is often plainly stamped upon the language of skalds. Certain poetic appellations were coined by particular skalds, who were remembered by name as the authors of those appellations: not only have we the direct testimony of Snorri to this effect, but we can see, in particular poems, individual peculiarities of expression. The poetic vocabulary of Egill is quite different from that of Kormakr or of Bragi. Cultural conditions in England were not so favorable to the development of individual modes of expression; nevertheless we can isolate compounds, and kinds of compound, peculiar to *Exodus,* to *Andreas,* or to *Elene;* the diction of any of these, or of *Genesis,* reveals specific points of difference from that of *Beowulf.* Many of these differences no doubt reflect differences in theme and purpose; many others seem to adumbrate differences in taste or in poetic power. We may readily concede that many compounds in any poem are stereotypes. But it is surely significant that the majority of compounds in *Beowulf* are peculiar to this one poem, and that a very great many of them are words which convey thought or feeling more freshly and vividly than the powers of other Anglo-Saxon poets ever compassed. They are, moreover, often used in telling combinations, in which the various elements of the sentence combine into a style more vigorous, stately, and beautiful than that of any other Old English poem.

II

VARIATION

Variation, "by far the most important rhetorical figure, in fact the very soul of the Old English poetical style, ... may be studied to perfection in the *Beowulf*."[1] Variation is indeed the chief characteristic of the poetic mode of expression; the poetic appellations, however striking in themselves, and however often they may serve as pure substitutions, find their most effective use as the materials of variations or of variation-like structures. Variation restrains the pace of Old English poetic narrative, gives to dialogue or monologue its leisurely or stately character, raises into high relief those concepts which the poet wishes to emphasize, and permits him to exhibit the object of his thought in all its aspects. But it could be a dangerous instrument in the hands of an inferior poet: it could impart on the one hand an effect of sheer redundancy, on the other an unpleasing jerkiness of pace; it could stiffen the flow of style, and clog the stream of thought.

Paetzel, in his very solid and careful study of variation, defines the figure in these terms: "... ein für das Verständnis genügend gekenn-

[1] Klaeber's edition, p. lxv.

zeichneter Begriff wird, entgegen dem Gebrauch der Prosa, noch einmal und zwar oft mit Unterbrechung des syntaktischen Zusammenhanges dem Hörer oder Leser vor die Seele gerückt. Diese Ausdrucksform nenne ich Variation. Ihre Hauptkennzeichen sind also 1) begriffliche, 2) syntaktische Entbehrlichkeit."[2] In his application of this definition he appears to me, on the one hand, to tend to excessive rigor, and on the other, to overlook the distinction between variation and parallelism. I have therefore undertaken to provide, in Appendix C, a correction of these shortcomings, with illustrations from the text of *Beowulf.*[3]

I should prefer to define variation as a double or multiple statement of the same concept or idea in different words, with a more or less perceptible shift in stress: one member of a variation may state the thought either more generally or more specifically than the other; or the second member, while restating essentially the same concept or idea, may do so in a manner which emphasizes a somewhat different aspect of it. When the members of a variation possess the same grammatical structure, they constitute a parallelism as well as a variation; but not all variations are parallelisms, nor are all parallelisms variations. I should insist that there are legitimate variations the members of which do not stand in the same grammatical construction: consider the opening lines of *Beowulf:*

> Hwæt, we Gar-Dena in geardagum,
> þeodcyninga þrym gefrunon,
> hu ða æþelingas ellen fremedon!

Since *Gar-Dena* is intended to apply, not to the whole Danish nation, but to the members of the royal house, it and *þeodcyninga* constitute a substantival variation, the two members of which stand in parallel structure. The clause *hu ða æþelingas ellen fremedon* is, like *þeodcyninga þrym,* the object of *gefrunon;* these two objects say the same thing in different terms, and form a variation, the first member of which is a substantive with qualifying genitive, the second a clause.

[2] Walther Paetzel, *Die Variationen in der altgermanischen Allitterationspoesie* (*Palaestra,* XLVIII; Berlin, 1913). The reference is to pp. 3, 4.

[3] Correction of so careful and systematic a work may seem presumptuous. Actually the limits of variation are not easy to define; but Paetzel's exclusions (see his p. 20) appear needlessly arbitrary.

Variation of substantive by clause is not uncommon; there is a fine instance in lines 350–353:

> . . . . . . 'Ic þæs wine Deniga,
> frean Scyldinga frinan wille,
> beaga bryttan, swa þu bena eart,
> þeoden mærne ymb þinne sið . . .'

Here we have, first, a multiple substantive variation *wine Deniga–frean Scyldinga–beaga bryttan–þeoden mærne,* with King Hrothgar as referent; but that which is to be asked of Hrothgar is also phrased in a variation—this time without parallelism: the first element is a pronoun in the genitive, the second a clause, the third a prepositional phrase. There is no identity of structure between *þæs–swa þu bena eart–ymb þinne sið;* but the identity of meaning is absolute. Identity of sense is more essential to variation than identity of structure.

In my first chapter I mentioned the fondness of the poet of *Beowulf* for grouping together different poetic appellations for a single referent in variations, each appellation expressing one aspect of the referent, so that the sum of the members of the variation presents a total description or characterization. An excellent instance is the sequence of terms applied to Hrothgar in Wulfgar's second speech, which I have just quoted (lines 350–353): the first appellation (*wine Deniga*) stresses the warm and affectionate relation between Hrothgar and his retainers; the second refers to him in terms of his lordship over them; the third emphasizes his generosity; the fourth, his renown. This is true variation: each member has the same referent as the others; the several members express it in somewhat different, and cumulative, terms. Unless each member of the sequence has the same referent, we have not a variation, but an enumeration—or, in certain cases, a progression. The distinction may be observed clearly in lines 333–335a, in which Wulfgar enumerates the offensive and defensive weapons of the Geats:

> 'Hwanon ferigeað ge fætte scyldas,
> græge syrcan ond grimhelmas,
> heresceafta heap? . . .'

This is an enumeration of different objects—shields, corselets, helmets, spears—which stresses, individually, distinct details that, taken together, present the total image of a company of splendidly armed men; but the several referents are different things: there is unity of effect but complete diversity of detail.

This passage is part of a larger and well-integrated block of narrative; it looks both backward and forward, and the whole of which it is a part reveals the great skill of the poet in utilizing variations to create a texture. In the lines closely preceding the last quoted the poet enumerates the weapons of the Geats, and his enumeration contains variation of its partials:

. . . . . . Guðbyrne scan
heard, hondlocen, hringiren scir
song in searwum, þa hie to sele furðum
in hyra gryregeatwum gangan cwomon.
Setton sæmeþe side scyldas,
rondas regnhearde wið þæs recedes weal;
bugon þa to bence,— byrnan hringdon,
guðsearo gumena; garas stodon,
sæmanna searo, samod ætgædere,
æscholt ufan græg; . . . (321b–330a)

These lines are separated from Wulfgar's opening words only by the poet's announcement of his speech and identification of the speaker; the thread of thought continues unbroken. The poet's enumeration of the details of Geatish armament—corselets, shields, spears—has sketched the image of a gallant band of men magnificently armed; now he communicates the effect of this impression as conveyed to Wulfgar,—the total effect of this fine armament upon a direct observer: 'that iron-clad company was well and worthily equipped with weapons' (lines 330a–331b). For Wulfgar's first words, meaning 'Who are ye and whence do ye come?' are framed in terms which repeat the poet's enumeration: 'Whence do ye bear the plate-bound shields, gray corselets and masked helmets, a heap of war-shafts?' In eleven words he pays compliment to each of the kinds of arms mentioned by the poet, for he has been as deeply impressed by the stately appearance of the Geats in their fine equipment as the poet's audience has been. This effect could not have been so vividly produced upon the audience without the variations which the poet has enclosed within his enumeration; for it is they which impart the excellence of the weapons of the Geats.

There are three of these variations: *guðbyrne–hringiren; scyldas–rondas; garas–searo;* the first of the three is reinforced by the terms *byrnan–guðsearo*. Appropriate adjectives, which do not stand in variation, enhance the effect by stressing typical and admirable qualities of corselets and shields: the former are *heard, hondlocen, scir;* the latter are *side, regnhearde*. There is no verb-variation: the various verbs denote different actions, each characteristic of its subject: the corselets *shone;* the ringed iron *sang;* the warriors *set* the shields against the wall, and themselves *bent* to the bench; the corselets *rang,* the spears *stood* together in a clump. The martial effect of the arrival of the Geats at Heorot, valiant men splendidly equipped, is presented dramatically, in a vivid, moving image.

In the creation of this effect the poet has used not only enumeration and variation, but summation as well (once in his own words, lines 330b–331a, and once in the respectful words with which Wulfgar closes his salutation, 336–339), and back-reference. The back-reference also is double: Wulfgar's first words hark back to the poet's description of the weapons of the Geats; and his mention of their helmets (*grimhelmas*), which are not mentioned in the enumeration of lines 321 ff., is intended to recall the poet's comment in 303 ff.:

. . . . . . Eoforlic scionon
ofer hleorber[g]an gehroden golde,
fah ond fyrheard, ferh wearde heold . . .

In this whole block of narrative, variation, with its attendant devices of enumeration and back-reference, is important out of all proportion to its frequency. It lends emphasis to the description of the arms of the Geats and gives force to the impression which the men in their armor make upon Wulfgar. Wulfgar at once transmits this impression to King Hrothgar:

'Hy on wiggetawum wyrðe þinceað
eorla geæhtlan . . .' (368–369a)

And the martial appearance of the hero and his men helps to motivate the quality of Beowulf's reception by the Danes. Wulfgar's enumeration of the weapons of the Geats recalls and reinforces the poet's enumeration, within which much of the effect of military might and magnificence is communicated by the enclosed variations. The whole passage raises in high relief the quality of the Geats as valiant men armed in a manner worthy of their courage. The continuity of this whole section of the poem is maintained by the repeated emphasis upon this quality, from the moment that the Geats begin to march toward Heorot until they enter Hrothgar's presence. Its texture is close and rich, its structure firm; its movement and sound are conveyed by verbs of shining, hastening, gleaming, singing, marching, ringing.

There is also a close unity of effect between this passage and that which describes the interchange between Beowulf and the Captain of the Shore, in which the stately appearance of the hero and his men, in their fine equipment, and the impression made upon the Captain by both, are similarly conveyed (lines 237–238a, 247–250a, 292).

Variation is but one of the devices through which this effect is produced and sustained; but it is the variations which lie at its center. The centrality, the focusing power, of variation becomes more apparent as the narrative advances. And it is in the use of variation that the superiority of the poet of *Beowulf* over all others of his age is most manifest: in other Old English poems the device is too often conventional, flat, and trite; in *Beowulf* it is an instrument of power and beauty.

In passages of great solemnity (as in very formal speeches), or of special dramatic tension, variations of three or more members are apt to occur; e.g., *sawlberendra–niþða bearna–grundbuendra* (1004b–06a). In some of these there seems to be a deliberate climactic arrangement, as in *feo–ealdgestreonum–wundini golde* (1380–82a), in which the first term is the most abstract, the last the most specific and vivid. In one such triple variation each of three substantives is modified by an adjective: all three nouns have the same meaning, as do two of the adjectives: *stige nearwe–enge anpaðas–uncuð gelad*. Here it is the connotation of the last adjective—'uncanny'—which raises the sequence to its climax.

The threefold variation often communicates a sense of deep emotional tension; the most striking illustration appears in lines 1644b ff.:

> Ða com in gan ealdor ðegna,
> dædcene mon dome gewurþad,
> hæle hildedeor . . .

The second and third members of the substantive variation are modified by varying adjectives, *dædcene–hildedeor; dome gewurþad* stands outside the variation, but serves to add a further touch of stateliness. This variation conveys and emphasizes the exceptional dramatic height and tension of the situation. The poet has prepared most carefully for this scene. We recall how the Danes, seeing the blood of Grendel's dam staining the mere, assumed that it was Beowulf who had perished, and returned to Heorot; the Geats, though without hope that their lord still lived, remained behind. Their joy at Beowulf's triumphant reappearance with the spoils of victory, and the pride with which they bore the head of Grendel to the royal hall, have been presented briefly, but with admirable power. Meantime the Danes sit despairing in Heorot, expecting that the coming of night will bring upon them further vengeful invasion by the she-troll. At this moment, when the Danes think him dead, Beowulf strides into the hall, bearing Grendel's severed head. His appearance creates an instant and complete emotional reversal: grief and fear are succeeded first by stupefaction, then by joy once the shock of astonishment has been dispelled. The shock is momentarily intensified when the Danes see the head of Grendel—

> Ða wæs be feaxe on flet boren
> Grendles heafod, þær guman druncon,
> egeslic for eorlum ond þære idese mid,
> wliteseon wrætlic; weras on sawon. (1647–50)

Here is the *structure* of variation; but the elements *Grendles heafod–egeslic–wliteseon wrætlic* do not constitute a variation in fact: the second and third members are descriptive of the first. The manner of description is unusual: the head is, literally, terrible to look upon (*egeslic*); the poet, having made the point that it is as frightening to the earls as to the queen, then ironically calls it 'a wondrous spectacle of beauty.' Yet the ironic words (*wliteseon wrætlic*) contain a statement of literal truth: the terrifying sight of horror was also, in a very real sense, a pleasing spectacle for those whom the living Grendel had so cruelly persecuted.

The whole scene, from the moment of Beowulf's entrance—announced in the triple variation quoted above—is presented with extraordinary dramatic force and great solemnity. If its significance is fully appreciated, one may perceive how completely it justifies Hrothgar's long and often misjudged monologue, for which it provides the motivation. As the scene develops, the role of variation in the communication of its tensity and emotional temper becomes almost incalculable: nowhere else in Old English poetry is there anything to compare with it. Indeed, we can find few instances of so perfect a transmission of feeling through language before Shakespeare.

Beowulf reports his victory at once, before the Danes can recover from their astonishment that he lives. Wisely, the poet employs little variation in his speech. The hero's words lack the touch of ironic lightness which had marked his announcement of his earlier victory over Grendel; they are sober to the point of grimness. This is right, for the fight with the she-troll had almost cost Beowulf his life. The speech is solemn in the extreme—as it should be, for it announces the completion of the errand of mercy which had brought him to Denmark. Even the assurance, at its close, that Hrothgar has no further need to fear for his men's lives is as sober as it is forceful. The speech is as simple and direct as any in the poem.

The cumulative proofs of Beowulf's triumph—his appearance, his speech, even the display of the monster's head—only deepen the astonishment of the Danes, without dispelling their shock. The hero then presents the hilt of the magic sword to Hrothgar; and in the old king's contemplation of it his emotional tension is gradually relaxed. The terms in which its transmission is reported are dense with variation:

Ða wæs gylden hilt gamelum rince,
harum hildfruman on hand gyfen,
enta ærgeweorc; hit on æht gehwearf
æfter deofla hryre Denigea frean,
wundorsmiþa geweorc; ond þa þas worold ofgeaf
gromheort guma, Godes andsaca,
morðres scyldig, ond his modor eac;
on geweald gehwearf woroldcyninga
ðæm selestan be sæm tweonum
ðara þe on Scedenigge sceattas dælde. (1677–86)

The concepts expressed in substantive variations are 'sword,' 'Hrothgar,' 'Grendel,' in the following sequences: *gylden hilt–enta ærgeweorc–wundorsmiþa geweorc; gamelum rince–harum hildfruman–Denigea frean–woroldcyninga ðæm selestan; gromheort guma–Godes andsaca.* In addition, the whole proposition 'the sword-hilt was given to Hrothgar' is set forth in a clausal variation of three members: *wæs on hand gyfen–on æht gehwearf–on geweald gehwearf;* the substantival variations are enclosed within the larger frame of the clausal variation. Moreover, *æfter deofla hryre* is varied in sense by the clause *ond þa þas worold ofgeaf gromheort guma ... ond his modor eac.* The appellation *Godes andsaca,* though it refers immediately to Grendel, also looks forward to the statement, in the immediately following account of God's destruction of the giants through the flood, *þæt wæs fremde þeod ecean Dryhtne.* Just as, after Beowulf's victory over Grendel, the monster's arm hung up in the hall, and later carried off by Grendel's dam, is a symbol of triumph and revenge, so now the golden hilt is a symbol of the final victory over monsters hateful to God: the symbolism becomes apparent in the account of the story of the Deluge inscribed on the hilt. Beowulf's victory is God's victory.

But that which is written on the hilt has another function: examination of it serves to give Hrothgar time to make the full transition from sorrow and shock to the joy that comes with the realization that all is gained rather than lost. This is obviously what the poet meant to convey by the wide separation of his first announcement of Hrothgar's speech (*Hrothgar maðelode,* line 1687a) from the actual utterance of his first words (1700), and by the quite exceptional parenthesis *swigedon ealle* (1699b). The other Danes are still gripped by emotional shock; Hrothgar has gained time, through his inspection of the hilt and the story engraved upon it, to recover and to formulate his thoughts. When words at last come to him, every thought expressed in his long monologue derives, with inexorable logic, from the circumstances which evoke the speech.

Moreover, the intensive and intricate variations in the account of Beowulf's gift of the sword-hilt to Hrothgar are so phrased as to communicate, fully and finally, the complete resolution of the central problem of Part I, and to mark the point of climax in the action. The monsters are slain, the Danes are safe; the hero has won matchless glory. From now on, although there are passages in which emotion is warmly and sensitively conveyed, the action slowly declines until it comes to rest in the last lines of the first part.

The scene we have been considering, the dramatic power of which is unmatched by any other in the literature of its age, illustrates certain of the larger aesthetic functions of variation. Paetzel, whose primary purpose was to establish a sound definition of the figure, and to examine and illustrate its structures and its formal characteristics, did not attempt to analyze its artistic effects; he tells us only that the psychological basis of variation is "Erregung der dichterischen Phantasie": "die Phantasie des Dichters ist so von einem Gegenstande erfüllt, dass sie ihn gar nicht aufgeben kann und sich in gewissen Abständen ihm immer wider zuwendet."[4] Now that which so fills the poet's imagination may be much more than an exciting concept: it may be a moving idea, a tragic situation, a clash of interest. Since out of tragic situations and clashes of interest dramatic action, and yet more tragic consequence, may develop, a poet who fully senses and deeply feels what he himself has to relate, and who participates sympathetically in the emotions of his personages, would inevitably find in variation a flexible and potent instrument. We have seen how, in the scenes we have examined, the poet of *Beowulf* transmits his own excitement to the listener through his variations, and how variation

[4] Paetzel, *op. cit.,* pp. 11–12.

may carry the dramatic impact of an entire scene. It may indeed—as we shall see—carry over from scene to scene; even from one structural block of the poem to another. Our poet is given to comparatively heavy use of variation in passages charged with emotion; sometimes, indeed, in such contexts variation is reinforced by words and phrases which, not structurally members of the variations, yet attach themselves closely to the variational members, and load them so strongly as to become, in effect, part of them. The emotion thus communicated may dominate a long narrative passage; it may provide the point of departure for a new train of consequent action.

This may be observed in the development of the situation first introduced in lines 129b–131. After Grendel's first depredations, and their terrifying impact upon the Danes, have been reported, the poet imparts to us the grief of Hrothgar:

. . . . Mære þeoden,
æþeling ærgod, unbliðe sæt,
þolode ðryðswyð, þegnsorge dreah . . .

Mære þeoden–æþeling ærgod constitute a combination of adjective and substantive variation; in line 131 there is verb-variation (*þolode–dreah*); the adjective *ðryðswyð,* used substantivally, varies *mære þeoden–æþeling ærgod*. But semantically there is a third element in the verb-variation: *unbliðe sæt*. Without the adjective, the verb *sæt* would be too colorless to participate in a variation of verbs meaning 'suffer' and 'endure'; but 'sat unhappy' is, in all ways except pure structure, a sound variation of them.

This variation, giving forceful expression to the king's sorrow—a nobler emotion than the terror-stricken grief of his men,—is followed by an extended statement (lines 134b–164) of Grendel's savage and long-continued persecution: he haunts Heorot nightly for twelve years. Again and again, in and after this tragic account, the poet reverts to the king's sorrow; indeed, it is Hrothgar's grief for his thanes rather than their suffering that constitutes the major theme of this long section of narrative. And each time, the king's emotions are conveyed in variations, which express his feelings climactically as the monster's depredations increase the measure of his grief:

twelf wintra tid   torn geþolode
wine Scyldinga,   weana gehwelcne,
sidra sorga . . . (147–149a)
Þæt wæs wræc micel   wine Scyldinga,
modes brecða. (170–171a)

These revelations of Hrothgar's sufferings are presented each in turn as the consequence of each stage in the climactic ravages of Grendel; the second (lines 147 ff.) follows the second monstrous visitation, and is enclosed within the poet's exposition of Grendel's persistent and insatiable ferocity. This is followed by a summation containing a bitterly phrased triple variation:

Swa fela fyrena   feond mancynnes,
atol angengea   oft gefremede,
heardra hynða;   Heorot eardode,
sincfage sel   sweartum nihtum . . . (164 ff.)

Here, after the first variation (*feond mancynnes–atol angengea*), the second and third point an ironic contrast between the splendor of Heorot and the miseries which Grendel inflicts upon the Danes within it (*fyrena–heardra hynða; Heorot–sincfage sel*). The irony deepens in the following lines, in the magnificent, all too generally undervalued 'Christian Excursus,' which makes clear that in their heathenism the Danes have brought this tribulation upon themselves, and that there is no hope for them save in God's mercy—which, in the natural order of things, only Christians can expect (lines 168–188). Here is the sharpest tragic irony: in their efforts to gain deliverance through sacrifices to their pagan gods, the Danes not only increase their present affliction, but also hazard the penalty of eternal damnation.

This whole narrative of hopeless suffering and sorrow is keyed by the first statement of Hrothgar's grief, with its multiple variation. Variation is heavy throughout this whole tragic section of the poem; it recurs abundantly in every statement of emotion; every instance increases the weight of pity and terror. It reaches a thundering climax at the end of the Excursus, with its declaration of the hopeless condition of the Danes:

. . . . Metod hie ne cuþon,
dæda Demend, ne wiston hie Drihten God,
ne hie huru heofena Helm herian ne cuþon,
wuldres Waldend. (180b–183a)

These lines set forth the impelling cause of all the affliction undergone by Hrothgar and his people, the reason for its long and implacable continuance. The sentence is a massive clausal variation enclosing a fivefold substantive variation and a threefold verb-variation. The lines which immediately follow the conclusion of the Excursus contain the sharpest restatement of the misery of Hrothgar; the whole terrible story of the haunting of Heorot ends on this note:

Swa þa mælceare maga Healfdenes
singala seað; ne mihte snotor hæleð
wean onwendan; wæs þæt gewin to swyð,
lað ond longsum, þe on ða leode becom,
nydwracu niþgrim, nihtbealwa mæst. (189–193)

Then, immediately, with that fondness for dramatic reversal which he frequently displays, the poet suddenly introduces the hero: the note of impending deliverance sounds like a trumpet. The sense of ineluctable tragedy has attained a tremendous climax; but it is instantly dispersed. The curtain has been lowered, as it were, upon a first act tense with terror, and swiftly rises upon a new setting, with new characters, who bring with them hope of happy consequence.

Throughout this first act of *Beowulf,* the cruel facts of Grendel's ravages have been narrated directly; but their impact has been imparted chiefly through their effect upon the emotions of Hrothgar. The primary vehicle of emotion is variation. Since variation, by its very nature, slows the pace of narrative,[5] and at the same time gives it specific force and sharpness, its use enables the author to communicate emotion with intensity and depth, and thereby impresses upon the listener the heroism and the tragic magnitude of the personages. The first part of *Beowulf* is heroic poetry so managed that it has the impact of drama: it gives the impression of a sequence of scenes upon the stage, connected by passages of transitional narrative. The first

[5] Klaeber's edition, p. lxv.

eighty-five lines are the Prologue to the play; in every ensuing scene the speeches are dramatic; the action falls naturally into several scenes, the tone of which is set by a dominant emotion. Thus the chief vehicle of emotion, variation, gives to each scene its quality and its continuity. Moreover the poet, in all the more tragic situations, is not content to convey the emotions of his characters in a single statement; he expresses them again and again, ever more forcefully, as the incidents of the action stimulate them afresh. In each restatement variation plays its central part. The consequences are, first, an increasingly developing awareness in the listener of the tragic situation; secondly, a deepening perception of the universality of its meaning; thirdly, appreciation of a continuous texture in the dramatic narrative.

Through variation, then, the representation of a dramatically significant emotion is emphasized and expanded; and its significance links together all the elements in a large narrative block. Yet, within the scene dominated by such an emotion, the poet, conscious of the complexity of human relationships, occasionally reveals cross-currents of interest, and uses their interactions toward that single effect which the character of the dominant emotion demands. Such a cross-current may make itself felt quietly and with subtle irony (as in the words of Wealhtheow to Hrothgar and to Beowulf, where emotion is controlled); or stormily, as in the interchange between Unferth and Beowulf.

That interchange, again, is the consequence of a powerfully felt emotion, the very quality of which is conveyed in variations. Its importance lies in the fact that it precipitates that very course of action toward which the dominant emotion of the scene—Hrothgar's passionate desire for Grendel's death—is directed. Beowulf has offered to venture his own life as Hrothgar's champion against Grendel; Hrothgar's reply is warmly friendly, but he does not immediately accept the offer. Near the close of his answer, Hrothgar expresses directly to Beowulf the horrors of the persecutions which the Danes have experienced, and the bloody outcome of the struggles of his thanes to defend the hall against the monster. This passage is the bitterest report of all: it communicates the sufferings of king and court far more sharply than the earlier statements of the king's grief; in it is focused, with terrible vividness, all the horror that has gone before:

> 'Đonne wæs þeos medoheal on morgentid,
> drihtsele dreorfah, þonne dæg lixte,
> eal bencþelu blode bestymed,
> heall heorudreore; ahte ic holdra þy læs,
> deorre duguðe, þe þa deað fornam.' (484–488)

In this deeply passionate utterance, variation, dense and interlocked, is used to carry the force of the king's emotion.

The closing words of the king's speech imply—as he had said more explicitly in lines 381b–384a—that he sees in Beowulf's coming some prospect of deliverance. After he has spoken, the feasting and mirth in the hall are reported briefly; then, with explosive force, the conflict of interest declares itself. Unferth, a famous warrior and a favorite of the king's, is angered by the warm welcome given Beowulf, and envious of any man who presumes to undertake an exploit which he himself recognizes as beyond his powers. He directs against the hero a speech which—to the modern reader at least—seems shockingly insulting, and utterly out of harmony with the extreme courtesy which Hrothgar has shown Beowulf. This challenge, and Beowulf's vigorous reply, seem to interrupt the main narrative; but in actuality they advance it. For Unferth's words spur Beowulf to claim for himself the right to confront Grendel, and to prove his competence to do so; and when the hero has spoken, there is no longer any question that Hrothgar will grant his request.[6] Thus the clash between Unferth and Beowulf becomes the mechanism which triggers all the ensuing action of Part I.

The conflict between the two men, to be effective, must be charged with emotion. Unferth's challenge is emotional from first to last, pervasively bitter with the speaker's envy; Beowulf's reply is calm and dignified so long as he is explaining the actual course of events in his adventure with Breca, which Unferth has misrepresented. Beowulf's words become angry only when, rounding on Unferth, he accuses him of want of courage to face Grendel, and attributes the monster's

[6] This has been demonstrated convincingly by Adrien Bonjour, in "The Digressions in *Beowulf*," *Medium Ævum Monographs,* V (Oxford, 1950), pp. 20–22.

successes to the military incompetence of Unferth himself and of the other Danes as well. It is therefore significant that, whereas Unferth's speech is filled with variations from beginning to end, Beowulf's reply contains only minor variations until the last sixteen lines,—and that these lines, edged with Beowulf's indignation and resolution, are heavy with variation. I need not discuss the variations in detail; the reader can see them for himself. Those in Unferth's speech are most marked in lines 513–518a and 520–522a. In lines 513–518, verb-variations predominate: they convey admirably the niggling scorn in Unferth's words. In 517–518 variation shifts from purely verbal to clausal; in 520–522a, lines in which Unferth asserts Breca's victory over Beowulf, the variation is substantival. Through much of the speech, the exciting, sneering misrepresentation is communicated chiefly through variation of verbs of action.

The more significant variations in Beowulf's retort appear in lines 590–606:

> 'Secge ic þe to soðe, sunu Ecglafes,
> þæt næfre Grendel swa fela gryra gefremede,
> atol æglæca ealdre þinum,
> hynðo on Heorote, gif þin hige wære,
> sefa swa searogrim, swa þu self talast;
> ac he hafað onfunden, þæt he þa fæhðe ne þearf,
> atole ecgþræce eower leode,
> swiðe onsittan, Sige-Scyldinga;
> nymeð nydbade, nænegum arað
> leode Deniga, ac he lust wigeð,
> swefeð ond sendeð, secce ne weneþ
> to Gar-Denum. Ac ic him Geata sceal
> eafoð ond ellen ungeara nu,
> guðe gebeodan. Gæþ eft se þe mot
> to medo modig, siþþan morgenleoht
> ofer ylda bearn oþres dogores,
> sunne sweglwered suþan scineð!'

The concepts stressed in these variations are: the terror and humiliation wrought by Grendel; the insufficient courage of Unferth; the inadequate martial power of the Danes as a whole (with ironic emphasis on the first element of the compound *Sige-Scyldinga*); and, by contrast, the warlike might of the Geats; and the bright morning of the next day, which will shine upon the triumph of Beowulf. Those particular elements of the speech most effective in convincing the Danes that they can expect Beowulf's victory are the concepts chosen for variation; and it is the variations which give Beowulf's words their bite and power. That they did carry conviction is demonstrated in the lines immediately following, which assert Hrothgar's joy over Beowulf's assurance, and his confidence that the hero will give him effective help. Those lines, quite appropriately, contain a threefold substantive variation, each member of which is the subject of its own clause; the referent of all three members is Hrothgar: he is king, with sole authority to appoint Beowulf champion of the Danes; and it is he whose state of mind is important at this point.

The scene is continued for some fifty-one lines, devoted to the pleasures enjoyed by Danes and Geats in the hall, the formal entry of Wealhtheow, Beowulf's vaunt that he will conquer or die, and Hrothgar's speech charging Beowulf with the defense of Heorot. These lines do not materially advance the action: they are partly setting, partly preparation for weighty matters to come; and they contain little variation. There is, however, one progression—a device admirably adapted to the conclusion of a scene—which sums up the account of the joys of the hall and serves as transition:

> Đa wæs eft swa ær inne on healle
> þryðword sprecen, ðeod on sælum,
> sigefolca sweg, oþ þæt semninga
> sunu Healfdenes secean wolde
> æfenræste. (642–46a)

The situation has been static since line 610, at which point the poet has established the complete emotional reversal experienced by Hrothgar. His sorrow and despair had received repeated emphasis from line 129b through line 488; now, filled with confidence and joy by the assurance contained in Beowulf's reply to Unferth, he is ready to entrust defense of the hall to Beowulf. Thus the dominant emotion—Hrothgar's suffering, lingering long, and suddenly transmuted into its joyful opposite—extends through, and unites, what we may call the first act of the drama. It is an act of two scenes, with two short narrative links, and one longer narrative passage which reports Beowulf's expedition to Denmark and his arrival at Heorot. The emotional cross-current set up by Unferth's challenge and Beowulf's reply precipitates the king's reversal of feeling, motivates his appointment of Beowulf as defender of the hall, and so makes possible all that follows. It is through the variations that the full force and acuity of these emotions is transmitted.

In one situation the poet uses variation with exceptional deftness and restraint, to suggest the tragedy impending over the House of the Shieldings. Wealhtheow's speech to Hrothgar, intended to remind Hrothulf of his obligations and ensure his loyalty (lines 1180b–87), contains very little variation: although her heart is filled with anxiety for her sons, her emotion is restrained. When, in the next moment, after giving gifts to Beowulf, she appeals to him to protect her sons, the depth of her feeling is disclosed in heavier variations (lines 1216–18; 1221b–24a; 1227).

Klaeber speaks of variation as "ubiquitous," and implies that it retards the action.[7] It is certainly pervasive; but in passages of vigorous action, such as the accounts of the hero's combats with monsters, it is relatively rare in lines that report the action itself, and heavier in those that communicate the feelings of the participants. In the narrative of Beowulf's fight with Grendel, variations are few and comparatively slight between the announcement of Grendel's advance on the hall and the moment when Grendel feels the power of the hero's grip; the first one of consequence occurs in lines 750 ff.:

> Sona þæt onfunde fyrena hyrde,
> þæt he ne mette middangeardes,
> eorþan sceata on elran men
> mundgripe maran; he on mode wearð
> forht, on ferhðe; no þy ær fram meahte.

[7] Edition, p. lxv. The retarding effect of variation accounts, of course, for its relative infrequency in the passages of swift action in *Beowulf*, as Brandl pointed out (Paul's *Grundriss der germanischen Philologie*, 2d ed., Strassburg, 1901–1909, II, 1, p. 1014).

Hyge wæs him hinfus, wolde on heolster fleon,
secan deofla gedræg; ne wæs his drohtoð þær
swylce he on ealderdagum ær gemette.

Here the variational pattern is remarkably complex; but it does not retard the action at all; indeed, it conveys, with unique vividness and force, the outstanding elements in that action, and the panic of Grendel. We have here a group of variations enclosed in a larger one, which extends beyond the bounds of a single sentence. The first of the enclosed variations is adverbial: *middangeardes–eorþan sceata–on elran men;* the third member, though it shifts from the sense 'anywhere' to that of 'in anyone,' nonetheless participates in the general sense 'in any quarter.' The periodic structure enhances the force of the whole, the most important member of the variation coming at the end. The second variation is phrasal: *on mode–on ferhðe:* the first member suggests a fear which fills the mind; the second, the sharp, sudden increase of that fear till it overwhelms the heart. The positive assertion of Grendel's helplessness (*no þy ær fram meahte*) is followed by a clausal variation declaring his desperate eagerness to break free: *Hyge wæs him hinfus–wolde on heolster fleon–*(*wolde*) *secan deofla gedræg.* Then the whole sequence is closed by the same affirmation—though in more general terms—with which it opened: *ne wæs his drohtoð þær swylce he on ealderdagum ær gemette* repeats the sense of *Sona þæt onfunde . . . þæt he ne mette middangeardes* etc. The variations convey Grendel's sudden, acute terror, contrasting with his earlier exultation in the expectation of a full meal on human flesh, and anticipating his anguished cries at the climax of his struggle to escape. If anything, the action gains in power through this revelation of its progress by means of the disclosure of Grendel's terror. Later the monster's lamentation is also set forth in variation (lines 785–788a): *wop–sigeleasne sang;* (*gryreleoð*) *galan–sar wanigean; Godes andsacan–helle hæfton.*

In narrating this combat the poet was confronted with a practical difficulty: wishing to preserve the dramatic contrast between the ease with which Grendel disposed of Hondscio and his helplessness in Beowulf's grip, and the emotional contrast between the monster's hideous joy at the sight of so many prospective victims and his agony of fear once the hero has laid hold on him, the author found it necessary to convey the power and the menace of Grendel's gigantic strength without permitting him a moment's advantage over the hero. He accomplished this by making much of the noise of combat and the damage wrought upon the furnishings of the hall by the impact of the struggling contestants, and through the effect of these upon the onlooking Geats and the Danes who hear the tumult. The emotions of both Danes and Geats are sharply represented: the Geats make heroic, if vain, attempts to help their lord; and the Danes are filled with terror at the shaking of the house, the crashing of benches, and the hideous wails of Grendel. The feelings of both are set forth in variations. Each of the Geatish thanes

> wolde freadrihtnes   feorh ealgian,
> mæres þeodnes;

they all

> ... on healfa gehwone   heawan þohton,
> sawle secan;

but they did not know that

> . . . . . .   þone synscaðan
> ænig ofer eorþan   irenna cyst,
> guðbilla nan   gretan nolde ...

The three concepts chosen for variation are those most basic to the poet's meaning and purpose: the devoted loyalty of the Geats impelled them to defend *their lord;* they meant to *kill* his foe; but even the *finest weapon* would not penetrate the giant's hide. The less noble emotions of the Danes are represented in another periodic variation:

> . . . . . .   Denum eallum wearð,
> ceasterbuendum,   cenra gehwylcum,
> eorlum ealuscerwen.   (767b–769a)

The irony of the situation—the fear of the Danes is excited not by any real peril, but by the din of the fight which is to deliver them—is underlined by the ironic term *ealuscerwen.*[8]

The lines with which the combat with Grendel ends, converted by the poet into a kind of chant of triumph, contain a substantival variation which recalls the emphatic and repeated statements of the anguish suffered by the Danes under Grendel's repeated attacks:

> . . . . . . Hæfde East-Denum
> Geatmecga leod gilp gelæsted,
> swylce oncyþðe ealle gebette,

[8] All but the most recent interpretations of this word are discussed by J. Hoops (*Kommentar zum Beowulf,* Heidelberg, 1932, pp. 97 ff.; see also his "Altenglisch *ealuscerwen, meoduscerwen,*" *Englische Studien,* LXV, 1931, pp. 177–180). The translation 'deprivation of ale,' favored by Hoops and others, was long rejected by Klaeber: "*-scerwen,* related to **scerwan* 'grant,' 'allot' (*bescerwan* = 'deprive'). 'Dispensing of ale,' or, in a pregnant sense, of 'bitter or fateful drink' might have come to be used as a figurative expression for 'distress'... It is to be noted that the author of *Andreas* (a better judge than modern scholars) understood the corresponding formation *meoduscerwen* (1526) in a sense which precludes the rendering 'taking away of (strong) drink'; to him it was 'plenty of (fateful) drink' ..."(Klaeber's edition, p. 156). Now there is no evidence whatever that the simplex **scerwan* meant 'grant' or 'allot'; the prefix *be-* (*bescerwan*) does not negate the meaning of the simplex with which it is compounded. In *Ps. Cott.* 50, 98 the compound *bescerwan* means 'take away,' 'deprive' (*Ne ðinra arna me bescerwe*); the simplex must have had the same meaning as the compound—to deprive. I do not agree that the author of *Andreas* understood *meoduscerwen* as 'plenty of (fateful) drink'; that interpretation stems from a false association of the word with *biter beorþegu* in line 1532; and it ignores the context in which the word occurs. The poet tells us that when the flood descended upon the Mermedonians, *meoduscerwen wearð æfter symbeldæge*—'deprivation of mead after a day of feasting.' Here is one of the typical contrasts so common in Old English poetry; the word *meoduscerwen* was chosen to contrast with *symbeldæge.* We have no right to interpret *meoduscerwen* in terms of *biter beorþegu,* which is neither a parallel nor a variation for it, but is rather a variation of *sorgbyrþen.* The author of *Andreas,* who knew *Beowulf,* simply imitated the Beowulfian *ealuscerwen* when he found himself in need of a word to contrast with *symbeldæg.* In both *Beowulf* and *Andreas* the term is figurative and ironic.

In the Second Supplement to his latest revision (1950), Klaeber (Edition, p. 466) cites Holthausen's view (*Anglia Beiblatt,* LIV–LV, 1943, pp. 27–30) that the first element in *ealuscerwen* is the same word *alu* "frequently met with in runic inscriptions and apparently meaning 'good luck,' 'safety.' Thus *ealuscerwen* 'taking away of good luck.'... Thus the annoying riddle of *ealuscerwen* ... seems to be happily solved by a twofold misunderstanding: 1) (taking away of good luck: ale; 2) dispensing (of ale, mead). The actual meaning of the noun in l. 769 is, most likely, 'disaster,' with a subaudition of 'terror.' "—Not at all: *alu* in the Prehistoric Norse runic inscriptions *may* mean 'good luck,' but there is no evidence that it does; it is found, for the most part, on bracteates in very short inscriptions. Its meaning is neither clear nor—apparently—uniform: on the stone of Orstad it seems to mean 'Denkmal,' 'Gedenkstein'; see A. Jóhannesson, *Grammatik der urnordischen Runeninschriften* (Heidelberg, 1923), pp. 76–77. Moreover there is no evidence that the word was used in Old English in the same sense as in Prehistoric Norse. I hold that *ealuscerwen* in *Beowulf* is used ironically: the Danes experience a terror such as they would have felt at deprivation of ale.

inwitsorge, þe hie ær drugon,
ond for þreanydum þolian scoldon,
torn unlytel. (828b–833a)

Thus the poet rounds out and places period to the first great stage of the action: in a clear statement that Beowulf has delivered the Danes from their long-endured persecution.

In this narrative of the first of Beowulf's three great adventures, the stages of the struggle, and its desperate nature, are communicated not so much by the direct statement of the action as through the revelation of emotions: of Beowulf's determination, Grendel's sudden and mounting fear once Beowulf has laid hold of him, and the emotions of Danes and Geats. In those lines which directly report the action there is very little variation, and that of the simplest; the variations are employed to express, explicitly and vividly, the emotions of the personages and of the onlookers. This revelation of emotion inspired by what happens, rather than the report of what happens, constitutes the active element in the management of the story.

In short, the author of *Beowulf* made use of the revelation of emotion as a major narrative principle; and perceiving the value of variation as a means of presenting emotion, he used it quite consistently, both to express the dominant emotion of a scene or a sequence of scenes, and to give depth and force to a single poignant situation. He used the figure also to reveal the conflicting emotions of different personages, the clash of feeling which gives rise to action; and to emphasize moments of dramatic reversal.

I have not found such consciously artistic use of variation in any other Old English poem. As we should expect, the author of *Beowulf* does, not infrequently, employ the device in more conventional ways. Its use in formal speeches is too familiar to require much comment. Its value in such speeches is that it imparts stateliness and courtesy to what is said. For this very reason its ironic use in Unferth's challenging speech to Beowulf is all the more pungent. The most obvious instance of variation in formal address is, of course, the dialogue between Wulfgar and Beowulf. In less formal speeches, such as the dying hero's first words to Wiglaf—speeches in which the relation of speaker to hearer is so close as to make formality unnecessary,—there is very little variation, unless the words are uttered under stress of emotion. Thus Hrothgar's speech to Beowulf, committing Heorot to his care, and uttered after the friendship between the two has been established, is quite free from variation. On the other hand, the Danish king's parting words to Beowulf, colored as they are by his love for the hero and his regret at Beowulf's departure, contain a number of striking variations.

The poet also uses variation to mark transition between one major phase of the action and another. Thus we find variation increasing in incidence and in density at the point at which Beowulf and his men set out for Denmark (lines 210 ff.); when the Geats, having passed inspection by the Captain of the Shore, march toward Heorot (301 ff., 320 ff.); in the account of the jubilation of the Danes over Grendel's bloody tracks and the water stained with his blood (841–850); at the point of Beowulf's dramatic entry into Heorot with the golden hilt and the head of Grendel (1644 ff.); and the still more dramatic moment when Hrothgar receives the hilt (1677–86); and—most momentous of all—at the opening of the second part of the poem.

In Part II there is considerably less variation than in Part I. The action of Part II is concentrated in time and place: there are but two scenes, that of Beowulf's last combat and death and that of his cremation and burial. The settings are, first, the dragon's barrow and the region adjacent to it; and secondly, the place of Beowulf's burning. The action is focused upon the fight with the dragon and the hero's death; all else that is told—the circumstances which made the combat necessary, the summary of events over more than fifty years of Beowulf's regency and his quietly glorious reign, the accounts of the stages of the wars between Geats and Svear, and the fates of the Hrethling kings—all these are necessary background to the main action, and at the same time furnish the elements of the subplot, the decline and destruction of the Geatish nation. These things are unfolded partly through direct narrative by the poet, but chiefly in monologue placed in the mouths of Beowulf himself, of the Messenger, and in lesser degree of Wiglaf. Subsidiary as they are to the main action, their importance is none the less great; for the theme of Part

II is double: the heroic death of Beowulf, and the overthrow of his people, who cannot long survive his fall.

The states of mind exhibited in Part II are, first and principally, those of Beowulf himself: his grief at the thought that some offense of his against God has brought down the dragon's fury upon his people; his resolute and enduring courage; his tender and mournful recollections of his dead kinsmen; and his care for his people in his last moments. The poet is also concerned, though less deeply, with the feelings of the faithful Wiglaf and the cowardice of Beowulf's ten faithless thanes, and with the sorrow of the Geatish people at the king's death. At all points until the end, the actions and emotions of Beowulf are central: the grief of the Geatish warriors becomes a tribute to him; Wiglaf's importance lies in the help he could give Beowulf; the Messenger is a mere voice—a kind of Chorus—through whom the coming overthrow of his lordless people is forecast.

In Part II, moreover, there are virtually no dramatic reversals: the poet makes it clear to us, from the very opening lines, that his hero, and the Geatish nation, are doomed; and the action marches relentlessly on toward catastrophe. The mood is almost uniformly dark and melancholy; there are no major shifts in emotional tone. Part II is elegy, as Part I is drama.

As we should expect, we find variation in the transitional passage with which the second part opens:

> Eft þæt geiode   ufaran dogrum
> hildehlæmmum,   syððan Hygelac læg,
> ond Heardrede   hildemeceas
> under bordhreoðan   to bonan wurdon,
> ða hyne gesohtan   on sigeþeode
> hearde hildfrecan,   Heaðo-Scilfingas,
> niða genægdan   nefan Hererices—   (2200–06)

The variations are restricted to the most significant elements of the thought: the long lapse of time between the events of Part I and those about to be communicated (*eft–ufaran dogrum*); attack by the Svear (*hyne gesohtan–niða genægdan*); the slain Heardred (*hyne–nefan Hererices*), whose fall brings Beowulf to the throne. *Heaðo-*

Scilfingas is rather an explanatory appositional to *hearde hildfrecan* than a variation of it. These seven lines are one long temporal clause; the circumstance which they place in time, Beowulf's accession, stands outside its scope. The next variation stresses the hero's advanced age: he was then *frod cyning, eald eþelweard* (lines 2209b–10). After this, so far as we can tell from the damaged text, there are no variations of much consequence until we come to the Lament of the Last Survivor (lines 2247–66). We might expect this speech, which sets forth the emotions of the lonely wanderer, to be heavy with variation; actually the variations are few: *guðdeað–feorhbealo frecne; fæted wæge–dryncfæt deore; æfter wigfruman–hæleðum be healfe; hearpan wyn–gomen gleobeames.* It should not be surprising, however, that variation should be so little in evidence in a speech which is really an elegiac set piece, not the expression of the actual emotion of any of the personages of the poem, nor in any way significant to the action. The value of the speech, apart from its intrinsic beauty, is the contribution which it makes to the prevailingly melancholy mood of Part II.

As in Part I, so here: variation has as its principal function the revelation and illumination of emotion. Even a dragon is permitted to feel passionately—as he must, if the tale of his ravages is to carry conviction:

> Wæs þæs wyrmes wig   wide gesyne,
> nearofages nið   nean ond feorran,
> hu se guðsceaða   Geata leode
> hatode ond hynde;   hord eft gesceat,
> dryhtsele dyrnne   ær dæges hwile.
> Hæfde landwara   lige befangen,
> bæle ond bronde;   beorges getruwode,
> wiges ond wealles;   him seo wen geleah. (2316 ff.)

There is substantival variation in *wyrmes wig–nearofages nið;* the following clause repeats the sense in different structure. *Bæle ond bronde* varies *lige*. The other sequences are enumerations rather than variations.

These lines state the motivation for Beowulf's expedition against the dragon: he undertakes his last exploit, as he had ventured against the monsters of the mere, not from any selfish motive, but to defend a people. The burning of his hall would certainly supply a strong personal motive; but it is secondary. The terms *sylfes ham–bolda selest–gifstol Geata* (2325b–27a) are something less than a true variation: though they have the same referent, they really constitute an enumeration of the functions and qualities of the hall.

The first really complex variations in Part II appear in the lines which describe Beowulf's state of mind when he learns of the dragon's ravages, and makes his preparations for battle. In this passage the first variation is purely emotional: *hreow on hreðre–hygesorga mæst* (line 2328); the second is *Wealdende–ecean Dryhtne* (2329b–30b). The following lines, in which the death of both combatants is forecast, are rather heavy with variation: *leoda fæsten–eorðweard ðone; guðcyning–Wedera þeoden; wigendra hleo–eorla dryhten; holtwudu–lind; lændaga–worulde lifes* (2333–43). Beowulf's contempt for the dragon is likewise expressed in variations (lines 2345 ff.).

This exposition of Beowulf's emotions is followed by the second of four accounts of Hygelac's death, introduced as 'not the least' of Beowulf's experiences of perilous fights. Its immediate function is to account for the hero's want of fear; but—as I shall show in a later chapter—its role is one of much greater importance: Hygelac's significance in the poem is much larger than his single appearance in person would lead us to expect. Accordingly in these lines his name is followed by a threefold variation upon it: *Geata dryhten–freawine folca–Hreðles eafora.*

The explanation of Beowulf's fearlessness—his invariable success in battle—is stated again, briefly and in general terms, in another variation (lines 2397–99a):

> Swa he niða gehwane genesen hæfde,
> sliðra geslyhta, sunu Ecgðiowes,
> ellenweorca, oð ðone anne dæg...

It appears once more at the opening of Beowulf's first speech in Part II (lines 2426 ff.); but in Beowulf's mouth it ceases to be justification of confidence, and becomes occasion for reminiscence. For though he remains fearless, he is no longer confident: his change of mood is prepared for in the account of his progress with his men toward the scene of battle. Premonition of death has touched the invincible hero; its coming is foreshadowed in the lines which describe the advance upon the dragon's lair:

> . . . . . .   He [the guide] ofer willan giong
> to ðæs ðe he eorðsele   anne wisse,
> hlæw under hrusan   holmwylme neh,
> yðgewinne;   se wæs innan full
> wrætta ond wira.   Weard unhiore,
> gearo guðfreca   goldmaðmas heold
> eald under eorðan;   næs þæt yðe ceap
> to gegangenne   gumena ænigum.
> Gesæt ða on næsse   niðheard cyning,
> þenden hælo abead   heorðgeneatum,
> goldwine Geata.   Him wæs geomor sefa,
> wæfre ond wælfus,   wyrd ungemete neah,
> se ðone gomelan   gretan sceolde,
> secean sawle hord,   sundur gedælan
> lif wið lice . . .   (2409b–23a)

The referents of the variations here are: the dragon's lair (*eorðsele–hlæw under hrusan*); the surging sea near which it stood (*holmwylme–yðgewinne*); the dragon lurking within it (*weard unhiore–gearo guðfreca*); Beowulf (*niðheard cyning–goldwine Geata*); the impending attack upon Beowulf's life by Fate, expressed in clausal variations. So far as we can judge, the shift in Beowulf's mood from confidence of victory to that state which can only be called feyness is induced by his contemplation of the scene itself, and his awareness of the terror lurking within the solitary mound by the sea. The oppression of the landscape, and understanding of the peril which it harbors, affect the hero's spirit. This is interesting: the ghastly scenery of the Haunted Mere had not so deeply shaken the young Beowulf; but now he has premonitions of doom. Behind these physical manifestations of danger lies the potency of Fate, which uses them to cast the shadow of death upon his spirit.

Throughout Beowulf's long monologue (lines 2426–2537), variations are scattered rather thinly; they appear in the opening lines slightly, in the brief account of Herebeald's death; and in the lines in which the hero recalls the vengeance he had taken upon Dæghrefn for the slaying of Hygelac (2501–27a). Two threads—one bright, one sombre—intertwine to form the fabric of this speech: that of Beowulf's valiant exploits in the past and his present resolution to confront the dragon bravely; and that of the deaths of his beloved kinsmen. The first flashes for a moment in lines 2426–27a, only to be overlaid by the second in 2427b; the second then prevails until line 2490; the intervening 64 lines recall with tender regret the tragic or heroic deaths of Herebeald, Hrethel, and Hæthcyn, and enclose the beautiful parable of the old warrior mourning for his hanged son. The two threads combine in a contrasting pattern in lines 2490–2508a, in which Beowulf's love and loyalty to Hygelac, and the vengeance which he exacted for his uncle's death, are equally stressed. His remembrance of the slaying of Dæghrefn brings the bright thread of valor into dominance:

> '. . . . . . Nu sceall billes ecg,
> hond ond heard sweord ymb hord wigan';

and this thread remains dominant in the pattern to the end of the monologue.

This speech is sentimental—in the best sense of the word—rather than emotional: the emotions recalled, however poignant when bitter events evoked them, are now recollected in tranquillity. It is not surprising, therefore, that variation is scattered and light; the more noteworthy instances cluster about these referents: Beowulf's early combats (*guðræsa–orleghwila,* lines 2426b–27a); the memory of Hrethel (*sinca baldor–freawine folca,* 2428b–29a); the dead Herebeald (*hyne–his freawine–his mæg,* 2437–39); the invasion of the Svear after Hrethel's death (*synn ond sacu–wroht–herenið hearda,* 2472–74a); Beowulf's vengeance upon Dæghrefn. The variations on this last theme express two referents: the necklace given to Beowulf by Wealhtheow and worn by Hygelac in his last fight (*ða frætwe–breostweorðunge*), and Dæghrefn himself (*Huga cempan–*

cumbles hyrde–æþeling, 2502b–06a). From this point to the end of the speech variations are still fewer: they concern Beowulf's thanes; his sword; the impending combat with the dragon in its potentiality of death for the hero. If the speech is exceptional in the rarity of its variations, the concepts expressed in variational form are those most important in the mind of Beowulf and, for the audience, most evocative.

There is a sequence of rather simple variations in the speech in which Wiglaf exhorts his comrades to come to Beowulf's aid: nearly all are concentrated in lines 2633–48a. Their members emphasize the generous gifts which Beowulf had given his retainers, his own excellence as king and friend, and his need of help against the dragon—the essential elements in Wiglaf's appeal. The force of the young thane's feeling expresses itself admirably in his stress upon those considerations which should induce his companions to defend their lord to the death; and these are expressed in variations. On the other hand, Wiglaf's denunciation of the cowardly thanes after Beowulf's death contains very few variations: *maðmas–eoredgeatwe* (lines 2865b–66a); *healsittendum–þegnum* (2868a–69a); *God–sigora Waldend* (2874b–75a); *fleam–domleasan dæd* (2889b–90a). This is the only emotional passage in the poem in which expression of feeling is too intense for variation: Wiglaf's contempt bursts the bounds of form and erupts at the end in one of the most direct and passionate sentences in Old English poetry:

'. . . . . .   Deað bið sella
eorla gehwylcum   þonne edwitlif!'

There is much more variation in the speech of the Messenger. This is a singularly meaty passage: it brings together, in thoroughly explicit statement, all that has been implicit throughout the second part of the poem. It announces to the people Beowulf's victory and death; it predicts invasion by the Svear and the destruction of the Geatish nation; it motivates this forecast by recalling the fall of Hygelac and the war in which Hæthcyn and Ongentheow fell; and it gives instructions for Beowulf's funeral. All this is directly and vigorously set forth, and its significance is immediately apparent.

Through much of the speech, and most obviously in its conclusion, there is both warmth of emotion and irony; and here (lines 3007–27) the variations eloquently reveal the feelings of the speaker.

The last considerable use of variation in the poem appears in lines 3110–33: a passage which introduces and reports Wiglaf's last speech and narrates the plundering of the hoard. Here we find the variations *byre Wihstanes–hæle hildedior; hæleða–boldagendra; hie–folcagende; gled–wonna leg; stræla storm–sceft; dracan–wyrm; wég niman–flod fæðmian.*

Some looser variations cluster near the end of the poem: *Hi on beorg dydon beg ond siglu–forleton eorla gestreon eorðan healdan; wordgyd wrecan–ymb wer sprecan; eahtodan eorlscipe–ellenweorc demdon* (3163–74a). These variations express naturally and warmly the deep grief of the Geats for their lord's death.

The praise bestowed upon Beowulf by his thanes in the last three lines of the poem is cast not in the form of variation, but in an eloquent enumeration of his virtues. Three of the four terms are very close to one another in meaning: *manna mildust, mon(ðw)ærust, leodum liðost.* I take the first superlative as meaning 'most liberal of men': although *milde* has the sense of 'liberal' only rarely in Old English texts, its Old Norse and Old High German cognates commonly have this meaning, which survives in Danish *gavmild,* Swedish *givmild.* The marked emphasis upon the hero's gentler qualities is significant: it is quite as much in his protectiveness and love for lord and people as in his valor that the heroic virtue of Beowulf resides.

In both parts of the poem there are many variations which have no other function than that of an ornament of style. Variation had become a conventional figure in Old English poetry; this accounts for its "ubiquity." But in *Beowulf,* to a degree and with a power and richness unmatched in any other poem, it becomes an instrument of vividness and beauty; it lends force and eloquence to the expression of emotion; it is used to emphasize those moments of feeling most productive of action, or those emotions or situations in themselves most dramatic. One has only to compare the variations in *Beowulf* with those in any other poem to see how consciously and imaginatively the epic poet manages the device. In Old Saxon poetry variation is so abundant that it becomes colorless; in *Brunanburh* it is almost constant and mechanical; in *Genesis* it rarely rises above the commonplace. Perhaps the author of *Andreas* comes closer to the poet of *Beowulf* in his variational effects; but he quite lacks the magnificence of *Beowulf,* and there is in his work none of that pervasive texture which variation achieves in the first part of the epic. The use of variation to mark the dominant mood, the salient and productive elements in a significant situation, and to link the situation with that which precedes or follows, is unique in *Beowulf.*

With respect to variation, then, the poet of *Beowulf* developed the inherited techniques of poetic convention in new and nonconventional directions. He did so, in a sense, under compulsion—the compulsion of a new and difficult task. He had to construct a heroic poem on the grand scale, in the traditional manner and with traditional matter. There were no sufficient native models from which he could learn how to create a structure, to organize and shape a long and moving narrative. He may have learned something from the *Aeneid;*[9] but not much in the matter of style, for the elements of his style descended to him from Germanic antiquity. Quite obviously he applied an original and powerful intelligence, and a rich sensitiveness, to the development of the potentialities of those traditional elements which, in the hands of older scops, had resembled the effects of "a worker in mosaic, placing in new combinations pieces ready to his hand."

◇ ◇ ◇

The foregoing chapters have considered the major categories of content-words in the vocabulary of *Beowulf,* not as items in a glossary, but as the major stuff of the language of poetry. We have looked at them as the *specific* language of poetry, differing from that of prose now in dignity, now in figurative content, now in their connotations and associations. We have observed certain principles gov-

[9] See T. B. Haber, *A Comparative Study of the Beowulf and the Aeneid* (Princeton University Press, 1931); R. W. Chambers, *Beowulf: An Introduction* (2d ed.; Cambridge University Press, 1932), pp. 121–128; Fr. Klaeber, "Die christlichen Elemente im *Beowulf,*" *Anglia,* XXXV (1911), pp. 111–136, 249–270, 453–482, XXXVI (1912), pp. 169–199; and Brandl's study in Paul's *Grundriss,* for the best discussions of the possible relationship between *Beowulf* and the *Aeneid.*

erning their use: notably, periphrasis, substitution, and variation. We have seen these words—simplices as well as compounds and combinations—functioning in connected lines and passages. We have, moreover, sought to look behind the word and the word-group to the image, the figure, to discover the poet's imagination at work. We have seen one thing clearly: the language of *Beowulf,* making heavy use of traditional formulas, is yet by no means "totally formulaic."

The formulaic element in *Beowulf* is indeed large: it extends beyond the selection or the formation of words into the patterns of word-groups, occasionally of verses, now and then of lines or short groups of lines. This is the inevitable consequence of the poet's undertaking to compose a heroic poem in the vernacular. We are grateful to Magoun for bringing to our attention the pervasiveness of this traditional and formal element in the language of the poem. But it is much more significant that, both quantitatively and qualitatively, the language of *Beowulf* is something other and more than formulaic: the majority of its compound content-words—the principal element of its poetic diction—are not to be found in any other poem.

It is equally significant that, as these words combine in the common figures of variation, enumeration, and progression, they assume power and beauty, and are used with a precision, a vividness, and an eloquence not to be discovered in other poems. In fine, the poet of *Beowulf,* like Homer, was by no means independent of formula, but was its master and not its servant. Nowhere else in Old English do we find such splendor of language; its wealth and sureness attest that *Beowulf* is the work, not of an illiterate 'singer,' but of a great literary artist, dominating, expanding, and transcending the limits of the form in which he elected to compose.

III

THE STRUCTURE AND THE UNITY OF BEOWULF

The poem of *Beowulf,* Klaeber tells us, "consists of two distinct parts joined in a very loose manner and held together only by the person of the hero." Like W. P. Ker, Klaeber finds some reason to regard the second part as a late-conceived sequel to the first, rather than as integral with it in the poet's original plan.[1]

J. R. R. Tolkien, on the other hand, maintains that the structure of the poem, "simple and static, solid and strong," is "not really difficult to perceive, if we look to the main points, the strategy, and neglect the many points of minor tactics. We must dismiss, of course, from mind the notion that *Beowulf* is a 'narrative poem,' that it tells a tale or intends to tell a tale sequentially . . . the poem was not meant to advance, steadily or unsteadily. It is essentially a balance, an opposition of ends and beginnings. In its simplest terms it is a contrasted description of two moments in a great life, rising and setting; an

[1] Klaeber's edition, pp. li, cvii; Ker, *Epic and Romance* (2d ed.; London, 1922), pp. 90, 117, 160–161.

elaboration of the ancient and intensely moving contrast between youth and age, first achievement and final death." Tolkien has won the assent of R. W. Chambers; and his view of the structure of the poem has received the weighty approval of Kemp Malone: "More striking is the originality of *Beowulf* in structure.... The two main parts balance each other admirably, exemplifying and contrasting as they do the heroic life in youth and age."[2]

Tolkien's symbolical interpretation, moreover—lately challenged by T. M. Gang and ably defended by Adrien Bonjour,—supplies us with a new and pleasing theory of the unity of the poem. Chambers' tribute is well deserved: "Towards the study of *Beowulf* as a work of art, Professor Tolkien has made a contribution of the utmost importance."[3] Whether or not we accept Tolkien's symbolism, he is certainly right with respect to the structure; and matters which he may have regarded as "points of minor tactics" clearly indicate that the poet was aware of the problems of unity posed by his balanced structure, and elaborated a carefully considered and effective design for the whole.

The poem seems to break in two only if we think of it exclusively in terms of its main action. At the end of Part I we leave the hero in his uncle Hygelac's court, a young champion who has done glorious deeds in Denmark, and whose loyal love for Hygelac is warmly returned; at the beginning of Part II we find him an old man, about to crown his own fifty-year reign with a final heroic sacrifice. The breach of continuity is not adequately bridged—indeed, it is made all the more apparent—by the brevity and swiftness of the transitional passage (lines 2200–10a) at the beginning of Part II. Obviously, if he had wished, the poet might have gone far to bridge this gap: whether or not he had traditional basis for any exploits of his hero during the fifty-year reign, he surely knew—for in lines 2354–96 he tells us—of Beowulf's gallant stand in Frisia, his slaying of Dæghrefn

[2] Tolkien, "Beowulf: The Monsters and the Critics," *Proceedings of the British Academy,* XXII (1936), pp. 271–272; Chambers, *Man's Unconquerable Mind* (London, 1939), pp. 68–69; Malone, "The Old English Period," in *A Literary History of England,* ed. Albert C. Baugh (New York and London, 1948), Bk. I, Pt. I, p. 94.

[3] Gang, "Approaches to *Beowulf,*" *Review of English Studies,* N.S., III (1952), pp. 1–12; Bonjour, "Monsters Crouching and Critics Rampant," *PMLA,* LXVIII (1953), pp. 304–312; Chambers, *op. cit.* (note 2, *supra*), p. 68.

and his escape, his refusal of the crown, his protection of the boy-king Heardred, and his expedition against Onela. This is God's plenty; and it is exactly the kind of stuff of which heroic lays were made. The poet could have made much of all this if he had wished; and he might easily have accounted for the long reign without revealed incident as the direct result of the power won by Beowulf in his alliance with Eadgils and through the defeat of Onela. Indeed, he seems to have conceived it so: for Beowulf, as he lies dying, asserts that 'there has not been a king of any neighboring people who has dared approach me with weapons' (lines 2733b–35).

If we compare the treatment, in *Grettissaga,* of the Icelandic outlaw's fight against the trolls of the waterfall with Beowulf's triumphs over Grendel and his dam, we see at once how capable our poet was of transforming into noble epic narrative the thinner stuff of folk-tale. How much more, then, might he have made of the hero's deeds in those middle years, from his valiant fight in Frisia through his magnanimous service to Heardred, and his retaliation for Heardred's death! He preferred to present them in a summary of intervening action; and this must have been his deliberate choice.

What determined that choice was evidently his judgment as an artist—a sound judgment; for to have treated these intervening events at length would have been to destroy his calculated balance, the exemplification of the heroic ideal in its two contrasted and most meaningful stages—first and last—of his hero's life. We are forever indebted to Tolkien for his perception of this. The poet wisely elected to subordinate, but *not* to sacrifice, such record as tradition gave him of his hero's exploits in the wars of peoples, and to use as his major theme the victories over monsters too formidable for any other champion to encounter. Through these he has revealed to us the matchless young hero, wise and loyal, brave and strong, beyond the measure of other men; and on the other hand, the old man still mightiest, facing certain death with unshrinking fortitude to save his people from the fury of the dragon. The sacrificial and triumphant death of Beowulf derives its meaning from this contrast. Had the poet stuffed his story with Beowulf's conquests of mortal foes, the incomparable "opposition of ends and beginnings" would have been lost: we should have gained a kind of English *chanson de geste,* and lost the world's noblest *Heldenleben.*

The poet carefully reinforces and points his "opposition of ends and beginnings": at the end of each part he has summed up the character and the *ethos* of his hero as revealed in the preceding narrative. Beowulf's loyalty to his lord, readiness to help the distressed, and magnanimity are emphasized in the fifty-five lines with which Part I concludes; his matchless courage despite the weight of years, his generosity and kindness to his followers, his devotion to his people, and his desire to deserve the esteem of men are expressed in the comment of Wiglaf and the Messenger in Part II, and in the eulogy uttered by his bereaved retainers as they perform his funeral rites. Most appropriately, the author places in Beowulf's own mouth the just and modest appraisal of his life: 'I have ruled this people fifty winters; there has been no king among the neighboring nations who has dared approach me with weapons, to threaten me with terror. I have awaited my appointed destiny in my own homeland, have held my own well; I have not sought strife, nor sworn oaths unrighteously. For all this, though sick with mortal wounds, I can rejoice; for the Ruler of Men will have no cause to reproach me with murder of kin when my life departs from the body.' (Lines 2732–43a.)

Herein lies the only *advance:* in the first part of the poem Beowulf has been presented as the ideal retainer and champion; in the second, he is the ideal king. In his passage from the lesser role to the greater, his heroic virtues inevitably find larger, though similar, modes of expression. We do not see his temper change, or his character develop: we see them reveal themselves appropriately and consistently in every action and situation.

In a heroic poem so conceived and constructed as "an opposition of ends and beginnings," the person of the hero must provide the essential bond between the balanced parts. It is so in the *Iliad,* the structure of which is very different from that of *Beowulf:* it is the person of Achilles through which the inner unity is maintained. But the hero functions within a very complex action, which must not be allowed to escape his domination. Therefore Homer confines all the action within the period of the wrath and reconciliation of Achilles: the fortunes of all the Greeks and Trojans depend upon *his* action or inaction, so that we feel the portent of his spirit behind all that is said or done; all that occurs falls within the few days of the wrath and in the period immediately following its resolution. The fate of Troy lies in the heart of Achilles, and is decided with the death of Patroclus.

There is no such unity of time or place in the *Odyssey;* though here also the resourceful, indomitable hero makes himself continuously felt. The structure of the poem arises out of the person of the hero: all the sorrows and wanderings of Odysseus result from a single act of his—the blinding of Polyphemus; and the story is brought together as Odysseus himself tells his toils and buffetings to Alcinous and the Phaeacian court. The resolution comes as the direct consequence of this narration by the hero; and in that moment the poet makes his hero appear to Homer's audience at his greatest and most sympathetic, through the eyes of the Phaeacian audience of Odysseus himself.

The nature of the main action of *Beowulf,* split as it is by a time-gap of more than fifty years, confronted its poet with a problem more difficult than Homer had to face. Beowulf's return home after his victories in Denmark, and the beautiful scene at the Geatish court, successfully avert a breach of the unity of place; but the very need to maintain a calculated balance compelled discontinuity of action. But it is only the main plot which suffers discontinuity; the action of the subplot is continuous, and is made, in all its parts, to pivot upon a single historical event. This event has the most decisive effect upon the hero's career, and upon the fates both of his people and of the Danes. It is through the poet's management of the death of Hygelac, and of Beowulf's relations to Hygelac, that the effect of discontinuity in the main action is overcome, and unity achieved.

I think that Klaeber—who has seen quite clearly the pertinence and the effectiveness of the legendary "episodes" in the first part of *Beowulf*—has failed to perceive the significance of the historical traditions which occupy so much of the second part. He thinks of these as "a little too much in evidence"; he feels that they "retard the narrative . . . rather seriously" (pp. liii–liv).

Now these historical stories are not episodes, at least not in the same sense as the tale of Finn and Hengest, of Sigemund, or of Offa and Thryð. They have a function much deeper and more vital than the mere supplying of background and setting. Unlike most of the episodes of Part I, they are conceived as falling, not in a heroic age anterior to the events of the poem, but within the hero's lifetime and personal observation or experience. Though they are more "in evidence" in Part II, they are present, and important, in Part I as well. Although Beowulf is not thought of as participating in all the events concerned in them, they all have intense and immediate meaning for him; they affect his life and the destiny of his people. They are, moreover, carefully distributed: in Part I we find historical stories dealing with the fates of the Danes; in Part II, historical stories of the wars between Geats and Svear.

They are, indeed, an essential part of the drama of the hero's life; they deal with situations and relationships which the poet had scarcely less at heart than he had the monster-quellings of the main action. It has been observed repeatedly, and by no one more acutely than by Klaeber,[4] that Beowulf is a hero of finer mold and nobler spirit than other champions of Germanic story; that he lives and dies as the selfless protector of those who suffer beyond their power to resist or to bear. In all this he has God's help; in the triumphant monster-slayings of Part I—as the poet tells us plainly—God, and the hero's courage, averted fate.

But at the very beginning of Part II, in the first twelve lines, we are made aware that doom impends over the hero and his people: the season of youth and conquest is long past. A theme which had been sounded in Part I now becomes dominant, and brings to our full understanding the nature of the poet's conception of his hero. It is more than the death of Beowulf which constitutes the tragedy of Part II, and so of the whole work: in death he is victorious; and he is old enough, and sufficiently full of honors, to die happily. His tragedy is that he dies in vain—indeed, that his death brings in its train the overthrow of his people.

[4] Edition, pp. l-li, cxviii, cxx–cxxi.

For the poet clearly conceives Beowulf, the noble champion and happy warrior unconquerable in personal encounter, as born to fight a losing battle against destiny. He has saved the Danes from the kin of Grendel, and he saves his own people from the dragon; but in each exploit all he has accomplished is the postponement of their destruction. Part I divulges, by skillful implication, the failure of the alliance between Danes and Geats which Beowulf and Hrothgar had hoped to promote: because of its failure, civil war will bring about the murder of Hrethric (and presumably that of Hrothgar as well), and in due course the fall of Hrothulf and the extinction of the Danish kingdom.[5]

Part II reveals the stages by which the power of the Geats declines through a succession of conflicts and the fall of kings, until only Beowulf remains to save them from conquest. When he dies, their last hope perishes with him. And so, justly, in Part II the allusions to fate (*Wyrd*) are to a power which God is no longer concerned to forestall, and which sweeps away both the hero and his nation.

The historical traditions which so deeply interested the poet do not impede the action; they are part of it. The downfall of the Danish and Geatish kingdoms, and Beowulf's involvement in the tragedies of nations, constitute the matter of the subplot. No one has failed to see how steadily and specifically Beowulf's last fight and death are related to the ruin of the Geats; but it has not been fully perceived how significantly this relation parallels Beowulf's frustrated hope of saving Hrethric and the integrity of Shielding rule. The ultimate and impelling cause of both national catastrophes, in the poet's eyes, was a historical event: the defeat and death of Hygelac in Frisia.

Beowulf's qualities of mind and heart, no less than those of body, are established before he is first required to act before our eyes. They

[5] Although the poet's allusions to the dynastic quarrels of the Shieldings (lines 1013–19; 1162b–68a; 1180b ff.; 1219–31) concern only Hrothulf's usurpation and the murder of Hrethric, he and his audience must have known of, and borne in mind, the later attack by Heoroweard (Hjörvarðr) on Hrothulf (Hrólf Kraki). This was certainly Chambers' view: see his *Beowulf: An Introduction*, pp. 29–30, 426–429, 448. It is, moreover, possible (I should think probable) that—as Chambers suggested in his revision of A. J. Wyatt's edition (*Beowulf with the Finnsburg Fragment*, Cambridge University Press, 1914, note to lines 82–85)—lines 82b-83a are an allusion to the burning of Hrólf's hall by Hjörvarðr, as lines 83b–85 allude to the fight at Heorot between Ingeld and the Danes under Hrothgar and Hrothulf.

are fixed and constant; they govern, and are exhibited with complete consistence in, all that he says and does. This consonance between the man and all his actions, in youth and age, in life or death, establishes the inner unity of his *Heldenleben;* and it is through the steady exhibition of those qualities in him which impel his actions and speak in his words that the heroic ideal is so admirably illustrated throughout the poem. It is delightful to observe how pellucidly Beowulf's character discloses itself on first meeting: not only to the audience, but to the personages of the poem—to the Captain of the Shore, to Wulfgar, Hrothgar, and Wealhtheow. It is this recognition of the character of the man that makes it possible for the Danes so easily to accept this foreigner as their champion. The surest evidence of his transparent nobility is Wealhtheow's appeal to him to protect her sons.

His selfless loyalty is exhibited in Part I in the scene at Hygelac's court after the return from Denmark. Early in Part II, it is illustrated most finely in the poet's summary of the events intervening between Hygelac's death and Beowulf's accession to the throne: through his rejection of the crown and his protection of Heardred. This is the point of transition between the hero's role as retainer and his role as king. When the action of Part II begins, the devoted thane has become the devoted monarch, all of whose acts are motivated by his love for his people and by his recollection of their rulers who had been his kinsmen. Through all that has changed, the heart of Beowulf has not changed; and this constitutes the binding unity of the poem.

His heroic qualities—that is, the sum of all those qualities which make him what he is, not merely matchless strength and courage—are displayed most beautifully and significantly in his personal relationships. These are the mainspring and the inspiration of his actions. The most important of all these relationships, from first to last, is that with his uncle Hygelac.

Although Hygelac appears in person only once, the poet manages to make him almost constantly felt throughout the poem. The hero himself is first mentioned not by name, but as *Higelaces þegn;* this, and *mæg Higelaces,* are the most frequent substitutions for the name *Beowulf* in Part I. Hygelac's name occurs 55 per cent as often as Beowulf's in Part I, and 69 per cent as often in Part II, where the requirements of alliteration do not materially affect its frequency.

More significantly, both the poet and his hero seem almost constantly preoccupied with Hygelac. In six of Beowulf's fifteen speeches Hygelac is mentioned tenderly and with deep affection; the poet also several times affirms or strongly suggests their mutual love. The story of Hygelac's last raid and death is told four times (once in Part I, three times in Part II)—more often than any other event; it is also briefly announced at the beginning of Part II. Each of the four accounts occurs at a highly dramatic moment; each has its peculiar emphasis, tone, and function.

Klaeber reminds us that here, and elsewhere as well, "different parts of a story are sometimes told in different places, or substantially the same incident is related several times from different points of view" (pp. lvii–lviii). This is a favorite narrative device of our poet's, not unlike the recurrence of a theme in music. But the exceptional prominence of the theme of Hygelac's death in *Beowulf,* the dramatic character of its use, and the emotion with which it is charged, justify us in regarding it as the equivalent of what we know in music as the *Leitmotiv.*

The poet's *Leitmotiv* was evoked by his concern for that balanced structure which Tolkien so clearly discerned. The young Beowulf is the hero as loyal thane; the old dragon-slayer is the hero as devoted monarch. And he was both these things because he was Hygelac's nephew. It was Hygelac's death which led to the overthrow of two peoples, both of whom Beowulf was concerned to save. It is Hygelac who supplies the *Leitmotiv,* which is the interwoven harmony of Hygelac's death and Beowulf's love for him.

Indeed, the poet makes much more of Hygelac, and of his relationship with Beowulf, than the main plot requires. Nothing in the *action* of Part I depends upon this relationship; only in Part II, in which the main action unfolds against the background of the Geatish wars, does Beowulf's kinship to Hygelac visibly affect his career. If the poet had presented it less richly, and had explained Beowulf's accession to the throne by a single statement of Hygelac's death, the main action could have been related quite as lucidly.

But so could the action of the *Odyssey* have been told without extensive treatment of the voyage of Telemachus; and the fortunes of its hero are not affected directly by the Greek poet's warm delineations of Nestor, Helen, and Menelaus. Both *Beowulf* and the *Odyssey* derive their main plots from folk-tale; and as W. P. Ker has said, "it is difficult to give individuality or epic dignity to commonplaces of this sort."[6] The poets were as conscious of this difficulty as the modern critics. The author of *Beowulf,* like Homer, recognized the necessity of grounding his hero's great actions firmly in place and time, and giving them emotional and ethical value through association with events and personages familiar and significant to the audience.

Indeed, our English poet goes beyond Homer in the constancy and purposefulness of his use of his hero's personal relations. It was not enough that Beowulf should display unequaled strength and courage in his victories over formidable monsters: the value of these exploits must be enhanced by the revelation of his deep and emotionally justified concern for those in whose interest he fought. Moreover, the demonstrations of his physical power and valor do not in themselves suffice to give Beowulf the roundness, the moral dimensions, and the human warmth of an epic hero. It is loyalty and unselfishness that make him unique as a hero, and constitute the essence of his heroic personality. These nobler attributes are exhibited—as they must be—in his relations with the other human personages of the poem: with Hrothgar and Wealhtheow; and most notably and constantly with Hygelac.

His associations with all the other persons of Part I (except, briefly, with Hygd) necessarily terminate with the close of the action of the first part; but his love and loyalty to his uncle rule his heart throughout his life; and Hygelac lives on to the end in both the poet's and Beowulf's recollection. Indeed, Hygelac dead is almost more alive than Hygelac living: nowhere is the poet so careful to express the impact of Beowulf's love for him upon the hero's emotions and actions as in the first two of the three reports of Hygelac's fall in Part II.

Outside the climate of the mutual love between these two, Beowulf

[6] *Epic and Romance,* p. 165.

would be little more than the monster-queller and marvelous swimmer of folk-tale. All the acts and events of his quasi-historical role in the epic flow from his relation to his uncle. It was as Hygelac's kinsman that he confidently pledged his own aid, and the military resources of the Geats, to Hrothgar and Hrethric; that he fought mightily in Hygelac's defense, and avenged him, in Frisia; that thereafter he refused the crown, acted as Heardred's protector, and as Eadgils' ally sought vengeance for Heardred; and that he himself became king. These details of his career are all revealed in direct connection with the first, and in the second and third accounts of Hygelac's fall.

The first report of Hygelac's end is given in the context of the feast in Heorot after Beowulf's victory over Grendel. Wealhtheow, who has perceived Hrothulf's ambition and is fearful for her sons, makes a moving appeal to Hrothulf's gratitude and loyalty. Then, knowing that conscience may weigh less than a crown, she turns to Beowulf, gives him a precious circlet, and asks his protection for her children. He withholds his answer until the hour of his departure; then (lines 1822–39) he promises his own aid, and Hygelac's military support, to Hrothgar against any foe, and offers Hrethric asylum at the Geatish court. That this speech and Hrothgar's answer (lines 1855–65) constitute an offer, and an acceptance, of a firm military alliance, is plain enough. If all had gone as Beowulf expected, Hrethric's life and crown could have been saved; and with a king who owed both to Geatish help once on the Danish throne, the Geats in turn might have had Danish aid against the Svear. But the poet's audience knew that Hrethric perished, and that Hrothulf usurped the crown; and the poet could not reverse the course of history. Therefore he carefully makes it plain, *before* Beowulf offers his support, that the Geats, though powerful at the moment of Beowulf's pledge, will be too weak to aid Hrothgar or Hrethric effectively in their hour of need. He has done this by telling us, immediately after Wealhtheow gives Beowulf the circlet, and just before her appeal to him, that Hygelac wore 'that neck-ring' on his last expedition, in which he and his host were destroyed. Hygelac's fall brings in its train Hrothulf's triumph and Hrethric's death; and with Hrothulf on the Danish throne, the Geats will be left isolated against the Svear.

The dramatic irony is deliberate and sharp. Against the major theme of Beowulf's triumph and the joy of the Danes in their deliverance from Grendel, there runs (to use Lawrence's figure) the counterpoint[7] of the tragedy of the Shieldings, which Beowulf confidently but vainly hopes to avert. This scene in Heorot, and its continuation in the last dialogue between Beowulf and Hrothgar, represent the poet's highest achievement in dramatic invention. Utilizing the known tradition that Geatish forces supported Hrethric in his unsuccessful resistance to Hrothulf, he avails himself of the traditional recollection of Hygelac's fall not only to account for Hrothulf's success and the future weakness of the Geats, but also to illustrate Beowulf's personal relations with Hygelac. The hero's last words to Hrothgar display his complete trust in Hygelac's support for whatever course of action he may propose. The poet's audience, recognizing the justice of this confidence, nevertheless knew, in this moment of recognition, that Hygelac's death would make it meaningless. It is grounded in the mutual love between Beowulf and his uncle, which has already been demonstrated in two earlier speeches by the hero, each uttered shortly before his combat with one of the monsters of the mere. In the first (lines 435–436, 452 ff.), Beowulf swears by his hope for Hygelac's continued love and favor that he will face Grendel without weapons, and implores Hrothgar, if he should fall, to send his corselet to Hygelac. In the second (lines 1482–87), just before he plunges into the mere, he asks that, in the event of his death, the gifts given him by Hrothgar be sent to Hygelac. These words bear testimony to his dependence on his uncle's trust and affection, as well as to his own great love for Hygelac.

The long scene at Hygelac's court, with which Part I concludes, carries farther the demonstration of their love, and displays it dramatically; it confronts us with the figure of Hygelac himself; and it prepares us for the concrete and striking evidences of Beowulf's devotion to Hygelac in Part II. In this scene the Geatish king speaks once: briefly, but nobly expressing his affection for Beowulf, his painful

[7] *Beowulf and Epic Tradition*, p. 27.

anxiety for Beowulf's safety in Denmark, and his thanks to God for his nephew's safe return. Beowulf in turn conveys the fullness of his admiration and love for Hygelac through his gift of the treasures bestowed on him by Hrothgar, and in the words that accompany it: 'These, O warrior king, I desire to transmit to thee, to give unto thee gladly. All my comforts still come from thee; I have few close kinsmen, Hygelac, save thee!' (Lines 2147–51.)

The poet then dwells on Beowulf's utter loyalty to his royal uncle, and strongly asserts the close and reciprocal affection between them. The last lines of Part I emphasize Hygelac's munificence toward Beowulf, and appropriately recognize his own well-deserved rulership.

Thus, from Beowulf's first speech to Hrothgar to the end of Part I, the poet repeatedly stresses, both through the hero's mouth and in his own person as author, the beauty and strength of the bond between these two noble kinsmen. In the closing scene, moreover, he imparts to the figure of Hygelac a remarkable vividness: we see the Geatish king as a powerful and noble person, and perceive that Beowulf's admiring love for him is well deserved and ardently returned. The demonstration of this love through Beowulf's words and acts gives warmth and depth to the hero's personality, and an additional dimension to his actions. It is his strongest and most enduring emotion, and exerts its influence as long as he lives. In Part I, Hygelac is the center of Beowulf's world; in Part II, the recollection of Hygelac remains, a living, moving force, in his heart.

When the action of Part II begins, only Beowulf, out of all the persons of Part I, survives. But it is otherwise with Hygelac than with Hrothgar and Heardred: they are dead and forgotten; Hygelac lives on in our memory, and compellingly in Beowulf's. Hygelac's death has so weakened the Geats that, even with Beowulf, they are defeated by Onela. Only Beowulf stands between them and conquest. Because at last, after a fifty-year reign, he too must fall, and they with him, the second part of the poem is dark with the shadow of ineluctable doom. The aged hero is a symbol of his people: in him they live, and after him they perish.

The second narrative of Hygelac's fall occurs early in Part II (lines

2354b ff.), and stresses Beowulf's valor in Frisia, and its consequences. Hygd offered him the throne; but he would not be lord to Hygelac's son, preferring to protect his young cousin until Heardred came of age to rule. Then Heardred too fell in battle; Beowulf became king, and took measures to avenge his cousin.

Here Beowulf's loyalty and love for Hygelac are set forth objectively, through the statement of his acts. His magnanimity toward Hygelac's son is motivated not only by his sense of duty toward the boy prince, but also by that same devotion to Hygelac which impelled him to defend his uncle to the last. It is an act of piety rooted less in obligation than in undeviating love.

The third report is in Beowulf's own words, and forms part of his long monologue (lines 2426–2537) spoken just before his challenge summons the dragon from its barrow. It is much more eloquent, and more subjective, than the other accounts. The old king, about to bid his men farewell, is without fear; but he is fey: *Wyrd* is 'immeasurably nigh.' Naturally, then, his thoughts dwell on the past: he recalls his youth, his love for his grandsire Hrethel and for each prince of Hrethel's line. He recalls Herebeald's fate, Hrethel's broken heart, and the swift attack by the Svear when they learned of Hrethel's death. He recounts Hæthcyn's fall at Ravenswood, and Hygelac's vengeful victory over Ongentheow; he speaks with strong emotion of the great love he had borne Hygelac, of his uncle's favors to him, and of his own devoted service. Always he had stood before Hygelac in battle; and so he means now to stand first in fight while sword and life shall last. So it had been 'ever since before the hosts I slew Dæghrefn, champion of the Franks, with my hands; not at all was he allowed to bring the precious breast-ornament to the Frisian king, but in the fight he fell, . . . the grip of war crushed his breast, the pulsings of his heart.'

In this speech the poet lets his hero establish his place in the royal dynasty, and reveal his devotion to his kinsmen. Beowulf's reminiscences begin with a tender acknowledgment of Hrethel's loving care: 'I was seven winters old when the lord of treasures, kindly ruler of the people, received me from my father; King Hrethel protected and maintained me, gave me gifts and feasting, was mindful of kinship.

Never in life was I a whit less dear to him . . . than any of his children, Herebeald and Hæthcyn, or *my Hygelac.*' This 'my Hygelac' strikes the keynote of the speech: in recalling his kinsmen one by one, and all with deep and warm affection, Beowulf is yet thinking first and always of Hygelac. Therefore he does not need to speak his uncle's name again; when, sixty-six lines later, he declares: 'I repaid him for those treasures as occasion was granted me,' we know he is speaking of his service to Hygelac, who, living or dead, had always had his fondest love. Beowulf's loyalty and admiration for his uncle had thrice found utterance in Hrothgar's presence; they had filled his words and actions in Hygelac's hall; here they are most ardently stated at the focal point of his recollections of all his long-dead kinsmen. This speech is the strongest expression of human feeling in the whole poem; its climax is Beowulf's passionate resolve (lines 2497 ff.) to be worthy, in his last fight, of his beloved Hygelac. Old as he is, and king for fifty years, he is still, in his own heart, 'Hygelac's thane.' As Beowulf is the poet's hero, so Hygelac is Beowulf's.

The last account of Hygelac's fall (lines 2913b–21) is given briefly and objectively, by the Messenger sent by Wiglaf to announce that Beowulf and the dragon both lie dead. There will be no peace for the Geats, the Messenger predicts, once Franks, Frisians, and Svear hear of Beowulf's end: the Merovingian has had no love for the Geats since Hygelac's fateful raid. As Beowulf had done, the Messenger joins to his recollection of the catastrophe in Frisia an account of the great fight in which Hæthcyn and Ongentheow fell; but he makes much more of the battle in Ravenswood. This is proper, since it is the Svear who are soon to conquer the Geats. In the Messenger's narrative Hygelac looms large, as rescuer of Hæthcyn's broken men and conqueror of Ongentheow. This dual emphasis upon Hygelac's fall and his military greatness serves to point out that Hygelac's defeat and death were the primary cause of the decline of the Geats; and that Hygelac's overthrow of Ongentheow provided the motive, as Beowulf's end afforded the eagerly awaited opportunity, for the Svear to fall upon and crush the Geats. The poet thus underlines the tragic irony of Beowulf's death in victory over the dragon, only more immediately fatal to the people he perished to save than were Hygelac's triumph over Ongentheow and his death in Frisia.

The narratives of Hygelac's fall and of the wars between Geats and Svear are so placed, and so managed, that they lend to the dragon-fight, and to the figure of the hero as king, a reality and a meaning stronger and deeper than the hero or the narrative of Part I achieves. The poet makes us aware, in Part II, that, because of Hygelac's end, the Geats can survive as a people only while Beowulf lives; and he has shown us, one by one, the critical stages in those wars which were to destroy them. The dragon-slaying is thus completely—and justifiably—encompassed by the traditional recollection of Geatish glory and of Geatish downfall. Through the story of each clash between Geats and Svear runs a darker thread, the tale of Hygelac's fall; and these stories enclose the main action. At only one point do they interrupt it, and then most briefly: the slaying of Eanmund by Weohstan, told in twenty-three lines, is introduced to motivate Wiglaf's loyal resolve to aid Beowulf against the dragon, and to explain the provenience of Wiglaf's sword.

Part II is more than the story of Beowulf's last heroic deed and death: it is also the story of the passing of that people whose last king he is. And these two stories are inextricably fused; for the tragedy of Beowulf is the tragedy of his people.

Throughout the poem, the author places in his hero's mouth, just before each of his great exploits, a warm acknowledgment of his love for Hygelac. Love and loyalty are, indeed, Beowulf's dominant traits: the essential quality of his heroism is active, selfless *caritas.* Granted the courage and strength which any hero must possess, the constant, instinctive illustration in thought and action of loyal love toward lord and people makes of physical prowess a means to consistently noble ends. Through the pervasive and climactic representation of the relation between Beowulf and Hygelac the hero's *caritas* is most clearly and convincingly revealed. The poet has enveloped Beowulf's *Heldenleben* in the climate of his love for Hygelac; and thereby he accomplishes a satisfying fusion of the monster-slayer with the king, of the fabulous and the historical elements of the story, of subplot with main action.

This envelopment binds the two parts of the poem into an inseparable whole. The heroic ideal which Beowulf illustrates in each part, and as the embodiment of which he lives and dies, is the projection of his character in action; but it feeds on his love for Hygelac. Though he much exceeds the measure of Hygelac, he draws strength from him. The young Beowulf lays the fruits of his triumphs at his uncle's feet; the aged Beowulf, before his last fight, makes his resolve to conquer or die a tribute to Hygelac's memory. Through Hygelac's defeat and death, Fate deprived Beowulf (*hyne Wyrd fornam*, line 1205b) of the power to save Hrethric, and made the extinction of the Geatish nation inevitable once Beowulf was lost to them. Thus the hero's victories are counterpoised by defeat; and his last and greatest victory brings death and ruin. I think, with Tolkien, that the poet meant to remind us that this is life's way with men.[8] The most heroic life must close in death, as Beowulf reminded Hrothgar; he who is permitted to 'achieve some share of renown before death,' and to face his last hour with fortitude, conquers, though he perishes. And however nobly man may strive toward noble ends, unless those be God's ends, man strives in vain. But it is the courage to strive, not success, which marks and ennobles the hero.

But the poet, who, as a good Christian, meant us to perceive this, was also conscious of the pity of such success in failure. The tragic irony that is so evident in the frustration of Beowulf's confident promise of aid to Hrothgar and Hrethric is yet more pointed in Beowulf's outpouring of gratitude to God that he has been permitted to buy with his death the dragon's treasure for his people. The possession of that treasure brings with it a curse; and his people, not knowing of the curse, express their love for their dead lord by burying the treasure in his tomb. They know—for the Messenger has forecast it plainly for them—that doom is soon to fall upon themselves; and rather than reap profit from their king's death they consign the treasure to the earth with him—thereby ensuring that his last wish also is frustrated. A doomed king has died to save a doomed people; and thus the harmonious interplay of main action and subplot reaches perfect fusion in the final scenes.

[8] Tolkien, *op. cit.* (note 2, *supra*), pp. 264–265, 274; cf. p. 260.

IV

DESIGN FOR TERROR

Klaeber directs attention to "a remarkable gradation in the three great crises of the poem": Beowulf's fight with Grendel "is rather monotonous and seems altogether too short and easy to give much opportunity for excitement . . ."; his combat with Grendel's dam is so much more perilous that "only a kind of miracle saves him"; and "the dragon . . . is entirely too much for his assailant . . . the final victory is won only at the cost of the hero's own life."[1]

This amounts to a recognition that the poet had a sound sense of climax. Nevertheless Klaeber finds it "not a little remarkable that in the account of the three great fights of the hero, care has been taken to state the outcome of the struggle in advance. . . . Evidently disregard of the element of suspense was not considered a defect in story telling."[2]

[1] Edition, p. lii.—The relations of Beowulf's combats with monsters to folk-tale are most admirably discussed by W. W. Lawrence: see his paper "The Haunted Mere in *Beowulf*," *PMLA*, XXVII (1912), pp. 208–245, and *Beowulf and Epic Tradition*, pp. 175–187, 204–243. Cf. R. W. Chambers, *Beowulf: An Introduction*, pp. 62 ff., 451 ff.; and Klaeber's edition, pp. 154–155, 182–183, 185.

[2] Edition, pp. lii, lvii.

J. R. Hulbert and R. M. Lumiansky, who have advanced very significantly our understanding of the poet's procedures, do not share Klaeber's opinion that the narrative of the fight with Grendel is monotonous, unexciting, or devoid of suspense.[3] It seems to me obvious that the account of Beowulf's combats with both monsters of the mere reveals a deliberate design for terror, carefully planned and skillfully executed.

The several forecasts (lines 696 ff., 705b ff., 734 ff., and 805b ff.) of Beowulf's victory over Grendel, which Klaeber regards as destructive of suspense, are so blanketed by the oppressive sense of fear that the brief release from tension which each affords only increases the hearer's responsiveness to each succeeding shock. Suspense can be maintained without withholding all knowledge of an action's outcome until the final moment: it resides in the degree and quality of emotional tension imposed upon the listener; in the effective prolongation of the conflict between fear and hope. That conflict must engross the imagination, must tax its capacity to endure, but must never exceed its limits of toleration.[4] Too much unrelieved horror blunts the response, and induces incredulity or indifference.

Through much of the narrative that precedes Beowulf's encounter with Grendel, the bloody evidence of the ogre's power and ferocity had been piling up: approximately 170 of the first 700 lines of the poem present it in all its aspects. Grendel had ravaged Heorot for twelve years, haunting the hall each night and carrying off and devouring every Dane who lingered in it after dark. His ruthlessness and implacability are repeatedly stressed; the fearful consequences of his blood-thirst are emphasized most eloquently near the end of Hrothgar's first speech to Beowulf (lines 473–488). All this accumulated horror was vibrant in the recollection of the poet's hearers, who

[3] Hulbert, "Beowulf and the Classical Epic," *Modern Philology*, XLIV (1946), pp. 65–75; Lumiansky, "The Dramatic Audience in *Beowulf*," *Journal of English and Germanic Philology*, LI (1952), pp. 545–550.

[4] Hulbert (*op. cit.*, pp. 70–71) has an excellent discussion of suspense in *Beowulf*, and points out (p. 71) that "it is astonishingly naïve in the critics . . . to imply that . . . precognition destroys suspense. . . . But in the work of a skilful artist its use results in building suspense as to how the end will be reached, as to the motives of an action or the effect of it upon the characters, or as to some other element in the events."

had no need to exercise the "willing suspension of disbelief." For them, monsters of Grendel's kind lurked ever in the night shadows, waiting to ensnare and devour. After the repeated reports of his persecutions their nerves were stretched taut; and as Beowulf lay down to await the troll, they were subjected to fresh strain by the ominous statement of the controlled fear of the hero's men:

> Nænig heora þohte, þæt he þanon scolde
> eft eardlufan æfre gesecean,
> folc oþðe freoburh, þær he afeded wæs;
> ac hie hæfdon gefrunen, þæt hie ær to fela micles
> in þæm winsele wældeað fornam,
> Denigea leode. (691–696a)

At this point, when Grendel is merely expected, the poet offers his first assurance that Beowulf will prevail. It does not so much allay fear as it prepares the listener to experience freshly and keenly the dreadful impact of Grendel's advance on Heorot; it must have been all but forgotten in the course of the ogre's nerve-shredding progress (702b–724a).

"Some enthusiasts," Klaeber observes, "have found the threefold bell-like announcement of Grendel's approach a highly dramatic device."[5] Its purpose has been more clearly, if not fully, perceived by Miss Bartlett.[6] It is neither bell-like nor repetitive; it is a hair-raising depiction of death on the march. Its form is an extension of the variation,[7] transcending in every way the customary uses of that device. In each of the three statements of Grendel's movement toward the hall the verb *com*—the only purely repetitive element—is followed by a different infinitive of motion; the designation of the subject is also varied. Grendel's ruthless intent is implicit in the first statement (702b–703a), vigorously asserted in the second (712 ff.), and expanded into an appalling declaration of his delight in prospective

[5] Edition, p. 154.

[6] Adeline Courtney Bartlett, *The Larger Rhetorical Patterns in Anglo-Saxon Poetry* (Columbia University Press, 1935), pp. 49–50.

[7] This was pointed out by Hertha Marquardt, "Zur Entstehung des *Beowulf*," *Anglia*, LXIV (1940), pp. 152–153.

slaughter after the third (730b–734a). Three several, *distinct* stages of the action are here set forth. This is not the familiar static trick of poetic convention; it is dynamic and progressive. Each successive statement of Grendel's oncoming represents an advance in time, in forward movement, in emotional force; each shows an increase over the preceding in the use of horrific detail; each imposes increased strain upon the audience.

Grendel is first seen moving through the dark: four of the six words that announce him evoke fear: Com on *wanre niht scriðan sceadugenga* (702b–703a). Tension is then somewhat eased with the assurance that God could, if He would, thwart Grendel's purpose, and that Beowulf holds faithful vigil. Then, all at once, the monster is closer: he moves down from the mist-shrouded moor. His advance is emphasized by the vigorous verb *wod:* he strides with baleful haste and murder in his heart; he knows where the hall stands, with the knowledge of murderous experience.

Whatever comfort lies in the poet's comment (lines 718–719) that this time Grendel will meet resistance such as he has never before encountered is instantly and dreadfully stifled: Grendel reaches the hall itself, and lays hold on the door. At the touch of his palms the iron bars give way; 'meaning murder, he wrenched open the mouth of the dwelling.' He stands there, shockingly visible:

> . . . . . . Raþe æfter þon
> on fagne flor feond treddode,
> eode yrremod; him of eagum stod
> ligge gelicost leoht unfæger.
> Geseah he in recede rinca manige,
> swefan sibbegedriht samod ætgædere,
> magorinca heap. Ða his mod ahlog;
> mynte þæt he gedælde, ær þon dæg cwome,
> atol aglæca anra gehwylces
> lif wið lice, þa him alumpen wæs
> wistfylle wen. (724–734a)

As he towers there in his monstrous might, his eyes like flame, and laughter on his ugly lips, the poet once more reassures us:

> . . . . . . Ne wæs þæt wyrd þa gen,
> þæt he ma moste manna cynnes
> ðicgean ofer þa niht. (734b–736a)

Even this does not dissolve suspense; it scarcely softens the horror of the nightmare spectacle within the hall. Indeed, we are instantly plunged into horror almost unbearable:

> Né þæt se aglæca yldan þohte,
> ac he gefeng hraðe forman siðe
> slæpendne rinc, slat unwearnum,
> bat banlocan, blod edrum dranc,
> synsnædum swealh; sona hæfde
> unlyfigendes eal gefeormod,
> fet ond folma. (739–745a)

In the death of Hondscio we have one of those features of Beowulf's combats with the trolls of the mere which are generally thought to have assumed their form in the epic as a consequence of imperfect understanding, by the poet or his predecessors, of the situations and motivations of the underlying folk-tale. "Turn to the folk-tales, and the situation is clear: the younger hero had to wait until his older or more renowned companions had fought and failed."[8] This position, just or not, does not afford a reasonable basis for depreciation or undervaluation of the poet's narrative. Are we seriously to suppose that Beowulf callously permits Grendel to kill and devour his thane because the poet did not comprehend, or did not know how to control, a situation inherited—at very far remove—from folk-tale? From the aesthetic point of view, the author's comprehension of the logic of the folk-tale is unimportant; all that is relevant is the quality of the story as *he* has told it: its power to move the imagination strongly and truly.

No; we are weighing the poet's story, not the folk-tale which was its ultimate source. In the poet's story, the slaughter of Hondscio is

[8] Lawrence, *Beowulf and Epic Tradition*, p. 176.

the culminating horror in an ascending sequence, which has been carefully constructed, from the first announcement of Grendel's appearance, through the successive stages of his progress and with increasingly vivid revelations of his mounting fury, to his ghastly appearance in the hall. After all this, the poet could not permit Beowulf to come to grips with him at once. All this terror must find its climax in death; it demands a victim, lest we lose conviction of its reality. It does not matter that, in the folk-tale, the hero's companions must fall before he can attack; this is no longer folk-tale, but the poetry of art. In *Beowulf* Hondscio died so that the poet's audience might have final demonstration of the hideous power and fury of the foe whom the hero must now face. The adverbs *hraðe* and *sona* (lines 740, 743) are meant to convey the unexpected swiftness of Grendel's first attack: it was too swift to permit Beowulf's intervention.[9]

Once Beowulf seizes Grendel, the monster never regains the offensive; he struggles only to escape. At this point, as Lumiansky has shown, the poet finds new means to prolong suspense.[10] The locked combatants reel back and forth, smashing benches, shaking the very structure of the house, which resounds with fearful din. The Geats strive to help their lord; the Danes, unable to see the trend of conflict, are terrified by the tumult and by the anguished screams of Grendel. The fight now has two audiences: the Danes and Geats, who hear or behold directly; and those who, listening to the poet's lines, participate sympathetically in the sensations of the dramatic onlookers, but with clearer perception of the outcome. The poet plays upon the nerves of both audiences through the generalized effect of confused and violent movement and the frightening effects of sound. At last all strain is removed by the announcement of Beowulf's victory, as

[9] Lines 736b–738 cannot mean that Beowulf deliberately allowed Hondscio to die in order that he himself might observe Grendel's mode of attack. Such conduct would be utterly inconsistent with his character as the poet has disclosed it, and would have horrified the poet's audience. These lines must mean that Beowulf, expecting the first attack to be directed against himself, was waiting to see how Grendel would bear himself under Beowulf's sudden counterattack. *Gefaran* can mean 'conduct oneself' as well as 'proceed'; and *under* is never used in the poem in the sense of 'in the course of' (attending circumstances). This relation is expressed by the dative without preposition, e.g., *hwyder helrunan hwyrftum scriþað*, line 163.

[10] *Op. cit.* (note 3, *supra*), p. 546.

the giant's arm is torn from its socket. Grendel flees; Beowulf hangs up the arm in token of triumph.

Throughout the narrative, the forecasts of the hero's victory are almost completely overlaid by the effects of fear, until the clear statement of Grendel's mortal hurt merges with the chant of triumph (lines 815b–833a). Only the *last* of all these forecasts relieves the suspense; and it is made immediately before we are told of the tearing out of Grendel's arm. Suspense, then, is maintained until the last moment before the battle is decided.

Though the issue is not really in doubt after Grendel feels the power of Beowulf's grip, the rising horror of all that has gone before, culminating in the almost intolerable moment of Hondscio's death, extends its emotional force over the entire struggle, and thus prolongs the conflict between fear and hope. Even when Grendel's anguished howls should give us certainty, the very evidence of his imminent defeat is turned into a new source of terror through the panic it arouses among the Danes. The poet reinforces this effect by making much of the shattering impact of the combat upon the hall, which the Danes had thought too strongly built to be so shaken; and by stressing the futility of the efforts of the Geats to aid their lord against the invulnerable troll. These evidences of Grendel's awesome strength, coming as they do when the issue is almost decided, both prevent the sympathetic fear of the listener from subsiding and add to the glory of Beowulf's achievement.

The closeness of the resemblance between Beowulf's monster-slayings in Denmark and the corresponding exploits of Grettir renders their differences of special value for the study of our poet's treatment of his material; no other version of the folk-tale is sufficiently similar to be of comparable service. The more important points of contrast between *Beowulf* and *Grettissaga* are in the character of the second combat, in its setting, and in the nature of its connection with the first. Lawrence has shown that the saga preserves the primitive conception of the monster's lair: a cave behind a mountain waterfall.[11] In *Beowulf* this original conception is masked by the introduction of features of moorland, fen, and sea; the Anglo-Saxons were unfamiliar

[11] See note 1, *supra*.

with great waterfalls. Nevertheless the account of the Haunted Mere in *Beowulf* is, as Lawrence says, "one of the finest pieces of description in all Anglo-Saxon poetry."[12]

In *Beowulf* the scene is vivid and richly imagined: the poet has created a setting magnificently terrible, most appropriate to the savage adventure which it frames. Its very wealth and grouping of uncanny elements provides an atmosphere in which combat with supernatural and horrible creatures assumes an inevitable rightness. In Hulbert's words, the poet put together such details as "would arouse a feeling of gruesomeness, horror, and foreboding."[13] He presumably enriched, and certainly ordered, such descriptive detail as he found in his sources to this artistic end.

In *Grettissaga* the fight with the giant in the cave is lamely introduced and anticlimactic. The hero has no compelling reason for exploring the waterfall; he stumbles on the giant sitting in his den, and finishes him off without much trouble. The poet of *Beowulf* made his hero's second fight more perilous than the first, and gave it a logical and emotional justification admirably tight and strong. His handling of this second combat is skillfully linked with the killing of Grendel; the separation of the two fights by the long and beautifully imagined scene of the feast in Heorot lends the force of tragic contrast to the incursion of Grendel's dam and the killing of Æschere.

Deliverance from long affliction had given the Danes a new and relaxing sense of security, upon which the violence of fresh, unforeseen murder falls with greater horror. In its contrast to the slower, rising fearfulness of Grendel's approach, the ogress' swift, stealthy onslaught and instant departure, unhindered by the frantic resistance of the Danes, impose sudden, dreadful fear. The grief and despair of Hrothgar are finely represented; in face of them, the innocent irony of Beowulf's salutation imparts a shocking touch of felicitous infelicity. Entering Hrothgar's presence in ignorance of what has happened, he asks whether the king has had a good night's rest!

There is, further, most significant contrast in the circumstances of

[12] *Beowulf and Epic Tradition,* p. 183.

[13] J. R. Hulbert, "A Note on the Psychology of the *Beowulf* Poet," in *Studies in English Philology . . . in Honor of Frederick Klaeber* (University of Minnesota Press, 1929), p. 193.

the two combats: Grendel had been trapped in the hall; his dam must be sought out in her own uncanny realm. Hrothgar's account of the 'hidden land' ascribes to it every forbidding aspect of nature, and arrays these aspects to stress their terror and danger. The region is lonely, savage, the natural abode of powers of evil. The terrain protects its wicked denizens, and accords with their nature. Even the stag, pursued from afar, will die in the jaws of the hounds rather than seek refuge there. Every feature shocks the imagination; and that 'fearful wonder, fire in the flood,' deals the last shock to the rational mind. Hrothgar's speech ends with a kind of shudder:

'. . . . . .   Nu is se ræd gelang
eft æt þe anum.   Eard git ne const,
frecne stowe,   ðær þu findan miht
sinnigne secg;   sec gif þu dyrre!
Ic þe þa fæhðe   feo leanige,
ealdgestreonum,   swa ic ær dyde,
wundini golde,   gyf þu on weg cymest!'   (1376b–82)

Extending once more the principle of variation to larger narrative units, the poet reëmphasizes the fearful nature of the monsters' lair and its approaches in his account of the march to it—another exploitation of the dramatic audience. The frightening aspects of the setting are impressed upon the listener more vividly through the revelation of their impact on the Danes and Geats as they traverse the region. The climax is reached when they come suddenly upon 'mountain trees overhanging the hoary rock, a joyless wood,' with bloody, troubled water standing below—and encounter in this place of fear the head of Æschere. The dead man's head, the bloody water, the grisly creatures swimming in the mere, are features unanticipated in Hrothgar's description; they give the scene its final, unexampled terror. Even so, with sure sense for the right moment to administer shock, the poet had climaxed the horror of Grendel's coming with the ghastly dismembering and devouring of Hondscio.

The mood of dread which the poet has thus imposed upon his audience is the more successfully realized and maintained through its effect upon Beowulf, who, in traversing the haunted land, had felt its every terror. He has no fear; but he is now no longer the fully confident warrior who had said to Hrothgar:

> 'Aris, rices weard,   uton hraþe feran,
> Grendles magan   gang sceawigan.
> Ic hit þe gehate: no he on helm losaþ,
> né on foldan fæþm,   né on fyrgenholt,
> né on gyfenes grund,   ga þær he wille!' (1390–94)

His diminished confidence is shown in his careful preparations for battle—his assumption of full armor and his acceptance of Unferth's sword. This contrasts sharply with his earlier refusal to use weapons against Grendel. Clearly the poet meant to prepare his hearers for a struggle much more dangerous than that with Grendel. Beowulf's address to Hrothgar after he has armed likewise implies that he is less certain of victory than he had been before the earlier fight. Though he had then considered the possibility of death, his request that Hrothgar send his corselet to Hygelac if Grendel should prevail is far less urgent and moving than his plea to the king as he prepares to plunge into the mere:

> 'Geþenc nu, se mæra   maga Healfdenes,
> snottra fengel,   nu ic eom siðes fus,
> goldwine gumena,   hwæt wit geo spræcon,
> gif ic æt þearfe   þinre scolde
> aldre linnan,   þæt ðu me a wære
> forðgewitenum   on fæder stæle.
> Wes þu mundbora   minum magoþegnum,
> hondgesellum,   gif mec hild nime;
> swylce þu ða madmas,   þe þu me sealdest,
> Hroðgar leofa,   Higelace onsend.
> Mæg þonne on þam golde ongitan   Geata dryhten,
> geseon sunu Hrædles,   þonne he on þæt sinc starað,
> þæt ic gumcystum   godne funde
> beaga bryttan,   breac þonne moste.' (1474–87)

Thus the poet sought to arouse in his hearers a more fearful apprehension for the hero's safety in the second fight than in the first; and

Grendel's mother indeed proved the more formidable adversary. Yet, in recounting her raid on Heorot, he had told us that she was less terrible than Grendel by just so much as a woman is weaker than a warrior. Klaeber finds this inconsistent with the facts, and explains it as "an endeavor to discredit the unbiblical notion of a woman's superiority."[14]

There is no inconsistency. *In herself,* Grendel's dam *is* weaker than her son; and so she shows herself in action—weaker, yet in her lair more dangerous. It is evidence of her lesser strength that, whereas Grendel had boldly broken into Heorot and, on his first raid, killed thirty thanes, she crept stealthily into the hall and killed but one. What made her dangerous to Beowulf was the conditions under which she must be met, the chances of a struggle that must be waged on her ground. The poet's twofold description of her realm, and his emphasis on Beowulf's arming, were intended to make the audience aware of these special dangers, and to underline their terrors.

They become sharply explicit in the narrative of the fight. Beowulf must dive into the gloomy depths and swim amidst their perils, his sight blurred by the water. His foe is in her element, and sees him clearly. Before he is aware of her she seizes him, and her talons grope for his flesh. He cannot free his arms; as she drags him down, sea-beasts assail him. Yet, when they reach her subaqueous hall, where firelight and the absence of water enable him to see and he can get footing, he breaks free and brings his sword down upon her head. His blade fails; he casts it aside and grapples with her. At once his superior strength is evident: he flings her down, and is having all the best of it until he stumbles and falls. Instantly she throws herself upon him and hacks at him with her knife. His mail protects him; yet he must have died if he had not thrown her off, and through God's grace caught sight of a marvelous sword, with which he cuts off her head.

So, although Grendel's dam is weaker than Grendel, the circumstances of the fight are so shaped that Beowulf's peril is greater, his victory harder won, than in his earlier combat with her mightier son. For all her ferocity and aggressiveness, the ogress' physical strength

[14] Edition, p. 181.

would have been insufficient to give him a hard fight if, like Grendel, she had had to meet him in Heorot. It is her initial advantage, gained by seizing him unaware in the water, and his stumble and fall when victory is almost in his grasp, that almost cost him his life; at all other stages of the fight, Beowulf has her on the defensive. What gives the combat its quality of singular danger, and brings the hero close to death, is that he must fight under conditions which, at two critical moments, make it impossible for him to exert his full strength. These are purely the conditions of the setting, the unfamiliar and dangerous aspects of the mere. In the narrative of the fight the poet makes practical use of them, as he had earlier used the visible awesomeness of the perilous region to instill terror. In the whole adventure, from Hrothgar's description of the monstrous realm to, and beyond, Beowulf's victory, there is perfect coherence and artistic unity.

Here again, as in the story of the fight with Grendel, the poet plays upon his two audiences. This time he avoids any forecast of victory until Beowulf throws the ogress off and sees the magic sword: he intended the sense of the hero's deadly danger to dominate the imagination of his hearers until the moment that the means of victory, and the victorious stroke, are at hand. Beowulf rises, sees the sword, snatches it, and slays in swift and immediate sequence, so that there is virtually no forecast at all. Even after Beowulf's triumph there is still, as Lumiansky has shown,[15] a secondary suspense. The Danes and Geats, who have long awaited the issue on the brink of the mere, unable to guess the course of combat, see the water stained with blood, and believe Beowulf has perished. Sick at heart, the Danes go back to Heorot; the Geats, though without hope, remain.[16]

Like the Danes in *Beowulf,* so in *Grettissaga* the priest Steinn, whom Grettir has left to guard the rope by which he means to climb to safety, sees blood in the stream, and thinking Grettir dead, goes

[15] See note 3, *supra.*

[16] C. W. von Sydow, in his concern to prove that Beowulf's monster-quellings do not derive from the Bear's Son tale, was forced to regard the departure of the Danes from the mere as a calculated effect: convinced of Beowulf's death by the blood-stained water, they experience a dramatic revulsion of feeling when Beowulf appears in Heorot alive and victorious ("Beowulf och Bjarke," *Studier i nordisk filologi,* XIV, 3 [Helsingfors, 1923], pp. 27–28).

home. His departure is later declared by Grettir, and admitted by himself, to be a rather shabby trick. In the "Bear's Son" folk-tale the hero's companions treacherously abandon him. The poet of *Beowulf* absolves the Danes of blame: since they can be of no help to the hero, no discredit attaches to their departure. Indeed, since they suppose their champion slain, they must be thought of as anticipating further persecution by the ogress, and so have a claim upon our sympathy. The desperate loyalty of the Geats affords an opportunity for dramatic contrast with their joy and pride when Beowulf swims to the surface, bearing Grendel's head and the hilt of the magic sword:

> Eodon him þa togeanes, Gode þancodon,
> ðryðlic þegna heap, þeodnes gefegon,
> þæs þe hi hyne gesundne geseon moston. (1626–28)

This contrast is followed by a second and a third. The exultant Geats enter Heorot with Beowulf's spoils, as the Danes sit in despair. Beowulf's appearance alive is so unexpected that, for a long moment after he has announced his victory, Hrothgar is speechless. The emotional reversal imparts an almost stricken solemnity to the king's grave speech of gratitude and admonition.

This is the veritable manner of epic, of the poetry of conscious art. The moment of Hrothgar's silence[17] is like the spellbound silence of Alcinous and his court at the close of Odysseus' narrative. It derives its impressiveness, and Beowulf's exploit gains immeasurably in lustre, from the poet's lofty conception of the motives and the conduct of the Danes.

Obviously we cannot describe with confidence the precise relation of the poet's narrative to its sources, since we do not know what these sources were, or in what form they reached him. We know only that the monster-slayings of Part I derive ultimately from a folk-tale, to which "both the 'Bear's Son' story and the 'Hand and the Child'

[17] The long break between *Hroðgar maðelode* (line 1687) and the first words of the speech (line 1700) is unprecedented in the poem, and is surely intended to convey more than the king's interest in the sword-hilt. The rephrasing of the formula for speaking (*ða se wisa spræc,* line 1698b) and the parenthetical *swigedon ealle* (line 1699b) suggest that the poet was concerned to impress upon his audience the emotional shock of Beowulf's appearance on the scene.

story show certain resemblances,"[18] and that the version known to the poet of *Beowulf,* or one very close to it, also lies behind the Sandhaugar adventure in *Grettissaga.* The saga has reversed the roles of the two monsters, and made the female troll the invader of the hall; but it preserves the original conception of the female as the more dangerous adversary. In consequence the saga narrative ends in anticlimax, as the story in *Beowulf* does not. This may account, in some degree, for the preservation in *Grettissaga* of the simpler and more primitive waterfall setting of the second combat. A fight so little dangerous to the hero as Grettir's struggle with the male troll demands no imagery of terror.

The whole quality of Beowulf's adventures in Denmark reflects the taste and power of a distinguished poet. Whether or not he understood the situations and motivations of folk-tale, he knew how to shape them into a noble story. The means by which he sustains the conflict between fear and hope in the two combats are surely in large part of his own devising: the peculiar terror which envelops Beowulf's combats is his creation. Such of its elements as are found in analogues have there no comparable force or concentration. We may surely regard as the epic poet's contribution the dreadful march of Grendel on the hall in its three stages, the dramatic utilization of Grendel's appearance within the door, the horrific exploitation of the devouring of Hondscio, and the fine use of the dramatic audience. Since his sources must have been comparatively brief, many of the details of the landscape of the mere must have been original with him; certainly their excellent ordering to induce terror, the discovery of Æschere's head just where the horror of the scene culminates, and the effect of these things upon the hero's mood, must be original with the poet. The very scope of epic permitted him to make the most of his story; but his clear perception of the possibilities latent in his material, and the skill with which he developed them, justify the high praise accorded his artistic power by Professor Malone.[19]

In marked contrast to Beowulf's monster-slayings in Denmark, his fight with the dragon is told not only with total disregard for

[18] Chambers, *Beowulf: An Introduction,* p. 484.

[19] In a review in *Modern Language Notes,* LXIV (1949), p. 191.

suspense, but with insistent emphasis upon the certainty of a tragic outcome. This does not mean that the poet who had shown, in Part I, such skill in the techniques of terror had become indifferent to them; he simply concentrates the effects of terror in the dragon itself. This monster is a much more deadly antagonist than Grendel or Grendel's dam: it is so formidable in its threefold armament of teeth, venom, and fire, so ruthless in its determined advance and in the mechanics of its attack, that death is the inevitable consequence of combat with it. If the dragon falls short, in any particular, of imposing that special quality of horror which is imposed upon the listener by Grendel and his dam, it is because the dragon is not, like them, a troll: it has not that loathsome perversion of human shape, that distorted exaggeration of human fashion and power, which so repel us in the monsters of the mere. It is more terrible, but less horrible.

But the edge of the terror with which the dragon inspires us is somewhat dulled by our awareness that, even in victory, Beowulf must perish. In the absence of hope, we cannot feel the extreme of fear. In his account of the combat with Grendel the poet used the several forecasts of Beowulf's victory to nourish a degree of hope, so that the listener might experience with more vivid excitement each new effect of fear. In the fight with Grendel's dam every advantage gained by the ogress is immediately followed by the hero's effective counterattack; therefore the only forecast of victory can be delayed until the very moment before Beowulf's discovery and use of the magic sword. But in the third and final conflict we are not even allowed to hope for Beowulf's survival: though he twice repels the dragon's onrush, the advantage is always with the monster. In its first assault its hide resists the edge of his sword, and the hero is borne back; in the second, Nægling shatters, though it finds lodgment in the dragon's head. Beowulf is now disarmed except for his sax; his death is certain. Though Wiglaf's valiant help enables Beowulf to 'cut the serpent in two in the middle,' the hero is fatally hurt. The listener, aware of the advantage gained by the dragon in each stage of the fight, knows that Beowulf cannot survive; and with honesty and justice the poet deliberately and repeatedly forewarns of his inevitable end.

The first hint that Beowulf is to die comes at the very beginning of Part II, before the issue is joined: '. . . Then the broad realm passed into Beowulf's hand; he maintained it well for fifty winters (he was then an old king, an aged land-ward) *until one began, a dragon,* to tyrannize on dark nights . . .' (lines 2207–11). In the very breath in which we are told of Beowulf's accession, and of his long and goodly reign, we are notified that that reign will end in consequence of the dragon's fury.

The poet never ceases—once he has reported the ravages of the dragon—to remind us of the inevitably fatal outcome. 'That beginning was terrible to the people in the land, even as it was to be grievously ended upon the person of their treasure-giver' (lines 2309b–11). Immediately after describing Beowulf's careful preparations against the dragon's fiery breath, the poet tells us: 'The prince, good from of old, was destined to experience the end of his allotted days, of life in the world—and the serpent with him' (2341b–43). And again (2397–2400): 'So he had survived each one of battles, of cruel combats, . . . of deeds of valor, *until* that one day when he must fight against the serpent.'

These forecasts of Beowulf's death in victory recur just before his long monologue (lines 2419b–24); immediately upon its close (2516–17); at the beginning of his first clash with the dragon (2570b–75a); upon the failure of his sword (2586b–91a); and again, almost immediately, upon the dragon's second advance. This last forecast is subtly phrased: 'Then he endured anguish, encompassed by fire, he who *up to this time* (*ær*) had ruled the people.'

All these more or less direct predictions are reinforced by significant expositions of Beowulf's state of mind, and by the poet's explicit statement that fate, which in the hero's youthful adventures had been overruled or set aside by God, and by Beowulf's own might, was no longer to be denied: 'His spirit was gloomy within him, restless and ready for death; Fate immeasurably nigh, destined to visit itself upon the old man, to seek the treasury of the soul, to sunder life from body. Not for long was the chieftain's life to be clothed with flesh.' (2419b–24.) 'His shield afforded the illustrious king protection to life and body for a briefer space than his desire sought, there where he now, for the first time, was permitted to prevail in such wise as Fate had not prescribed for him triumph in battle.' (2570b–75a.)

This last, rather difficult sentence sums up the situation excellently: Beowulf was to be permitted to prevail over the dragon, but not in such a manner as to emerge from the struggle with complete triumph; he is to conquer, but not to survive. The agency which grants him victory but denies him life is Fate (*Wyrd*). Again there is a dramatic audience: Wiglaf and his ten companions. Wiglaf, seeing the course of the fight, recognizes that his lord is in such straits that he cannot survive without help; the panic-stricken flight of the ten less valiant thanes serves to emphasize Beowulf's extreme peril and imminent death.

In the narrative of the dragon-fight the poet has deliberately disregarded the element of suspense; and in this he is artistically justified. The poet of the *Chanson de Roland* similarly abandons suspense in his treatment of the catastrophe at Ronceval: in the tone and manner of his account of the fatal march of the rear guard, in Oliver's repeated pleas to Roland to sound the horn, and predictions of disaster if Roland persists in his reckless refusal, we are fully forewarned of the tragic consequence. In both epics the procedure of the poet is determined by the nature of the material, by the compelling hand of tradition. The poet of the *Roland* knew, and his hearers knew, that Charlemagne's rear guard had been wiped out in the Pyrenees, and Roland slain; the author's duty was not to arouse in his hearers an artificial and delusive hope that somehow, in spite of their knowledge of the tragic conclusion, a miracle might wipe out the actual past. His part was to show noble fortitude in the face of hopeless odds, and to impart its heroic grandeur. The poet of *Beowulf,* and his hearers, knew well that the Geats had been conquered by the Svear. If Beowulf had been conceived as surviving his fight with the dragon, the Svear could hardly have conquered them—but they *had* done so. Therefore Beowulf must die, since only his death could account for the known fact of his people's downfall. All the poet could do, therefore, was to make the circumstances and the manner of his hero's end as tragically glorious as possible. To this end he emphasized the terrible power of Beowulf's antagonist, the immutable decree of Fate, and Beowulf's heroic fortitude in a combat which no man could hope to survive. Since God had permitted the overthrow of the Geatish nation, God was not disposed to avert Fate's decree that Beowulf must die; Beowulf himself recognized clearly, in the hour of his death, that God had been gracious in permitting him to slay the dragon.

Through his very forecasts of Beowulf's inevitable end, the poet gives additional grandeur to the hero's heroism. In the contemplation of Beowulf's unshaken courage in the face of certain death and his full awareness that in death he achieves his greatest victory, we are moved by the old man's fortitude as we are never moved by the young Beowulf's triumphant conquests. And we are moved the more deeply as we recognize that his heroic sacrifice cannot avail to save his people from ultimate destruction.

Beowulf, unlike Roland, is a hero without a tragic flaw. His very valor, wisdom, and magnanimity, expended unstintedly, lead only to a hero's grave in a land soon to be conquered. The greatness of his deeds and his virtues is enhanced by their ironic futility. In preserving his people from the menace of the dragon, at the cost of his own life, he deprives them of the protection which only he can give them. His tragedy is theirs; the fate of neither can be averted. Man is mortal, and the good man can only face his responsibility and accept his destiny. Beowulf fights the good fight, and transforms tragedy into a glory in which he and his people participate.

If Beowulf required the help of Wiglaf to overcome the dragon, so, too, Odysseus overcame the suitors with the aid of Telemachus and the divine support of Pallas. In *Beowulf* there is a special beauty in the devotion of the young thane who defies death to aid his lord; this relationship, like that between Beowulf and Hygelac, was one especially appealing to the Anglo-Saxon. If none of Beowulf's followers had come to his support, we might indeed feel that he had thrown his life away; but Wiglaf's valor nobly complements and completes Beowulf's, and enables us to feel that, in dying for his people, Beowulf did not die in vain. Even though his end brings theirs in its train, we can feel that the Geatish people—all but the cowardly ten—died, like their lord, as men should die. It is the spirit of Wiglaf that speaks in the beautiful eulogy with which the poem concludes, the funeral-chant of Beowulf's retainers:

> eahtodan eorlscipe ond his ellenweorc
> duguðum demdon,— swa hit gede(fe) bið,
> þæt mon his winedryhten wordum herge,
> ferhðum freoge, þonne he forð scile
> of *li*chaman (læded) weorðan.
> Swa begnornodon Geata leode
> hlafordes (hry)re, heorðgeneatas;
> cwædon þæt he wære wyruldcyning[a]
> manna mildust ond mon(ðw)ærust,
> leodum liðost ond lofgeornost.

V

SETTING AND ACTION

It is a natural but not altogether safe assumption that Beowulf's fights with Grendel and his dam reached our poet's ears in the form of heroic lays. This may be so; but such themes are very rare, either in such lays as have survived or among the summaries of lays preserved by medieval writers such as Paul the Deacon or Saxo Grammaticus. Generally speaking, Germanic heroic lays were concerned with the deeds and the sufferings of heroes whose stories had at least a slight foundation in the traditional recollection of the clashes between peoples in the Migration Period; though not history, and often remote enough from historic fact, they at least embody traditions associated in the minds of poets with historical events.

Beowulf's slaying of the trolls that haunted Heorot is—as we have seen—the same sort of stuff that we find in Grettir's adventure at Sandhaugar: the female troll in *Grettissaga,* and Grendel's dam, are very like the hall-raiding, man-eating female troll slain by Arnljot Gellini.[1] We cannot assert that Germanic court poets would have

[1] See *Ólafs saga helga,* cap. 141, in Finnur Jónsson's edition of *Heimskringla* (København, 1911), pp. 332–333.

considered the defense of a hall against such creatures ill-suited as the subject of heroic lays; but this kind of theme is more likely to find its way into oral prose narrative—into saga—than into court poetry. It originates as folk-tale, is characteristically transmitted in folk-tales, and has thence been picked up and carried on a number of times in saga.[2]

The sources of *Beowulf* were no doubt various, and complex. Lays, oral tales, mnemonic verse, versified genealogies, and poetic encomiums of princes may all have lain in the poet's memory, to be drawn upon as needed. We have no evidence that the major elements of the story had been combined into a continuous narrative by any poet earlier than the author of our epic. It seems improbable that such a combination could have been made before the introduction of the Roman alphabet made composition in writing possible. The heroic lay of pagan times was necessarily short, for it had to be composed and transmitted orally.

It is a far cry from any extant heroic lay to the complex and well-ordered poem of *Beowulf*. If that poem rests upon a number of lays, each of which presented a portion of the hero's career, then its author faced and accomplished a task much more involved than the mere joining of their narratives into a single work.[3] He has so managed the substantially distinct parts of his hero's career that, though they constitute a deliberate balance, both exhibit the same heroic ideal; and in both parts, in triumphant death as in glorious victory, all the hero's words and deeds arise out of, and express, the same noble qualities of character.

The three great events of the main plot—the killing of Grendel, the victory over Grendel's dam, and the fight with the dragon—display striking structural similarities, and equally striking variety of narrative treatment. In each case, the inciting cause is very much the same: the destruction wrought by a monster; in each, the hero, after a hard and dangerous struggle, slays his foe—though the hero himself is fatally hurt in his last fight. In each, the fight is preceded

[2] There is a fine example in *Haralds saga harðráða,* capp. 80–81.

[3] See Lawrence, *Beowulf and Epic Tradition,* pp. 245–246, 262.

by an exposition of the hero's state of mind; the fights with Grendel and his dam are each followed by his report of the combat to Hrothgar, and by an account of the gratitude and praise heaped upon him by the Danish king. Each of Beowulf's monster-killings is undertaken to deliver a people sorely afflicted; and in each case the people involved, though saved from present affliction, is nevertheless doomed to suffer ultimate catastrophe.

Yet, within these similar frames there is wide diversity: diversity in setting, in attendant circumstance, and in manner of treatment. These differences have been discussed in the last chapter; but it will be necessary to touch upon them again. It will be sufficient at this point to recall briefly what has been said about the imagery of terror. In his narrative of the fight with Grendel, the poet several times assures us of a happy outcome; yet he overbalances each assurance with effects of horror so calculated and climactic, and imparts so vividly the impact of the terror of battle upon his dramatic audience, that the listeners' sense of fear and peril is maintained almost to the end. In the story of the fight with Grendel's dam he deliberately withholds any assurance that the hero will prevail; and through impressively fearful setting and vivid alternation of the fortunes of fight he keeps us anxiously uncertain of the hero's victory, or even of his survival, until the instant before the means of victory is discovered and used. It is—as we have seen—quite otherwise with the dragon-fight: here we are told repeatedly that both Beowulf and the dragon will perish; and these direct forecasts are reinforced by expositions of the hero's states of mind, from just before battle is joined through each phase in the movement of the fight to the very end.

Quite evidently these differences in mood and treatment represent the author's deliberate choice: we are dealing with the work of a poet "who subdued existing narrative material to a controlling artistic purpose of his own."[4] If what he told derives from popular and heroic tradition, the whole manner of the telling, the motivations, the characterization, the whole plan and direction of the story into a single heroic and ethical channel are the work of a fine craftsman and a great poet. Attempts to prove plural authorship, or to show that

[4] *Ibid.*, p. 19.

individual passages are interpolations, have shipwrecked on the tough cohesiveness of the work. The style of *Beowulf* is as nearly uniform as the style of so long a poem can be expected to be, and as varied as the effects at which the poet aims demanded: it is unique in power and beauty in the whole course of Old English poetry. As we have seen, so large a proportion of the vocabulary of the poem is elsewhere unmatched that it presents every appearance of striking originality within a highly developed conventional usage. The well-designed, balanced structure which Tolkien discerned, and the pervasive irony, no less than the magnificence of language, show the hand of an artist in complete command of his material and his medium. We have, then, no reason for surprise at the fine congruity between the major stages of the action and their settings.

If we compare the narrative of Beowulf's monster-slayings in Denmark with the corresponding action in any of the analogues, we discover two sharp differences: first, the settings of the combats in *Beowulf* are infinitely richer and more elaborate than the settings in any other version; and secondly, the settings in the epic are not only beautifully calculated to enhance the effect of the main action, but are also so contrived as to suggest something beyond it, something at once magnificent and tragic. The settings in the first part of the poem are at once dramatic and symbolic: they reveal a present splendor and intimate its imminent ruin.

These differences reflect, of course, dissimilar levels of tradition. Even in *Grettissaga* the underlying folk-tale of the purging of a hall still bears the stamp of its popular origin, although the story has been somewhat rationalized and elevated in consequence of its circulation among a logical-minded people and its attachment to the historical figure of Grettir. In *Beowulf* it has found its way into the poetry of art, and has been transformed through association with a royal court and princely personages—and finally through the genius of a great poet—into the stuff of heroic poetry.

The story of the purging of a hall of an invading monster or pair of monsters came to the author of *Beowulf*—as it later reached the compiler of *Grettissaga*—in a form which required two distinct though not widely separated settings: the haunted hall, and the lair of the trolls that ravaged it. The more formidable of the two trolls made a practice of raiding the hall for his victims; the hero's first fight therefore took place (or, as in *Grettissaga,* began) in the hall. The second troll had to be sought out and destroyed in its lair. For us it is a minor matter that, in *Grettissaga,* it is the female monster which raids the hall and is killed first; it is of greater importance that both in the saga and in *Beowulf* the she-troll is the more dangerous adversary.[5]

The differences in the action of these two versions concern us less than the differences in setting. In *Grettissaga* the hall is the house of a farmer; in *Beowulf* it is a royal residence. In *Grettissaga* the abode of the monsters is a cave behind a waterfall in a river-gorge near the house: the terrain is rough and mountainous, but it has none of the trappings of terror which envelop the Haunted Mere. Hrothgar's description of the region, and the poet's account of the march to it, seem to imply that a considerable distance separates it from Heorot.

These differences, to a degree, accurately reflect the differences between the cultural level, and the milieu, of the two versions: farmers' dwellings are common in Iceland, royal halls nonexistent; and, as we have seen, the Sandhaugar episode in *Grettissaga* is relatively close to the folk-tale. But the poet of *Beowulf* was not content to use Heorot simply as the scene of the fight with Grendel; it is also the splendid and luxurious home of Hrothgar, and the setting of nearly all of Part I. We see the personages—Beowulf and his followers as well as the Danes—inhabiting this royal residence, enjoying all its pleasures and amenities: it is, indeed, the most comprehensive and detailed picture of Germanic aristocratic life that has come down to us from any source. The scene as a royal court was supplied by the poet's source; its lavish embellishment, its luxury and splendor, the courtesy and charm of the life within it so vividly pictured, are the gift of the poet. So, too, many of the features of the Haunted Mere

[5] I cannot agree with Chambers (*Beowulf: An Introduction,* p. 49) that "in this the *Grettissaga* probably represents a corrupt tradition: for, that the female should remain at home whilst the male searches for his prey, is a rule which holds good for devils as well as for men." Grendel and his dam are Scandinavian trolls, and *Grettissaga* has inherited from Scandinavian tradition the superior aggressiveness of the female troll, while *Beowulf* has inherited the thoroughly Scandinavian belief in her special dangerousness.

may have been present in the poet's source; but it was certainly our poet who first perceived how admirably they could be used to envelop the fight with Grendel's dam in an atmosphere of terror.

Neither in *Grettissaga* nor in any of the folk-tale analogues is there any clear and logical link between the two monster-slayings: the second, where it exists, is motivated weakly or not at all. In *Grettissaga* the hero visits the gorge and finds the second troll merely out of curiosity: he does not expect to find another monster. The connection between the settings is the simplest possible: the house at Sandhaugar lies near the river. The two stages of the action are almost wholly unconnected.

In *Beowulf,* the motivation for the combat with Grendel's dam is her murder of Æschere; the link between the two fights is close and carefully wrought. As far back as line 149b—long before Beowulf makes his first appearance—Grendel's ravages had been represented, in almost legal terms, as the pursuit of a feud which could not be settled through the intervention of friends or the payment of wergeld. The Danes had fondly hoped that Beowulf had settled the feud by killing Grendel; but Grendel is survived by his dam, who steals into the hall and murders Æschere in revenge for her son's death. Hrothgar's words to Beowulf make specific use of the language of the blood-feud: 'She has avenged that feud in which thou yesternight didst slay Grendel.... He fell in battle, having forfeited his life; and now another wicked destroyer has come, has sought to avenge her kinsman, and has far advanced the feud.' (Lines 1333b–40.) Only Beowulf can bring the feud to an end; he must seek out the she-troll in her lair and destroy her. Thus the second stage of the action is launched.

We do not know how much of this the poet found in his sources; there is nothing, either in Old English nonreligious poetry or in folk-tale, to indicate that the management of motivation or transition in *Beowulf* owes much to his predecessors. And all that goes before the transition which we have just examined is equally well contrived and closely knit. We have seen how effectively the climactic horror of Grendel's ravages is built up, till his persecution of the Danes became known to men 'sadly, in songs.' Hearing—presumably through such songs, or through the reports of sailors, of Hrothgar's straits, Beowulf came from Geatland to aid him; but as the king's speech of welcome makes clear, Beowulf, in settling this 'feud' for Hrothgar, was acknowledging his obligation to Hrothgar for settling an earlier feud which otherwise might have brought death to Beowulf's father. Beowulf's resolve to act as Hrothgar's champion, already firm, is still farther settled in consequence of Unferth's discourteous challenge to his competence; and the hero pledges himself to kill Grendel with his hands or perish. The motivation for his fight with Grendel is elaborate and strong; the outcome of that fight provides the motive for the killing of Æschere, which in turn motivates the desperate combat with Grendel's dam.

The very nature of the theme—the purging of a hall—requires the fight with Grendel to be staged in Heorot; the fury of the struggle is dramatically conveyed through the poet's report of its terrific din, the breaking of benches, and the almost shattering effect of the struggle upon the building itself. It is in the hall, too, that Æschere is killed; there, too, that Beowulf and his men receive rich rewards at the feast in celebration of the victory over Grendel; there that Beowulf brings his trophies, after the second combat, to astonish the Danes who had thought him slain. The unity of the action is provided by the hall Heorot itself: "Its great importance as a motive in the action is at once apparent. It was regarded as the crowning achievement of a great nation, as the centre of national life; in size and splendor it was unparalleled; its joys and its gift-giving had never been equaled. No wonder, then, that it aroused the envy and hatred of the outcast Grendel, provoked his nightly attacks. It was for the cleansing of Heorot that Beowulf came to the Danes; and Heorot is thus the centre of the first part of the poem, the thing fought for, the exciting cause of all the action."[6]

It might seem somewhat surprising that this combat with Grendel, fought to purge Heorot, should prove so much less dangerous to the hero than the fight with Grendel's dam. Yet it is so as well in all those analogues which preserve the twofold fight: the female monster is

[6] Walter Morris Hart, *Ballad and Epic* (Harvard Studies and Notes in Philology and Literature, XI, 1907), p. 152.

a much more desperate adversary than the male.[7] Grettir, like Beowulf, is in grave danger of death in his fight with the she-troll, and has little difficulty disposing of her male companion. It is characteristic of stories of trolls that the female is the more aggressive and the more terrible opponent: few male monsters compare for sheer horror with the man-eating, hall-raiding she-troll killed by Arnljot Gellini; she is very like to her counterpart at Sandhaugar, and to Grendel's dam. The poet of *Beowulf,* in representing the male Grendel as the persistent and terrible raider of the hall, and permitting the female to invade Heorot only as her son's avenger, departed from an ancient and common pattern. We cannot tell whether this departure was of his own devising, or whether he found it in his source; at least, in the poet's hands the departure proved most fortunate, for it permitted him to order his hero's exploits climactically. It also involved him in a grave difficulty, which he resolved brilliantly.

The difficulty has left its marks on the story of the fight with Grendel: in spite of the long and horrific record of Grendel's ravages in Heorot, in spite of the carefully built effects of terror in Grendel's last march upon the hall, his horrible appearance within the door, and the devouring of Hondscio, Grendel does not give Beowulf a really good fight. Though capable of killing thirty Danish thanes in one night, there is no aggression left in him once he feels the power of Beowulf's grip; he struggles not to destroy, but to escape. Since there is little glory in an easy victory, the poet was compelled to find effective means of making Grendel *seem* a more dangerous enemy than he was. He achieved this precisely by making the most of Grendel's ruthless ravages among the Danes, by constructing for his last invasion of Heorot a tremendous machinery of terror, culminating in the ghastly devouring of Hondscio, and by imparting the sense of panic produced among the Danes by the din of the fight and Grendel's shrieks of pain. After the fight is over, the awesome power of Grendel is further communicated by the description of his monstrous

[7] For the major analogues see W. W. Lawrence, "The Haunted Mere in *Beowulf*," *PMLA,* XXVII (1912), pp. 208–245, and *Beowulf and Epic Tradition,* pp. 179–193; Margaret Schlauch, "Another Analogue of *Beowulf*," *Modern Language Notes,* XLV (1930), pp. 20–21; Chambers, *Beowulf: An Introduction,* pp. 451–485.

hand and arm. Very skillfully the poet has made the fight seem worthy of the prize; actually it is not.

The poet was sufficiently remote from popular tradition to feel compelled to represent Grendel's dam as inferior in strength to her son; but the compulsions of his story could not be wholly escaped. His hero *must* come closer to death in the second struggle than in the first. His artistic sense pushed him in that same direction; therefore, having committed himself to the untraditional but logical admission that the she-troll was not so strong as Grendel, he was obliged so to manage Beowulf's combat with her as to place him in mortal danger. This he accomplished, as we have seen, through his skillful management of the conditions of the fight: Beowulf is seized unaware in the water, taken by surprise, and dragged down into a milieu unfamiliar to him and favorable to his antagonist. The poet's representation of the Haunted Mere is not the consequence of failure to apprehend the nature of the setting in the folk-tale; it results from the necessity resting upon him to fashion the setting so that it will both oppress the hero's spirit and place in his way obstacles calculated to prevent him from using his strength to best advantage. This he has done, and done triumphantly: for his description of the region of the mere not only accounts for the terror of the combat, but also constitutes one of the glories of the poem.

Strictly speaking, of course, the two major settings in the epic derive from those of the folk-tale; but they have been greatly transformed and expanded in the epic. In Heorot the poet has given us "an idealized picture of royal splendor . . . obviously to give a proper setting to heroic narrative. . . . There is a subtler purpose, too, in emphasizing Hrothgar's apparent prosperity; it contrasts sharply with impending tragedy."[8]

Actually the poet brings before us a twofold dramatic contrast. Against the magnificence of Heorot, the very building of which was so glorious an act, the ruthless incursions of Grendel and his dam stand out with greater horror; and after Grendel's death, the future treachery and murder of kinsmen afford a still more tragic contrast with present pride and glory. The first of these contrasts gives vivid-

[8] Lawrence, *Beowulf and Epic Tradition,* pp. 72–73.

ness and shocking force to the main action; the second lends tragic pathos to the matter of the subplot. After the slaying of Grendel, the darker side of the first contrast is represented by the killing of Æschere; the second contrast is subtly suggested in the narrative of the feast in Heorot.

Six hundred and sixty lines separate the conclusion of the fight with Grendel from Beowulf's encounter with Grendel's dam. This lull in the main action is occupied by an account of the celebrations of Grendel's death by the jubilant Danish warriors, and by a much longer account of the feast. Within the first of these the episode of Sigemund and the first account of Heremod are enclosed—two contrasting studies of the theme of heroism. Within the second we hear the scop's lay of Finn and Hengest, and are told of Wealhtheow's appeals to Hrothulf and to Beowulf. The parallel surely intended between the sorrows of Hildeburg and those in store for Wealhtheow moves in the hearer's mind as the Danish queen speaks. We are more fully prepared for her words by the palpable hints of Hrothulf's future revolt which lie near the opening and just after the close of the lay of Finn and Hengest.

The scene, stately and splendid, is suffused with tragic irony, displayed in two contexts. First, against the joy, the seemliness, and the splendor of the feast and the gift-giving, the poet reminds us that these Danes, still united in fellowship and loyalty, and imagining neither treason nor rebellion, will one day be divided by civil war; secondly, even as Hrothgar and his men leave the banquet and go to bed with full confidence that their afflictions are ended, the poet warns us that they are to be tragically disillusioned. The warning in lines 1233b–37a and 1240b–41 points in both directions; the lines following it reinforce the irony with a ringing affirmation of the vigilant valor with which the Danish warriors, full-armed, guard the hall—in vain.

The feast is treated at great length and *con amore;* on the surface, it exhibits every outward aspect of noble and generous conduct; underneath, it is ominous and threatening. Whatever basis there may have been in the poet's sources for a scene of jubilation, these tragic undercurrents, and the dramatic irony which edges the poet's treatment of his minor theme, are certainly his own; for them there could have been no model. Much of the external splendor of the scene must also have been of his creation; and there can hardly have been any source other than the poet's perceptive imagination for the balancing, against that magnificent background, of the hidden clash of loyalty with ambition, the rising conflict of opposed interests, and the subtly dramatic use of the queen's attempt to forestall fate. It is not the pageantry of the feast, but the manner in which the author places his personages within its setting and invests them with tragic meaning, which gives the scene its greatness. As, in the *Odyssey,* Homer used the visit of Telemachus to the court of Menelaus to exhibit the unhappy fortunes of the great Achæan lords after the fall of Troy, so the poet of *Beowulf* employs the feast in Heorot to foreshadow the ruin of the noble house of the Shieldings.

The poet's love of contrast has been frequently remarked;[9] but it neither springs from a propensity to didacticism nor reflects undue preoccupation with "the unwar wo or harm that comth behynde." Contrast is the essence of all tragedy; and *Beowulf* is a tragedy. The tragedy of the hero becomes explicit in Part II, in his own death and in the destruction of his nation made inevitable by his death; it is implicit in Part I, in the fall of Hygelac and in the consequent failure of Beowulf's expressed intention to give aid to Hrothgar and to protect Hrethric. It resides in the imminent outbreak of internecine war among the Danes, and in the heartbreak in which the hopes of Hrothgar and Wealhtheow must end. The nobility with which the poet invests the figures of the Danish king and queen—of Hrothgar, who has adopted Beowulf as a son, and of Wealhtheow, who looks to Beowulf to save her sons—gives meaning to the tragedy of his helplessness to avert their fate. So, too, he is powerless to save Hygelac, or Heardred, or his people.

The most obvious contrast within Part I is that between the settings of the two combats: one, the stately and luxurious hall of Hrothgar and the gallant life of heroes for which it was designed; and the other, the terrible landscape of the Haunted Mere. The first envelops

[9] See especially Joan Blomfield's admirable paper, "The Style and Structure of *Beowulf,*" *Review of English Studies,* XIV (1938), pp. 396–403.

darker and deeper contrasts: first and most immediately important, that between the joys for which the hall was built and the bloody persecution of its inmates by Grendel; secondly, the contrast between the present solidarity and good-will among the Danes, and the treason and bloodshed to be enkindled by Hrothulf's ambition. The first warning of the troublous times in store for Hrothgar's realm occurs immediately after the announcement of his greatest peaceful triumph, the completion of Heorot and his munificence within it: 'The hall towered, lofty and wide-gabled; it awaited the surges of battle, hostile fire; nor was it long until that edged hate between father-in-law and son-in-law was destined to awaken in furtherance of murderous hostility.' Although Hrothgar and Hrothulf were to beat back the invasion of the Heaðobards, the stately hall was to be destroyed.[10]

The setting for the second combat contains no such contrasts; but, as we have seen, the perfect congruence between it and the action within it is followed by a swift succession of striking dramatic contrasts.

Besides the recurring balances of good and evil, there is a personal contrast as well: in the foreground of the feast stands the figure of Beowulf, balanced, in virtue of his unshakable loyalty, against Hrothulf—and destined, through circumstance and his own character, to become involved in the fortunes of his Danish hosts. It is within the setting of the feast in Heorot, and in consequence of what occurs there, that he becomes involved. The poet thus transforms what, functionally, might have been no more than a scene of transition between the two stages of the main action into the very heart and center of the developing subplot. In consequence of the management of this scene, Beowulf, the champion of the Danes against the kin of Grendel, becomes a protagonist in the tragedy of nations.

The manner of his involvement is subtle and moving. Just after Hrothgar has surveyed the bloody arm of Grendel, and shortly before the feast begins, the king has announced his adoption of the hero as a son. The first act of the feast is Hrothgar's presentation to Beowulf of a golden banner, a helmet, sword, and corselet: these are at one and the same time appropriate rewards for the slaying of

[10] See note 5 to chapter iii, *supra*.

Grendel and the material pledge of Beowulf's adoption. One of the eight horses that the king gives Beowulf carries Hrothgar's own war-saddle. Hrothgar rewards not Beowulf alone, but each of the Geats, and pays a generous wergeld for the ill-fated Hondscio. On the surface, these splendid gifts are a suitable recognition of the incomparable service which the hero has rendered; their full meaning is soon to be pointedly suggested by Wealhtheow. All this (indeed, all that happens at the feast) is calculated not only to increase the delight of the audience in noble acts nobly performed, and in the spectacle of a rich and glorious court, but also to prepare them for the enmeshment of Beowulf in the dynastic troubles of the Shieldings.

As Lawrence suggested, the lay of Finn and Hengest sung at the feast by Hrothgar's scop offers, in the tragedy of Hildeburg, a significant parallel to the suffering in store for Wealhtheow. Indeed, the thought of Wealhtheow's future sorrow may both have recalled Hildeburg's story to the poet and impelled him, in his treatment of the legend, to lay stress upon the passion and the griefs of the protagonists.[11] As the destiny of Wealhtheow is very like that of Hildeburg, so the motives and conduct of Hengest contrast dramatically with those of Hrothulf. Hengest, whose ultimate decision was to be true to his dead lord in spite of his oath to Finn, did his duty by the Germanic code; Hrothulf, whose ambition brought anguish to Wealhtheow and death to her son, violated that code most shamefully. If the poet intended this parallel and this contrast to be perceived by his hearers, then the Finn Episode is part of the design of the scene—at least as a symbol, and in the deliberate, slow creation of a mood which plays a solemn diapason to the dominant theme of Danish jubilation.

We cannot suppose that the poet did not calculate his effects, or that he was unaware that, for his listeners, things treated in sequence had some logical connection. At the very commencement of the feast he had warned his hearers that treachery would soon divide the Shieldings; forty-five lines later the scop sings of Finn and Hengest. Immediately after the conclusion of the lay, Wealhtheow advances and stands before Hrothgar and Beowulf. The poet then instantly

[11] *Beowulf and Epic Tradition*, pp. 126–127.

reminds us that the peace between Hrothulf and his royal uncle is *still* unbroken, that each is *as yet* faithful to the other. The implication is plain: the peace and good faith between them will soon be shattered, and Hrethric, and probably Hrothgar as well, will perish. The dramatic irony is yet more trenchant in Wealhtheow's speech to Hrothgar, actually directed not less to Hrothulf than to the king. She appeals eloquently, and most tactfully, to Hrothulf's loyalty and sense of gratitude; but her words to Hrothgar are very significant: 'Accept this cup, my noble lord, dispenser of treasure! Be joyous, O giver of gold to men, and speak to the Geats with gracious words, as is fitting.... It was told me that thou didst purpose to have this warrior for a son. Heorot is purged, the shining ring-hall. Make use of many rewards while it is yet permitted thee; when thou must depart to meet thy fate, leave to thine heirs people and sovereignty....' (Lines 1169 ff.) The full implications of this speech emerge only when the queen addresses Beowulf.

Turning to him, she fills the hero's cup. Her words to him are wisely calculated to ask much while seeming to ask little; and splendid gifts—including a circlet as precious as *Brosinga mene*—reinforce her request. Her petition, 'Be to these youths generous of counsel,' is of course a request for more than advice; it is phrased more explicitly after she has paid Beowulf a generous compliment: 'Thou hast brought it about through thy venture that far and near through all the world men esteem thee, even as widely as the sea, the court of the winds, encompasses its shores. Young prince, be thou prosperous as long as thou shalt live! I wish thee well of these treasures. Be thou to my son a gracious friend through thy deeds, possessing joy!' (Lines 1221–27.) Here is a clear appeal for help for her sons in the event that Hrothulf's ambition should prick him on to seek the crown.

The chivalrous Beowulf, who had already risked his life to deliver the Danes from Grendel, could hardly reject such a request; before he leaves Denmark he promises aid to Hrothgar and protection to Hrethric.

Wealhtheow's words to Beowulf supplement and explain the first part of her speech to the king. She reminds the king—and, by indirection, Beowulf as well—of his adoption of Beowulf, and urges Hrothgar to 'speak graciously to the Geats' and 'be mindful of gifts' to them; she asks him to 'make use of many rewards': that is, to reward Beowulf and his men yet more richly than he has already done; and almost immediately she gives Beowulf magnificent gifts, and speaks to him with the utmost graciousness. The words 'when thou must depart to meet thy fate, leave to thine heirs people and sovereignty' seem to carry the implication that, by binding the Geats yet more closely to him, Hrothgar can the more surely preserve the succession for his son Hrethric. Wealhtheow means to make certain, by reminding Hrothgar and Beowulf that the king has adopted Beowulf, and, through every courtesy and generous gift-giving, that the Geats are placed under obligation deep enough to ensure their aid and that of the matchless hero Beowulf.

I have shown in chapter iii how, through the promise given by Beowulf to Hrothgar just before he leaves Denmark, the dramatic irony of the scene at the feast is extended to the end of Beowulf's visit; and how the poet, through his first account of Hygelac's fall, reported immediately after Wealhtheow's gift of the necklace, makes it plain that the death of the Geatish king and the destruction of his host in Frisia explain the inability of the Geats to give Hrethric effective aid against his usurping cousin. Beowulf promises help in all sincerity; the poet underlines the fact that his failure to save Hrethric is not his fault, but is the work of Fate.

Twice, in his account of the feast in Heorot, the poet stresses the theme of human suffering directly, and emphasizes man's ignorance of the decrees of Fate (lines 1057–62; 1233 ff.)—with the intimation that woe must follow joy, and that God is man's only refuge. The immediate application is general, to the necessary dependence of man upon God in an uncertain world; the secondary application is to the imminent death of Æschere. But for Danes and Geats alike there is a deeper meaning, in those successive passages which report Hygelac's death and Wealhtheow's appeal to Beowulf.

In this scene, and in that of Beowulf's farewell to Hrothgar, the poet makes his most effective use of contrast. As the nobility of Beowulf is brought into high relief by contrast with the cruelty and niggardliness of Heremod and the disloyalty of Hrothulf; as the present splendor of Heorot contrasts with the impending disunity and civil strife in which its princes are to perish; so too the glory of Beowulf's victories is dramatically balanced against the mighty hero's helplessness to avert the ruin of Wealhtheow's hopes. Acting as champion of an afflicted king and people against those powers of evil which are the enemies of God, Beowulf achieves victory and undying fame, in virtue of God's help and his own proud strength. But in the larger ends of statecraft he fails: all his courage and strength cannot save Hygelac, Hrothgar, or Hrethric, for God is not concerned to intervene in their quarrels; and human might, without God's help, cannot contend against Fate. In the scene at the feast the poet reveals this not directly, but by suggestion and implication; for his primary theme is the triumph of Beowulf, as exhibited against the splendid setting of Hrothgar's court.

The contrast between present joy and future catastrophe in the narrative of Part I is afforded by the balance between the glorious events of the main action and the tragic subplot; by the underlying antithesis between the hero as God's instrument against the kin of Cain and the hero as prince and statesman vainly intervening in purely human affairs and frustrated by Fate. In Part II, Fate has tipped the balance against the hero, and this contrast vanishes; instead, the poet constantly confronts us with the contrast between past and present; between the heroic youth that has been and the heroic old age that has lost nothing of youth's courage and little of its strength, but well-nigh everything of its good fortune. Indeed, Part II is one long, mournful contrast to the splendor and glory of Part I. The mighty nation of the Geats has become weak; the hero is doomed to die, and his people to suffer conquest. This contrast is so swiftly introduced that it strikes us with sudden shock: immediately after the beautiful scene between Hygelac and Beowulf, the second part opens with these words: 'In time it came to pass, in later days, in clash of battle, when Hygelac fell, and war-swords slew Heardred...' The great war-king of the Geats is dead, and his son slain. Then, immediately after the announcement of Beowulf's accession to the throne, we are warned of his impending death (lines

2200–11). From this point on, we are never allowed to forget that Beowulf must shortly die. The decline of his nation is conveyed through the hero's recollection of the unhappy fates of the Hrethling princes; its ultimate overthrow in consequence of Beowulf's death is forecast by Wiglaf and the Messenger; the fates of hero and people are set off against the remembrance of the mighty deeds of Beowulf's earlier years. In Part II there is no present weal to afford a contrast with impending woe; instead, the unrelieved darkness of the theme contrasts bleakly with the recollected splendor and glory of Part I.

Klaeber, regarding Part II as a late-conceived sequel to Part I, finds "grave structural defects" in the narrative of Beowulf's fight with the dragon, and is convinced that, because of the separate and distinct character of the sources of the main action and those underlying the accounts of the wars between Geats and Svear, "a superior unity of structure was never achieved." This failure "to establish an organic relation between the two sets of sources" accounts, in Klaeber's view, for the absence from Part II of "what generally appears in 'Bēowulf's Adventures in Denmark' as an integral part of the story, natural setting, or pertinent allusion...."[12]

I have tried to show, in chapter iii, how mistaken this view of the structure of *Beowulf* is, and how artfully the poet has achieved "a superior unity." There *is* pertinent allusion in Part II: Beowulf's long monologue uttered just before his farewell to his warriors is full of it. We cannot expect, in the narrative of the dragon-fight, the same kind of setting as that within which the action of Part I unfolds, since the action itself is different in nature, circumstance, and significance.

It is true enough that, after Beowulf's departure from Denmark, situation and action are far less richly staged than in the earlier part of the poem. The royal hall of Hygelac, and the manner of life at the Geatish court, are merely sketched, with none of the fullness and magnificence of the scenes in Heorot. Hygelac and his queen are the only personages, apart from Beowulf; there is a watcher at the port, but the little said of him is intended only to convey his joy at Beowulf's safe return: in this he represents the entire court and

[12] Edition, pp. cvi, cvii.

people. Queen Hygd is a shadowy figure in comparison with Wealh-theow; she is characterized only by contrast with the Anglian Queen Thryð. Even Hygelac is far less vividly and circumstantially presented than Hrothgar, though we feel his influence throughout the hero's life.

But this is as it should be. We should not expect the poet to have concerned himself overmuch with the court of Hygelac, since it is the scene of no action. It is not, like Heorot, "the center of the first part of the poem, the thing fought for, the exciting cause of all the action." If the poet had represented the Geatish hall and its occupants as lavishly as he did the Danish court, the scene would have been expanded out of all proportion to the purpose for which it was designed. Its importance lies solely in the opportunity which it affords for Beowulf's report to his lord of his adventures in Denmark, and for the warm and meaningful demonstration of the mutual love and trust between Beowulf and Hygelac. Therefore the scene is almost wholly given over to the representation of these things: in a short but eloquent speech by Hygelac, in Beowulf's long reply, and in the poet's moving comment upon the nobility of the Geatish king and his nephew, and the devotion of each to the other. This is the function of the scene; and it is what the audience wished to hear. That audience needed no elaborate description of the physical setting, or of the joy within the house of Hygelac. We have been shown one Germanic court, the most glorious of all; surely we can transfer from that experience as much as we need to impart reality to another similar scene.

Again, there was no need to impart the personality of Hygd. She had no such part to play in the tragedy of a royal house as had Wealh-theow; it is the unhappy fate of the Danish queen, and her wise though unavailing efforts to avert that fate, which make her interesting and important. As for Hygelac, I have already shown the means which the poet uses to project his portentous figure over all the secondary action, in both parts of the poem. It is clear, as we read, that Hygelac's end kindled the poet's imagination and oppressed his spirit with special force. Therefore there is no need, when he is brought upon the scene, for more than a brief, suggestive characterization of him. But the terms in which this is effected are carefully chosen: he is renowned; he is conqueror and *bana* of the mighty Ongentheow, and 'goodly young war-king' (lines 1925, 1968–69). All this is rounded out and emphasized in the fine lines that conclude Part I.

In short, the poet, in avoiding a duplication of the extensive treatment of a royal court which he had already given as setting for the major action in Denmark, observed a wise and just proportion. It was necessary to bring Beowulf back to his home, to show the warmth and depth of the affection in which he and his uncle held each other. To enclose their meeting—devoid of action as it is—in a setting richer and more elaborate would have been to smother that which the scene was intended to disclose. Here setting is of small importance; its content of human feeling is everything.

The beautifully conceived interchange between Beowulf and Hygelac with which Part I concludes leaves the listener in precisely the state of mind which the poet must have intended. At this moment Beowulf is in the flower of youth and strength, and at the height of his renown; the Geatish kingdom is at the peak of its power. The great king has a matchless champion as his right-hand man, and they are united in a deep and abiding love. Hard upon this triumphant note comes, at once, the crashing dissonance of the opening of Part II. In a few breathless lines the poet announces the sequent fatalities which have weakened the Geats and left them ringed round with powerful enemies. Hygelac has fallen; his son Heardred has been slain in battle with the Svear. Beowulf has come to the throne, and has held it well for fifty winters—*until* a dragon ravages his land. The eleventh line, with its fateful *until,* forecasts the hero's own fall, which is to entail the ruin of his people. Of all the many contrasts in the poem, this is the most dramatic. Here, at the outset of the last action, the tragic close is anticipated.

It is a first principle of storytelling that setting must be appropriate to the action which unfolds within it. The major action of the second part of *Beowulf* is the dragon-fight; its causes are the theft of a precious vessel from the dragon's hoard, and the dragon's savage retaliation upon the Geats. Its vengeance is swift and terrible: 'it encompassed the people of the land with fire, with flame and burning.' At last Beowulf's own hall 'melted in waves of flame' (lines 2312–26). The hero must now meet the dragon, and both must die.

The matter of the subplot, the decline and downfall of the Geatish nation, is presented by the poet speaking in a role like that of the Greek Chorus (lines 2200–11; 2354b–96; 2611–25a); by Beowulf, recalling in personal reminiscence the deeds and fates of his royal kinsmen (2426–2509); and by Wiglaf and the Messenger, in the form of forecast (2884–91; 2910b–3027). These events, since they are disclosed as recollection of things past or as prediction of things to come, require no setting. The main action calls for one major setting: the barrow in which the dragon guards its treasure, with its immediate environs; and one minor setting, which is so barely sketched that one can hardly visualize it at all: that of Beowulf's cremation and entombment.

The major setting lacks the fullness, the complexity, and the vividness of detail which give brilliance to the settings of Part I (the hall Heorot, and the landscape of the mere). This is as it should be, in view of the singleness and the simple directness of the action of Part II. The second part of the poem concentrates upon the dragon-fight and its consequences for the hero and his people; there are no complicating factors. The tragic fates of the Hrethling kings, as recalled by Beowulf, afford the explanation for the complete dependence of the Geatish nation upon Beowulf's survival; its destruction is the consequence of his death. Accordingly the minor setting needs to be no more than indicated; the major setting is spare, austere, and well designed to accord with the tragic action.

The poet rightly refrained from cumbering his narrative with inessentials. A preliminary scene, showing Beowulf in his royal hall dispensing gifts, would be superfluous and out of tune. We have had plenty of that in Part I, where it was appropriate and necessary; here, now that the hero is old and near his end, there is no place for it. The hero's residence has a single function: it is to be burned by the dragon's flaming breath, and its destruction precipitates the combat.

Like Grendel's dam, the dragon must be sought out and confronted in its lair; but unlike the she-troll, it is not a *demonic* monster. Terrible as it is, it is not a descendant of Cain, not the hereditary enemy of God. Neither—with all respect to Tolkien—is it a projection from pagan myth of the Midgard Serpent. As Lawrence puts it, the dragon "was apparently regarded much as we look upon the hippopotamus or the rhinoceros—a strange animal, not met with every day, to be sure, but not outside the pale of ordinary human experience."[13] But it was a fearful and mysterious creature, to which Germanic story assigned a characteristic function, plainly stated in the Gnomic Verses of the Cotton MS (lines 26b–27a): *Draca sceal on hlæwe, frod, frætwum wlanc.* Accordingly there is no need to envelop its lair in the trappings of terror, as the poet had enveloped the Haunted Mere. Its setting does not require to be described as uncanny or horrible: by its very nature the dragon guards treasure secreted in caves, mounds, or barrows. It provides its own terror: terror of enormous size and serpentine strength, of teeth and flame and venom and impenetrable hide.

Our poet abides by this tradition: his dragon lives in the wasteland, at some distance from the Geatish court, in a barrow near the sea, 'alone, under the earth.' Rocky cliffs guard the approach to the barrow, which is supported on columnar stones on which rest stone arches (*stanbogan*). It seems, as the poet conceives it, to combine the actual features of a primitive barrow with those of a Roman ruin. The only suggestion of terror attaching to the scene is the brook which flows out from the barrow, flaming from the dragon's fiery breath. At no great distance stands a headland, on which Beowulf's followers stand to watch the action; close to it is a wood, in which the ten cowardly thanes take refuge when they see their king hard-pressed.

This is all; and it is enough. There is nothing mysterious about the scene; the dragon itself is a natural creature. The setting is stark and lonely; but terror resides only in the fearful armament of the dragon and the fury of its attack, before which even the invincible Beowulf must retreat. Its overwhelming might is evidenced by the hero's compulsion to give ground, by the failure of his sword, and by his triply mortal wound, deep, burning, and envenomed. Again and

[13] *Beowulf and Epic Tradition,* p. 207.

again the poet stresses the savage nature of the dragon's onslaught, and through the revelation of its power he displays Beowulf's fortitude:

> Gewat ða byrnende gebogen scriðan,
> to gescipe scyndan. Scyld wel gebearg
> life ond lice læssan hwile
> mærum þeodne, þonne his myne sohte,
> ðær he þy fyrste forman dogore
> wealdan moste, swa him wyrd ne gescraf
> hreð æt hilde. (2569–75a)

Each time the dragon charges, Beowulf suffers grievously from the shock of its attack and from its flame and venom; each time he meets it with unshrinking valor. Even after Wiglaf joins him, its heat forces both heroes back, and Beowulf receives his death-wound. Yet in this last, desperate moment, with Wiglaf's help he achieves victory.

The setting, then, is in its general outlines fixed by tradition; the poet elaborates the conventional aspects of a dragon's lair only by a somewhat detailed description of the barrow, and of the treasure contained in it as that treasure is examined by Wiglaf after the dragon's death. Those elements which impress one as of the poet's invention are the burning brook, the rocky approaches to the barrow, the stone 'seat' on which Wiglaf sits to gaze on the stone 'arches' of the barrow; and the account of the treasure (lines 2757–70). The rather detailed inventory of the treasure reflects its importance as a motive in the action: as hidden treasures are, it is guarded by a dragon; the dragon's wrath is kindled by the theft of a flagon from the hoard; the fight, and Beowulf's death, are inevitable consequences of the dragon's wrath. In lesser degree than the hall Heorot, but nonetheless deeply, the treasure engages the poet's interest; he gives us two distinct explanations of its presence in the barrow. It was, he tells us first (2231–66), the treasure of a people that had perished, and had been deposited in the barrow by the last survivor. Later (3069–75), he affirms that it had been placed there by 'illustrious kings,' who had set a curse upon it. Lawrence is certainly right in regarding this second explanation as the more original: the poet relies upon the curse for much of the irony which tinges the conclusion. Lines 3066 ff. clearly imply that the curse was accountable for Beowulf's death; before he dies, he gives thanks to God for permitting him to buy the treasure for his people with his life; their grief is too great to permit them to accept the fruits of his sacrifice, and they bury the gold with him. But the first explanation of the treasure plainly engaged the poet's fancy; he could not resist the temptation to supply an account of the origin of the treasure which would give him an opportunity for a lyrical passage which is, in fact, one of the beauties of the poem.[14] Here—as once before[15]—he allowed himself to depart from strict consistency for a purely poetic effect.

The narrative of the dragon-fight is swift and furious; except for the lines which set forth the flight of Beowulf's thanes and explain the role of Wiglaf and the origin of his sword, it is uninterrupted. This single break is essential: the desertion of the thanes is required, to give full plausibility to the representation of Beowulf's mortal peril. The hero's men had not deserted him in his fight with Grendel, nor even at the Haunted Mere, when they thought him slain. It is the panic of all but one of his bravest men which convinces us that, in the dragon, he faces a foe far more terrible than Grendel or Grendel's dam. The intervention of Wiglaf is equally necessary, both to demonstrate the extremity of the hero's peril and to supply him, in his darkest hour, with a companion as loyal as he himself had been to Hygelac. Moreover, it is the devoted gallantry of Wiglaf which justifies Beowulf's sacrifice: if none of the Geats had stood by him, we should feel that their impending conquest by the Svear was fully justified, and that Beowulf's death for them was a futile gesture. Moreover the poet wished to assure us that, fatal as it was to prove to his people, Beowulf's fall did not leave the Geats utterly leaderless.

The main action, then, vigorous and fierce, and in the main uninterrupted, is enclosed in a setting the major elements of which are traditional, but which the poet has elaborated in his description of

[14] *Beowulf and Epic Tradition*, pp. 213–220.

[15] In lines 2183b–89.

the barrow and the treasure. It remains, however, a setting appropriately lean and stark. This is to the good: in a more elaborate setting the action would have lost something of its fury and its force.

The minor setting, in the two scenes of Beowulf's burning and interment, is very lightly suggested. Poetic names adorn these scenes: the place of cremation is called *Hrones-næs;* the site of Beowulf's burial mound is *Earna-næs;* both are close to the sea. The mound is 'high and broad, widely visible to seafarers'; a seemly wall is wrought about the hero's ashes, and the treasure is buried with him. The fashion of his pyre, and the account of his burning, resemble rather closely the details of the burning of the warriors slain at Finnsburg (lines 1107–24); in both instances the pyre is hung with armor, and the dead placed amidst the helms and corselets; flame roars, and smoke ascends to heaven. In both, moreover, the principal mourner is a woman: Hildeburg in the one case, and apparently Beowulf's widow in the other.

The accounts of these two cremations are sufficiently similar to suggest that the pagan practice of burning the dead, no longer in use after the conversion to Christianity, had assumed a conventional manner of treatment in poetry. Stjerna and Chambers have pointed out discrepancies between actual pagan practice and the treatment of the cremations in *Beowulf:* "the evidence ... tends to show that the account of the funeral customs is not quite accurate, representing what later Christian times knew by tradition of the rite of cremation, rather than showing the observation of that rite by an eye-witness."[16]

Nevertheless the accounts of the burning of the dead Danish and Frisian warriors after Finnsburg and the cremation of Beowulf differ in two significant respects. First, although the ritual details are very similar, they are expressed in different terms: if the elements of the two descriptions are essentially conventional, the conventionality is not evident in the diction. Secondly, the lamentation of Hildeburg expresses simply her grief for those slain at Finnsburg; the grief of the woman who mourns for Beowulf is not only for his death, but for its consequences to herself and to the Geatish people:

[16] See Chambers, *Beowulf: An Introduction,* p. 125.

(song) sorgcearig, *sæde* geneahhe,
þæt hio hyre (hearmda)gas hearde (ondre)de,
wælfylla wo*r*n, (wigen)des egesan,
hy[n]ðo (ond) h(æftny)d. (3152–55a)

The mourning of "Beowulf's widow" reinforces the forecasts of Wiglaf and the Messenger with respect to the downfall of the Geatish nation; it is symbolic rather than personal. Klaeber is wrong, then, in believing that "she was introduced, awkwardly enough, merely in the interest of a conventional motive";[17] the fears expressed in her lamentation afford the last and strongest intimation of the ruin to fall upon Beowulf's people through his death. Justly enough, Beowulf's warriors chant around his ashes the praises of their dead lord; the woman clearly sees, and grieves for, the destruction of his people.

[17] Edition, p. 230.

VI

EPISODES AND DIGRESSIONS

Klaeber estimates that "about 450 verses in the first part [of *Beowulf*] and almost 250 in the second part are concerned with episodic matter. . . ." In his judgment, "most of the episodes are introduced in a skilful manner and are properly subordinated to the main narrative"; but "the facts of Geatish history . . . are a little too much in evidence and retard the narrative of the second part rather seriously."[1]

The digressive and episodic matter in the poem has been systematically examined by Adrien Bonjour, who finds that "each digression brings its distinct contribution to the organic structure and the artistic value of the poem . . . all of them, though in different degrees, are artistically justified."[2] I agree wholeheartedly with this conclusion.

Before we consider particular episodes, certain important distinctions require to be made. The poet has made extensive use of at least three kinds of material: folk-tale, heroic legend, and historical tradition. Folk-tale provides the matter of the main action: the hero's three major combats, and his qualities as a marvelous swimmer and

[1] Edition, pp. liii, liv.

[2] "The Digressions in *Beowulf*," *Medium Ævum Monographs*, V (1950), p. 75.

the possessor of the strength of thirty men. Heroic legend is the source of most of the episodic matter of Part I—matter which consists of allusions to, or summaries of, such heroic stories as those of Sigemund, Heremod, Hama, Ingeld, Finn and Hengest, and other great figures of Germanic antiquity. Historical tradition makes its appearance in both parts of the poem, most extensively in Part II. It presents the relevant portion of what the poet and his audience knew about the history of Denmark under the Shielding kings and the causes of the fall of the Shielding dynasty, and what was known about the wars of the Geats and Svear, from the proximate beginning of those struggles to the ultimate overthrow of the Geatish nation. The fall of Hygelac in Frisia, reported as soberly in *Beowulf* as in the *Historia Francorum* of Gregory of Tours, is the fact of central importance in this historical material. It seems likely that these reminiscences of history derived, at least for the most part, not from heroic lays, but from traditionally transmitted poetic eulogies, mnemonic verse—both genealogical and of the kind represented in the older portions of *Widsið*,—and oral prose narratives of a sort roughly comparable with the Icelandic royal sagas.

Broadly speaking, the allusive and summary matter derived from heroic legend, which is strictly confined to the first part of the poem, serves as enrichment or adornment, or affords characterization by way of compliment or contrast, or drives home a specific point, or—in Tolkien's words—gives the "sense of perspective, of antiquity with a greater and yet darker antiquity behind."[3] For the most part these legendary tales have little or nothing to do with the course of the action; yet none of them is actually foreign to the poet's main purpose. The partial summary of the legend of Sigemund, for example, is placed in the mouth of Hrothgar's scop, and ostensibly affords an illustration of that court poet's exceptional poetic skill which, in the lines immediately preceding, has been praised in terms that give us the clearest and most detailed account of a Germanic poet in action. But the Sigemund episode has two further functions. First, its telling is represented as a feature of the rejoicing of the Danish warriors at

[3] "Beowulf: The Monsters and the Critics," *Proceedings of the British Academy*, XXII (1936), p. 275.

the overthrow of Grendel: how can their deliverance from the persecutions of a horrible monster be better celebrated than by alternately racing their horses and listening to a heroic lay of the monster-slayings of an ancient hero? Secondly, the scop's choice of a song of Sigemund is complimentary to Beowulf: it implies that he is comparable with the greatest hero of legend.

A very brief legendary digression has to do with Hama's flight from Ermanaric with the necklace of the Brosings: this allusion is a more effective means of conveying the great value of the necklace given to Beowulf by Wealhtheow than any description of it could have been. The legend of Ingeld—which seems to me to be most subtly employed—both affords Hygelac, through Beowulf's report to him, a useful indication of the political involvement of the Danes and convinces us of the truth of the poet's and Hrothgar's affirmations of Beowulf's exceptional wisdom and political insight. The legendary episode of Offa's wife Thryð serves, by contrast, to establish the liberality, gentleness, and mature wisdom of Hygd.

These examples will serve as illustrations of the manner in which the poet uses his legendary material. The stories have a twofold value: they are fascinating in themselves, and they all contribute, in some specific way, to the vividness, the color, or the depth, of the main narrative. Since they must all have been well known to the poet's audience, he seldom troubled either to tell the whole story or to tell it in such a way that the modern reader can understand it as his hearers understood it. Indeed, some of the episodes—most notably that of Finn and Hengest—are told so elliptically or allusively that scholars have disputed over their interpretation since the beginning of serious study of the poem. Yet it is easy to perceive that, told as the poet has told them, they were deeply moving to those contemporary listeners who knew the stories well. In the Finn episode, misapprehend it as we may, the poet has told what his hearers certainly felt—and even we, in our comparative darkness, also feel—as a tragic masterpiece. These heroic episodes had for the Anglo-Saxon a double appeal: he was permitted to enjoy a fine story told in cunning allusion, so that he felt himself almost a participant in the telling; and he could relish the aptness of its use for a specific purpose at a particular moment in the main narrative.

The historical traditions, especially in Part II, are different not only in origin, but also in character and function, from the legendary matter that furnishes the episodes of Part I. The first and clearest difference lies in their relative place in the time-scale. The stories from heroic legend are conceived as the stuff of antiquity: with the single exception of the Ingeld episode, which looks forward as well as back, they are thought of as having happened before Beowulf's day; they give the "sense of perspective." The historical traditions, on the other hand, deal with events conceived as falling within Beowulf's lifetime and personal observation or experience, and as touching him or his kinsmen directly. Though he is not thought of as participating personally in all these historical events, they are all of intense concern to him; those in which he is not immediately involved affect the fates of personages who are his friends or his foes. These historical stories give background and setting for his later career; and their further function is dramatic and vital: they are part of Beowulf's life. They do not, as Klaeber believes, impede the main action of Part II; as I have pointed out in chapter v, only one of them—and that a brief one—interrupts the narrative of the dragon-fight; and it is directly pertinent to the intervention of Wiglaf in that fight. The others either precede or follow the narrative of the encounter with the dragon.

The historical traditions have to do with the downfall of the Danish and Geatish kingdoms, both of which Beowulf was concerned to uphold; their matter is the tragedies of nations with which he was emotionally as well as politically involved. They are the stuff of the subplot, which is unfolded through the eloquent speeches of Wealhtheow, through the poet's allusions to the troubles in store for the Danish realm, and through his treatment of the several stages of the wars of the Geats. Both these national catastrophes are the ultimate consequence of the defeat and death of Hygelac in Frisia.

I have already suggested another difference—one of distribution—between the legendary and the historical matter within the poem. The heroic legends appear only in Part I; except for the Ingeld episode, the allusions to Hrothulf's ambition and its tragic consequences, and the first account of Hygelac's fall, the matter of historical tradition is reserved for Part II. This distribution is just: the war between Ingeld and the Shieldings, the death of Hygelac and the consequent inability of the Geats to save Hrethric, the usurpation, the reign, and the fall of Hrothulf, were all accomplished before the action of Part II begins; the conquest of the Geats by the Svear is conceived as the direct consequence of Beowulf's death. Significantly, Hygelac's fall, the *ultimate* cause of the destruction of both kingdoms, is the one historic event which is treated in both parts of the poem.

Another, and an important, difference appears in the narrative manner of the heroic as against the historical matter. In contrast with the elliptical, allusive manner in which the legendary episodes are told, the events of historical tradition are reported clearly, and apparently completely. We have seen that, of all the episodes of Part I, only the Ingeld episode is thought of as approximately contemporary with the main action. Though it is heroic legend, it is placed, not in dark antiquity, but after Beowulf's return from Denmark; it is reported by Beowulf, and relates events which have not yet reached their tragic climax. Now the story of Ingeld is the only heroic legend intercalated in the poem which is told from its beginning almost to the end, and circumstantially. It is, in fact, told in the manner which the poet otherwise reserves for such historical events as the death of Hygelac or the battle of Ravenswood. It has, moreover, the same quality of verisimilitude which characterizes the treatment of the wars between Geats and Svear. However scholars may disagree with respect to the precise time and place of its preliminary action, or the meaning of certain lines of the text, the legend of Ingeld as the poet tells it is substantially clear; all of it except the last battle between Danes and Heaðobards is told with sufficient fullness. It, and it alone, falls between the category of heroic legend and that of historical tradition. Rightly so: though, to the poet and his audience, the story of Ingeld lay far in the past, it stands unique among all the heroic legends utilized in the epic in that its protagonists are contemporary with Beowulf himself. And it is part of that tragic story of the Shielding dynasty which belongs to the matter of the subplot.

A final difference between the heroic stories of Part I and the historical traditions is that the former for the most part deal with tales of heroes Germanic rather than specifically Scandinavian. The only exceptions are the story of Heremod and the Ingeld episode. In the stories of Ingeld and of Hrothulf, the motives of the personages are represented as personal as well as political; the political element in the motivation stamps them as closer to historical tradition than are most heroic legends. But this lies in the very nature of their themes. The struggle for the Danish throne resulted, as a matter of fact, from personal ambition. The Ingeld episode has the pattern of heroic legend, and derives from a lost lay or lays; yet it attaches itself easily to the historical tradition, and preserves the memory of a historical struggle between two peoples. The tale of Hygelac's fall, which we know to be solidly historic, may have been derived from oral prose tradition, or from poems of the type represented in Scandinavia by the *drápa*. The stories of Heremod, Ingeld, and Hrothulf belong to purely Scandinavian tradition; they appear to rest upon historical events, and their transformation into the stuff of heroic legend is incomplete.

Broadly speaking, then, the poet has made distinct and different uses of the legendary material on the one hand, and the historical on the other; only one legend—that of Ingeld, which has a sound historical basis—dealing with events occurring within Hrothgar's reign is made to serve a dual purpose.

One story, that of Heremod, is used twice in Part I; it is specifically Danish. It is told once by way of contrast to the story of Sigemund; the teller is apparently Hrothgar's scop, but may be the author of *Beowulf;* later it serves the purpose of a moral example, in the course of Hrothgar's long 'sermon' to Beowulf. The story belongs to antiquity; since its central figure is a Danish king who lived before Hrothgar, and who is nevertheless not included in the poet's genealogy of the Shielding dynasty, we must think of him as earlier than Scyld.

In the third chapter I have considered the poet's use of historical tradition in both parts of the poem. I shall now examine the artistic value of the major legendary episodes in Part I. To this end it will be sufficient to look briefly at the Finn episode, and to study more closely those of Ingeld and Unferth. These three are the longest, the most elaborate, and the most subtly managed of all; the others have been admirably discussed by Bonjour.

My views on the Finn episode have been expressed in two papers published in 1943;[4] they have not changed since then. Here I shall merely touch upon certain aspects of the story as the poet has told it, and indicate the probable reasons for his choice of this particular legend for extensive treatment, and for the manner of his use of it.

The Finn episode is introduced into the poet's account of the feast in Hrothgar's court in celebration of Beowulf's victory over Grendel. On the surface, the occasion for its telling, although more formal, is otherwise not unlike that for the earlier narrative of the exploits of Sigemund. Both episodes are presented as the content of lays sung by Hrothgar's scop; but the fact that the lay of Finn and Hengest is sung in the hall, at a banquet attended by Beowulf and King Hrothgar, prepares us for something more elaborate and meaningful than the lay chanted to the rejoicing thanes between bursts of horse-racing. The scop recites a number of lays at the feast, but only this one is specifically reported. The poet of *Beowulf* tells the story in his own terms: its theme is that of Danish vengeance for the slaying of King Hnæf. It is developed not directly and objectively, but in terms of the sufferings of the unhappy Queen Hildeburg, Finn's wife and Hnæf's sister, and the struggle in the heart of the dead king's chief thane Hengest. The principal emphasis is upon the states of mind of Hengest, who is responsible both for Danish acceptance of the terms of peace offered by Finn after a drawn battle with the Danes (in which Hnæf has fallen) and for the obligation to avenge Hnæf. In this moral and emotional dilemma in which Hengest finds himself we readily recognize a constantly recurring theme of Germanic heroic poetry which has been admirably defined by Lawrence: "The clash of conflicting duties with each other, and with the elemental passions of love and hatred and ambition, supplies the poet with his richest themes. Tribal law and tribal custom are the rocks against which the

[4] "The Climax of the Finn Episode," *University of California Publications in English,* III, No. 8 (1943), pp. 285–362; "Design and Motive in the Finn Episode," *ibid.,* XIV (1943), pp. 1–42.

lives of men and women are shattered, like surf on a storm-bound shore.... The more hampered a society is by convention, the more distressing become the cases where convention does not prove a safe guide, where the choice must be made between conflicting duties."[5] This is the tragic situation of Hengest, torn between his duty to keep his oath to Finn and his moral obligation—reinforced by his own desire—to avenge Hnæf, who has fallen in combat with Finn's men.

The poet tells us only briefly and obscurely how the fighting first broke out, or what was Hengest's actual role in the final battle which satisfied the desire of the Danes for vengeance and resulted in Finn's death. Those elements of the story to which he accords longest and most detailed treatment are: (1) the terms of the compact which Finn offers Hengest after the slaying of Hnæf; (2) the funeral rites for the slain warriors; and (3) Hengest's emotional turmoil between the beginning of winter and the accomplishment of Danish vengeance in the spring. The special care with which the poet develops these three features of his story makes it evident that he found them the most compelling to his spirit, and that we should see in them the clues to the interpretation of the tragic story.

In a very real sense these three elements, together, constitute the Finn episode. The seventeen and one-half lines which precede the account of the compact state the theme, and summarize the action antecedent to Finn's offer of peace. The funeral scene directly follows the detailed exposition of the compact. Only a two-and-a-half-line transition separates the funeral scene from the poet's analysis of Hengest's states of mind; this is immediately followed by a highly compressed fourteen-line conclusion, in which the theme of vengeance is triumphantly restated in terms of its accomplishment. The analysis of Hengest's inner conflict and its resolution is the climax of the story; for this racking conflict in the hero's heart the exposition of the compact and the moving account of the funeral rites furnish the emotional background and the essential motivation.

The episode observes a most rigorous economy of action. The initial statement of the theme (revenge for Hnæf) is confined to three lines;

[5] *Beowulf and Epic Tradition,* pp. 28–29, 58. See also Andreas Heusler, *Die altgermanische Dichtung* (Berlin-Neubabelsberg, 1923), pp. 157–158.

the action antecedent to the making of the compact is very briefly summarized. The account of the means by which Hengest's dilemma is finally resolved, though it constitutes the climax of the story, is highly compressed (lines 1142–45); it derives its force from its position, and from its heavy load of implication. The final restatement of the theme—vengeance accomplished—is swift, terse, bare of unessential detail. From first to last the theme of revenge is treated, not in and for itself, but as it beats upon the mind and tears the heart of the hero upon whom the duty of avenging rests.

A vivid but unhappily fragmentary lay, the so-called *Fight at Finnsburg,* preserves the first part of this tragic story, except that it tells us nothing of the cause of that first action in which Hnæf fell, and breaks off before the moment of his death. This lay shows no concern with motives or with emotional struggle; it deals exclusively with the attack upon Hnæf and his men, and their valiant resistance. It is all vigorous action. If we may judge by this lay, the poet of *Beowulf* could not have found in his sources more than the merest hint of the tone and manner of treatment which distinguish his interpretation of the theme. We may with confidence credit him with something new: the management of an old heroic theme in terms of character and human suffering. Later in time and on foreign soil we find, in those lays of the *Poetic Edda* which Ker called the "Northern Heroides," a comparable interest in the motives and the passions of heroic figures, rather than in the action which induced or resulted from them; but in Anglo-Saxon England the closest approach to the tone, the emphasis, and the manner of the Finn episode is to be found in the so-called elegiac poems and in the elegiac passages of *Beowulf;* and in them the emotions represented, however eloquently, are those of hypothetical figures rather than of the personages of heroic legend.[6]

The Finn episode is the longest of all the episodic stories in *Beowulf,* the most pitiful and tragic. It is self-contained, and in itself is quite independent of the main story. Yet it is highly appropriate in its context: it is fitting that, at the banquet in celebration of Danish deliverance from Grendel, Hrothgar's scop should display his art, and

[6] The elegiac passages in *Beowulf* serve principally to emphasize the pathos or the tragedy of the situation which evoked them (so lines 2444–62a) through an imagined parallel, or to create a mood appropriate to a situation (as in lines 2232b–70a).

that the poet's illustration of that art should be as impressive as are his representations of the transcendent splendor of Heorot, with its 'gold-bright tapestries along the walls, a multitude of wondrous sights,' its towering gables, its concourse of gallant men, and its wise, munificent ruler.

But the episode bears significantly upon the matter of the subplot, as Lawrence has pointed out. I agree with him that "the story of Queen Hildeburg was here designedly brought into connection with the tragedy in store for Queen Wealhtheow"; that "the telling of the story of Hildeburg in the presence of a queen who was herself of another people than that of her husband, whose efforts to keep the peace were destined to come to naught, and whose daughter Freawaru was to experience much the same melancholy destiny as the wife of King Finn, is surely not without significance."[7] There is strong support for this judgment: the feast in Heorot, at which the lay of Finn and Hengest is sung, is introduced by the poet's warning that, in the not distant future, dynastic feud and treachery among the Shieldings will bring catastrophe and sorrow; and the warning is repeated, more specifically, as soon as the scop has finished his lay (lines 1013–19; 1163b–68a). The noble speech in which Wealhtheow—only a few lines after the conclusion of the lay—tactfully reminds Hrothulf, the future rebel and murderer of her son, of all the favors he has received from Hrothgar and herself, is shadowed by the knowledge of the poet's audience that neither gratitude nor loyalty will avail to save her from a fate like that of Hildeburg. These close juxtapositions are evidence that the poet's version of the lay of the scop was deliberately designed to awaken pity and terror for the future destiny of the innocent Wealhtheow and her son and husband, as the legend of Finn brings before us the fate of the innocent Hildeburg and her son and husband. The parallel is not perfect; but the poet of *Beowulf* is fond of such parallels, and of illuminating contrasts as well. The faithful Hengest, avenging his lord at the cost of great suffering to himself, affords a striking contrast to the faithless Hrothulf. The scop's lay of Finn and Hengest is a beautiful example of the poet's gift of tragic irony.

[7] *Beowulf and Epic Tradition*, pp. 126–127.

The altercation between Unferth and Beowulf is not, in any proper sense, a digression. The interchange is not sufficiently self-contained to be considered an episode: it is but the initial stage in a continuing relationship, which manifests itself at various points during Beowulf's visit to Heorot. It constitutes an integral part of the main narrative of Part I, and affects its course; it has importance for the subplot as well. The dramatic quality and the violent tone of Unferth's challenge and Beowulf's answer can easily seduce us into a dangerous unawareness of the later relations between the two men; these relations, and the strangely undervalued contrast between Beowulf's attitude toward Unferth and that of the poet, give the clues to one of the minor mysteries of the poem. Unferth is a personage of greater importance than has been generally appreciated; if we are to understand his significance we cannot confine our attention to what Klaeber has called "The Unferth Intermezzo"; we must seek an explanation for everything the poet tells us of a singular personage.

As soon as Beowulf has been admitted to Hrothgar's presence, the hero announces the purpose of his visit, and asks the king's consent to pit his strength against Grendel. As soon as Wulfgar had announced Beowulf's arrival, Hrothgar had perceived that 'holy God has sent him to us out of His mercy . . . against the terror of Grendel'; yet, although the king's reply to Beowulf's opening speech is in the highest degree gracious and friendly, he does not at once reply to Beowulf's petition to be permitted to act as champion of the Danes against the monster: all that we can make of Hrothgar's answer (lines 489–490) is that he is inclined to accede. Then, suddenly, in the midst of mirth and feasting, Unferth addresses to the hero a speech of unprovoked insult. He recalls a youthful adventure in which—as he alleges—Beowulf vied with Breca, lord of the Brondings, in a swimming-match in the wintry sea, and was decisively beaten. Unferth represents the affair as an act of headlong folly; his conclusion is a complete denial of Beowulf's competence to meet Grendel on equal terms: 'Therefore I expect of thee worse results—though thou hast everywhere shown valor in press of battle—if thou darest await Grendel close at hand throughout the night' (lines 525 ff.).

Unferth's words seem shockingly offensive; their impropriety is all the greater against the extreme courtesy of Beowulf's reception by the Captain of the Shore and by Wulfgar and the warm friendliness of Hrothgar's welcome.

Beowulf at once replies, at first with calm politeness: Unferth, he answers, has said quite enough about Breca and his exploit, and drunkenness has clouded his judgment. He then corrects Unferth's distorted version of the adventure: after frankly admitting the charge of youthful rashness, he demonstrates that he had shown matchless courage and endurance. Breca had not strength enough to outdistance him; and though he could have left Breca behind, he had no wish to do so. When a furious tempest separated them, Beowulf suffered the full violence of the storm, and the assaults of sea-monsters, which he slew with his sword. At length he came safe to land, after enduring greater hardship, and performing greater feats of valor in the waves, than any other man.

Thus far Beowulf has merely justified himself, and has spoken with marked restraint. Now he turns fiercely on Unferth, and declares that neither the latter nor Breca ever performed such deeds—'though thou didst become slayer of thy brothers, thy closest kinsmen; for that thou shalt suffer damnation in hell, keen as thy wit may be.' This concessive clause savagely echoes and answers that which closes Unferth's speech: 'Therefore I expect of thee worse results—though thou hast everywhere shown valor in press of battle...' His anger mounting, Beowulf concludes his retort with words much more biting than Unferth's:

'I tell thee truly, son of Ecglaf, that Grendel would never have wrought such terrors... upon thy lord, such humiliation in Heorot, if thy spirit were as valiant in battle as thou thyself dost reckon it. But he has discovered that he has no need to fear overmuch this feud, the savage assault of thy people, the victorious Shieldings: he takes forced toll, he spares none of the folk of the Danes; nay, he murders and devours in mirth of spirit; he has no cause to expect resistance from the Spear-Danes. But I shall show him shortly now the strength and courage, the might in battle, of the Geats. Thereafter he who is permitted will go in pride to the mead-bench, when the morning light of another day, the sun clothed in radiance, shines from the south over the sons of men!' (Lines 590–606.)

This violent interchange contrasts so jarringly with the warm graciousness and seemliness of the preceding speeches as to cry aloud for explanation. The poet attributes Unferth's offensive words to jealousy: 'The undertaking of Beowulf, the brave sea-farer, was to him a great vexation; for he did not admit that any other man on earth had ever ventured upon more glorious deeds under heaven than he himself' (lines 501b–505). But this is something less than satisfying; for Unferth's position was such that his first speech to Beowulf must have something of an official rather than of a purely personal character. He was obviously a high official of the Danish court: he is called *ðyle Hroðgares* (line 1456); he sits at the feet of the lord of the Shieldings (1166); he enjoys the confidence of Hrothgar and Hrothulf (1166b ff.). Although we do not know the precise meaning of the title *ðyle,* it seems to imply that he was the king's official spokesman. In view of the cordiality of Hrothgar's welcome to Beowulf, we should expect the king's spokesman to utter a formal echo of Hrothgar's own gracious greeting. Instead, Unferth directs at Beowulf a decidedly unfriendly speech. However envy and injured vanity might have affected his own feelings toward Beowulf, it seems strange that he should have dared to violate his official duty and flout the plain intention of his lord.

We can hardly regard this interchange as a mere flyting: flytings are either exchanges of rude wit, rough games, or invective preceding a fight. Here no fight can conceivably occur, since Beowulf is the honored guest of the king; and the encounter between Beowulf and Unferth is certainly no game. Both men mean what they say; both speak in anger.

Lawrence's explanation of Unferth's outburst is equally unsatisfying: "It irritates him [Unferth] that a distinguished foreigner has come to slay the demon which no Dane has been able to dispose of . . ."[8] Bonjour agrees: "Beowulf's arrival to fight a monster that they themselves were entirely unable to get rid of, and the acceptance of foreign help for this purpose, contained the possibility of wound-

[8] *Beowulf and Epic Tradition,* p. 153.

ing the pride of the Danes."'[9] This view of the feelings of the Danes is not only unsupported by the text; it is effectively denied by the poet's own words. He makes it quite clear that none of the Danes except Unferth felt the slightest resentment at Beowulf's taking their quarrel upon himself; to the contrary, they are delighted to have him do so. Again and again: in the words of the Captain of the Shore (lines 287b–300), in Hrothgar's answer to Wulfgar (372–389), and in the king's words to Beowulf (esp. 473–490), it is made abundantly plain that Beowulf's offer to deliver the Danes from Grendel was received with unmixed joy. These Danes had suffered too much and too long to nurse a pride of which few shreds were left them. Unferth's speech expresses his own irritation only; the lines which follow the conclusion of Beowulf's retort assert that Hrothgar and his men heard Beowulf's resolve to confront Grendel with happy relief: 'Then was the dispenser of treasure, gray-haired and war-fierce, joyous; the prince of the Bright-Danes was confident of help; the guardian of the people had heard Beowulf's resolute purpose. There was the laughter of heroes; mirthful din resounded; words were joyous.'

The function of the debate between Unferth and Beowulf is obvious: it is intended—as Bonjour perceived[10]—to convince the Danes beyond the possibility of doubt that Beowulf has sufficient strength, as well as sufficient courage, to deliver them from Grendel. Hitherto, in spite of Hrothgar's clearly expressed hope that God had sent the hero to save them, the Danes had had no adequate ground for complete confidence in the hero. Hrothgar had, indeed, heard that Beowulf had 'the strength of thirty men in his handgrip'; but this was only hearsay. In his first speech to the king, Beowulf had supported his request to confront Grendel alone, 'with the band of my warriors,' by citing his victories over 'the kin of giants' and 'nicors by night'; but the evidence for this is his own word. The Danes were indeed moved to gratitude and hope by his offer to undertake their cause; but in view of their own repeated failures against Grendel, they may

[9] "The Digressions in Beowulf," *Medium Ævum Monographs,* V, pp. 15–16.
[10] *Ibid.,* pp. 20–22.

well have felt more than a little doubt that Beowulf, brave and willing as he might be, could destroy the monster.

But Unferth's misrepresentation of the adventure with Breca gave Beowulf a priceless opportunity to establish beyond question his superlative strength and valor, and his ability to defend Heorot. His own account of his swimming-exploit, of his victorious struggle against fearful sea-beasts and the stormy sea of winter, carries complete conviction; his very vehemence lends weight to the demonstration of his might. That is the meaning and the justification of the lines quoted above (607 ff.), which immediately follow the end of his speech: 'Then was the dispenser of treasure joyous . . . the king . . . *had confidence in* help . . .'

Unferth's challenge, rooted in jealousy, and Beowulf's crushing reply, had the effect of implanting in every Danish heart full conviction that Beowulf could and would accomplish their deliverance; and in consequence Hrothgar grants Beowulf's petition to face the monster. The complete trust which the Danes now have in him is further expressed, in indirect discourse, by the queen (lines 625–628a; 639–640a).

The debate between Unferth and Beowulf is, then, amply justified as a narrative device. It is justified also by its own magnificent effectiveness; indeed, both speeches are admirably constructed and phrased. It would be a grievous error to regard the terms in which Unferth taunts the hero as conventional: they are most cunningly conceived, with vivid and violent verbal figures designed to stress and to ridicule the vehement efforts in the sea of two young men frantically striving to make good a foolish boast.

The calm condescension of Beowulf's opening words; his clear, detailed exposition of the actual nature of the exploit, of his sufferings and his victory over the stormy sea and its monsters; the edged but restrained anger with which he throws the murder of kin in Unferth's face as the latter's greatest achievement; and the storm of fury that reminds Unferth of his want of courage to face Grendel—all these make the hero's answer a masterpiece. The two speeches together create a dramatic moment of superb force and intensity.

But this is no mere dramatic interlude, and it does much more than accomplish its primary function. Even in isolation, it raises problems yet unanswered: How did the official spokesman dare insult a guest whom his king had warmly welcomed, and through that insult risk offending the king himself? And why did Hrothgar not instantly rebuke his spokesman for this seemingly unpardonable act?

Moreover, the incident is *not* isolated. The relations between Beowulf and Unferth continue until the hero leaves Denmark; but they undergo a striking change. Unferth's envy of Beowulf vanishes; the two become friends. Is this natural, after the virulence of the spokesman's original attack and of Beowulf's reply? Is it possible that the poet's hearers perceived, in Unferth's speech, something more than envy and gratuitous insult? They knew, better than we, what the duties of a *ðyle* were. They may have felt that envy and injured vanity alone did not fully account for Unferth's conduct: if so, they could understand both Hrothgar's reason for failure to rebuke him, and Beowulf's ready acceptance of his friendship once it was proffered.

Unferth had heard of Beowulf's youthful adventure with Breca; but we do not know what version of it he had heard. If he had known the actual facts, as Beowulf reports them in his reply, and had nonetheless perverted the truth, then Beowulf's later acceptance of his friendship would hardly have been possible. But Beowulf *does* accept his friendship; moreover, in confuting Unferth's version of the adventure, Beowulf charges him with drunkenness, but not with deliberate falsehood. The poet may well have intended his hearers to understand that Unferth reported the adventure, in good faith, in a version distorted before it reached his ears, and that Unferth was responsible not for the misrepresentation but only for the malice with which he repeated a tale he had heard and honestly accepted as fact. Beowulf's reply contains no suggestion that Unferth knew he was distorting the facts.

As Hrothgar's spokesman, Unferth had certain duties and obligations. If the Danes were to accept Beowulf as their champion against Grendel, he must be equal to his task; for them, everything was staked on the issue of the combat. Therefore, if Unferth had heard a version of the swimming-exploit which represented Beowulf as soundly beaten in a foolhardy undertaking, then it became his duty to bring the matter into the open and force Beowulf either to prove his competence or to confess himself guilty a second time of undertaking what he could not perform. Unferth would then have acted quite properly in asking, 'Were you beaten by Breca, as I have heard?' Instead, in his pride and envy, he asks, 'Are you THAT Beowulf who WAS beaten by Breca?' The form of his question, and the tone of his whole speech, are dictated by his personal jealousy; but his fault may have lain, not in deliberate perversion of the truth, but in his eager acceptance of a story the truth of which he was not in a position to test. He is guilty of gross discourtesy, but not of willful slander. His motives may have been mixed beyond his own comprehension: a proper desire to prevent his king from entrusting the defense of Heorot to one who might prove foolhardy and incompetent is pricked by his own envy. Beowulf admits the charge of youthful folly (lines 535–537a), and then shows how his strength and courage turned folly into glorious achievement. The confession of folly serves as a sop to Unferth's injured vanity; he can thereafter stomach the rebuke to his discourtesy.

This assumption—for which there is admittedly no positive evidence—has the merit of making both the immediate situation and the later relations between Beowulf and Unferth reasonable and intelligible. Unferth's question is prompted by his sense of duty; its tone and manner are the expression of his jealous vanity, which the poet stresses: he is a man to make what personal capital he can out of the performance of his duty. Hrothgar understands him, and recognizes that he must do his duty in his own disagreeable way. For this reason, and because Beowulf's answer to Unferth's question is important to the Danes, the king does not reprove his spokesman. Beowulf's retort validates his qualifications to meet Grendel to the satisfaction and joy of the Danes. Unferth himself, once convinced that Beowulf is a match for Grendel, can forget and forgive the hero's sharp words and respect Beowulf's superiority. An envious man is much more apt to cherish rancor against an equal, or one slightly superior to himself, than against one whom he knows to be immeasurably greater. As Klaeber observes: "Unferth evinces a spirit of generosity, courtesy, and sportsmanlike fairness toward Beowulf when the latter has demonstrated his superiority."[11]

I think we must acquit Unferth of deliberate perversion of fact, in view of Beowulf's later acceptance of his friendship. His reply to Unferth has emptied the hero's heart of the just resentment first roused in him, as it could not have done if Unferth had compounded discourtesy with deliberate falsehood. One might, of course, raise the question whether Unferth's friendship was sincere; and the question deserves consideration.

After Beowulf's victory over Grendel has made him the idol of the Geatish court, Unferth might well be glad to curry favor with him, and shrewd enough to see that a show of generosity would give himself greater popularity and firmer favor with the king. Some support for such a view of his conduct could be derived from the fact that he was not an overscrupulous man: he had not shrunk from murder or betrayal of his brothers; and later he was to have some part in the conspiracy of Hrothulf. A man evidently lacking in principle might well see advantage to himself in counterfeiting friendliness toward one for whom he had previously exhibited envy and hostility. Unferth's character as disclosed by the poet lends color to such a hypothesis. But only an honestly felt good-will toward Beowulf could have prompted Unferth to lend him a sword as valuable as Hrunting: 'never had it failed in battle any man who grasped it.' The poet, who never fails to show his distaste for Unferth, does not so much as hint that his motive in lending the sword was anything but good. Even a man jealous and unscrupulous may be moved to honest admiration and friendship by the courage and magnanimity of a Beowulf.

The direct evidence of Unferth's change of heart is contained in three passages. The first (lines 980 ff.) tells us only that, when the Danes saw Grendel's arm hung up in token of Beowulf's victory, *Þa wæs swigra secg sunu Ecglafes.* To Klaeber this implies that Unferth felt compunction for his former conduct: "er schämte sich."[12] Lawrence translates, "the son of Ecglaf was pretty silent";[13] the implications of this rendering are rather different. The poet tells us only

[11] Edition, p. 150.

[12] "Unferðs Verhalten im *Beowulf,*" *Anglia Beiblatt,* LII (1942), p. 271.

[13] *Beowulf and Epic Tradition,* p. 154.

that Unferth was *silent;* he does not say whether shame or continued envy made him silent. But if we regard the sentence as a whole, we see clearly that it contains a deliberate thrust: Unferth *wæs swigra secg ... on gylpspræce guðgeweorca.* If he was ashamed, it was not for his initial discourtesy, but because of his now proved inferiority to Beowulf.

The second passage (lines 1465–71a) reflects a curiously dual attitude: the poet admits the generosity of Unferth's gift of his sword to Beowulf, but cannot refrain from barbing his statement of it: 'Indeed the son of Ecglaf, mighty of strength, did not remember what he had formerly said, drunk with wine, when he lent the weapon to a better warrior; he himself did not dare to risk his life, to engage in brave adventure under the turmoil of the waves; there he lost his glory, his renown for valor.' This is a little more favorable: if it reflects upon Unferth's courage, it concedes that his original quarrel with Beowulf *was not in Unferth's mind* when he lent his sword to the hero. It suggests strongly that Unferth's attitude toward Beowulf had become genuinely friendly, and that all rancor was past. Certainly Beowulf so regards it; for he not only accepts Unferth's sword, but in his last words before his descent into the mere he offers Unferth his own sword in return.

There is, finally, an ambiguous passage (lines 1807–09), which may mean either that Beowulf, departing from Denmark, gave Hrunting back to Unferth, with generous words of thanks; or that Unferth, in that last scene between them, gave Hrunting to Beowulf as a permanent gift. In either case the lines attest that the two men were good friends, and that each had esteem for the other. In the light of this we must believe that Unferth's good-will was genuine.

But this only confronts us with another problem—one that has been somewhat neglected by the critics, although it bears significantly upon the role and the function of Unferth in the poet's design. For we can hardly doubt that the spokesman had a part to play in the drama of Heorot, although the poet chose to suggest it rather than to let it be acted out upon the stage. The problem is this: What is the meaning of the complete cleavage between Beowulf's attitude toward Unferth, and that of the poet?

Beowulf has accepted Unferth's friendship no later than the moment in which the exchange of swords is made—perhaps earlier; the hero's parting words to Unferth (lines 1809b–12) suggest that the friendship was genuine and warm. The poet, on the other hand, maintains his dislike of Unferth stubbornly; whenever he expresses his opinion of the man, he does so with marked acerbity. He attributes Unferth's first words to Beowulf to envy and vanity; he reaffirms (lines 1167b–68a) Beowulf's charge that Unferth had been responsible for the death of his brothers; he exults grimly over Unferth's silence at the sight of Grendel's arm. Even when he records the loan of Unferth's sword, he emphasizes the spokesman's lack of courage to encounter Grendel's dam, and asserts that he 'lost his glory' in leaving the adventure to another. Finally, he plainly intimates (lines 1165 ff.) that Unferth was to play a mischievous and evil part in Hrothulf's conspiracy against Hrothgar and Hrethric. In short, the author represents his hero as accepting and returning the friendship of a man whom the poet himself consistently and sharply reprobates.

The manner in which the poet regularly manages his minor characters suggests that his treatment of Unferth is quite deliberate and calculated. It is his invariable practice to introduce these lesser personages only for a specific purpose, and to let them disappear from the scene when that purpose is fulfilled. Wulfgar is never mentioned after Beowulf has been admitted to Hrothgar's presence; the Captain of the Shore necessarily appears a second time when Beowulf boards his ship to leave Denmark. Wealhtheow, apart from two brief and casual allusions (lines 1649b, 2173b–74a), is neither on the stage nor spoken of after her appeal to Beowulf to protect her sons. Although Hygelac—for very good reasons—casts his shadow over the entire epic, he appears in person only to receive Beowulf's report and to exchange gifts with him. Wiglaf, introduced as Beowulf's most wholly faithful thane, fulfills his role in the dragon-fight, and remains on stage only until he has ordered the preparations for the hero's funeral rites. The Messenger appears only long enough to carry out the part assigned him by Wiglaf, and to utter his forecast of national calamity.

It is most unlikely that the author departed from his usual procedure in the single case of Unferth. Between Beowulf's first speech to Hrothgar and his departure from Denmark, the only Danes who have speaking or acting parts are the king himself, Queen Wealhtheow, and Unferth. Beowulf's parting words to the spokesman (given in indirect discourse) are separated by only four lines from his farewell speech to Hrothgar. It seems probable, therefore, that the poet meant us to think of Unferth as playing a part of considerable importance to the Danes after Beowulf's departure.

Moreover, he reminds us of Unferth's presence at every larger stage of the narrative except during the actual combats with Grendel and his dam: immediately after Hrothgar's reply to Beowulf's first speech; at the close of Beowulf's report to Hrothgar of his victory over Grendel; at the king's feet during the great feast in Heorot; beside the mere when Beowulf prepares to meet Grendel's dam; and in the king's presence when Beowulf takes his leave. Even the formidable Hrothulf appears less frequently, and neither speaks nor is spoken to. Except in the hour of Beowulf's farewell, the poet reveals his disapprobation of Unferth whenever he mentions him.

We cannot escape the conclusion that every appearance of Unferth, every direct or indirect revelation of his character, had significance in the poet's design. If this had not been so, Unferth would never have been mentioned again after Beowulf's retort to him had fulfilled its function of convincing the Danes that Beowulf should be accepted as their champion. Both Beowulf's acceptance of his friendship and the poet's consistent dispraise of him must have their place and meaning in the drama of the first part of the poem.

Part I is concerned with more than the hero's triumphs over the monsters of the mere. In Lawrence's words: "... the adventures with Grendel and his dam are the main theme of the first part of the epic; and the tragedies of the Danish house of the Scyldings, the chief of the secondary themes."[14] Again and again[15] the poet reverts to this chief secondary theme, the importance of which is underlined by his glorification of the Shielding kings in the introductory lines of the poem (lines 1–85). In the development of that theme—which

[14] *Beowulf and Epic Tradition*, p. 27.
[15] See chapter iii, *supra*.

the poet manages by allusion, but, from the point of view of his contemporary hearers, quite clearly—Unferth was an important figure. At best he played the mischief-maker or evil counselor; at worst he may have had a more active role in Hrothulf's insurrection and the killing of Hrethric. The elliptical character of the passages in which the impending civil war and Unferth's part in it are foreshadowed shows that the poet's audience was familiar with the traditions of Hrothulf's revolt and with the degree of Unferth's complicity.

It was presumably Unferth's role in those tragic events of the subplot which motivated the poet's unconcealed dislike of him. His clash with Beowulf could be forgiven, as it was forgiven by Beowulf; his guilt toward his brothers, though scarcely pardonable, had been overlooked by Hrothgar. But the poet, who made his hero the model of loyalty, and closed the first part of his epic with a glorification of loyalty, could not forgive Unferth that disloyalty to his king which evidently stained him in tradition, and which was to make him in the end a traitor to the noblest of Danish monarchs.

The fact of Unferth's ultimate treachery cannot be doubted: the poet establishes beyond question his complicity in Hrothulf's treason (lines 1164b–68a).[16] Since Beowulf had promised help to Hrothgar against any foe, and suggested that Geatish aid would be forthcoming at need for Hrethric also, the hero himself is deeply concerned for their security. That the Geats did attempt to aid Hrethric in his struggle against Hrothulf is implied in Scandinavian tradition. The poet has capitalized on his knowledge of this tradition, and carefully introduced his first account of Hygelac's death (lines 1202–14a) to explain Beowulf's inability to help Hrothgar's heir more effectively. It appears probable that, in his treatment of Unferth, the author intended to suggest that the evil in the spokesman's nature was to precipitate a tragedy that Beowulf would have prevented if he had been able.

Beowulf could not foresee the part Unferth was to play in this tragedy; but the poet and his hearers were familiar with it. This accounts for the cleavage between the hero's attitude toward Unferth

[16] Kemp Malone, "Hrethric," *PMLA,* XLII (1927), p. 269; Fr. Klaeber, "Hrothulf," *Modern Language Notes,* XX (1905), pp. 9–11.

and the poet's. In Unferth the poet shows us "a man with an evil temper and a bad reputation,"[17] and with a future consistent with his past. Treacherous to his kin, he was to become a traitor to his king. But he was also a man of some generous instincts, and apparently of considerable charm, like "honest Iago." It is his better or more attractive qualities that induce Beowulf to accept his friendship—actually, of course, it is these very traits that make the man so dangerous. His moral instability, enviousness, and love of intrigue make him a rascal in the end. In him the poet has achieved a sound piece of characterization, by the very device of permitting us to see the man through the eyes of the hero on the one hand and those of the author on the other.

It is part of the pervasive irony of the poet's temper that he could represent his hero—who undertook to aid and protect Hrothgar and his heir against whatever foe—as accepting the friendship of that counselor who was to have a share in the blood-guilt of Hrethric's murder, and most probably in Hrothgar's as well. The irony here is almost but not quite matched by that of the later part of the poem, in the desertion of Beowulf by those thanes whom he had trusted most, and to whom he had given costliest gifts.

The view of Unferth which I have presented here is not shared by Bonjour, whose discussion of the "Unferth Intermezzo" is in so many ways rich and illuminating.[18] He sees, as I do, that the poet's continuing concern with Unferth is clear evidence of the importance of the spokesman's role; but he follows Klaeber in the latter's more kindly estimate of Unferth's character.[19]

Although he admits that "Unferth's first reaction was naturally enough spite and jealousy," Bonjour is at some pains to rehabilitate him. He assumes, without any support from the text, that Unferth

[17] Lawrence, *Beowulf and Epic Tradition,* p. 77.

[18] "The Digressions in *Beowulf,*" pp. 19–20.

[19] Klaeber's edition, pp. 147–150; see also his "Unferðs Verhalten im *Beowulf.*"—It is important to observe that there is no evidence whatever, in the poem, to support Bonjour's argument that Unferth was a man of exceptional valor, and greatest of Danish champions. The poet does not suggest that Unferth ever participated in any attempt to defend the hall against Grendel, and plainly tells us that he lacked courage to face Grendel's dam. He is called *eafoþes cræftig* (line 1466); we are told that Hrothgar and Hrothulf believed in his courage (lines 1166–67); Beowulf calls him *widcuðne man* (line 1489). There is not, however, the slightest indication that he had ever distinguished himself for valor.

was "foremost of Danish warriors"; he excuses his resentment of Beowulf on the ground that "as long as no one proved able to meet Grendel in fight, Unferth—who apparently did not venture to measure himself against the monster—could still enjoy the position of undisputed superiority which he was eager to maintain." And he refers to Unferth as, after Beowulf, "the first and foremost fighter, second to none."

The poet does indeed attribute to Unferth great strength (line 1466a); he does *not* say, as Bonjour asserts, that *he hæfde mod micel.* His statement is that Hrothgar and Hrothulf *believed þæt he hæfde mod micel, þeah he his magum nære arfæst æt ecga gelacum.* This reminds us of Beowulf's mention of Unferth's murder or betrayal of his brothers as the spokesman's greatest claim to courage. Both passages are ironic. The allegation that Unferth's unwillingness to face Grendel, or Grendel's dam, does not reflect on his valor because "the monster simply transcended human powers"[20] ignores the fact that there had been Danes who dared pit their strength against Grendel, and bravely perished (lines 480–488). So far as the evidence goes, Unferth seems to have been both strong and courageous in the face of ordinary foes, but prudent enough—like those other thanes who sought refuge from Grendel among the bowers—to avoid facing probable death. The poet nowhere suggests that his courage exceeded that of other members of Hrothgar's *comitatus.*

Bonjour even attempts to salvage Unferth's reputation in the matter of his murdered or betrayed brothers: "The fact that Unferth did not 'lose his glory,' or at least kept his prominent position, though he is said to have killed his brother, makes it likely that he did not act as a coward in that particular (and quite obscure) drama."[21] The implication of the parenthesis seems to be that, if we only knew the facts of that "obscure drama," we might hold Unferth excusable. Perhaps; but no one can blink the significance of the poet's resurrection, in a significant context, of Beowulf's charge, or ignore the weight of Beowulf's assertion that the penalty Unferth must pay for his brothers' death is damnation in hell.

[20] Bonjour, "The Digressions in *Beowulf,*" p. 18.

[21] *Ibid.*, p. 19, n. 5.

Bonjour quite illogically uses Unferth's loan of his sword to Beowulf as evidence against his complicity in Hrothulf's treachery. The loan, he says, "is the more effective, coming from a man of great valour, and enhances all the more Beowulf's extraordinary capacities. At the same time, and by this very attitude, Unferth gains our sympathy and we cannot but applaud the final friendly scene. We may add, therefore, that the attempts to represent Unferth in a way as the villain of the piece are wide of the mark in *Beowulf*—artistically they lack any firm basis."[22]

They do not lack a firm basis, for a pretty solid foundation has been laid by the poet. In lines 1017b–19, he has told us that no treachery had *as yet* been committed by the Shieldings—that is, that Hrothulf was not *yet* conspiring against Hrothgar and Hrethric. Lines 1163b ff. make the point clearer: 'There sat the goodly twain, uncle and nephew; their friendship was *yet unbroken,* each loyal to the other. Likewise there sat Unferth the spokesman at the feet of the lord of the Shieldings; each of them had confidence in his spirit, that he had great courage, *though he had not been faithful to his kinsmen at the play of edges.*'

No one doubts that these two passages forecast allusively the impending revolt of Hrothulf against his uncle and cousin, his murder of them, and his usurpation of the throne. The immediate adjunction of the statement about Unferth, *in this context,* can be nothing else than a clear intimation that he is to have a hand in fomenting the revolt, and perhaps in its bloody consequences.

This was pointed out long ago by Olrik;[23] it has been stressed again and again, by Chambers,[24] by Malone,[25] and by Lawrence.[26] Klaeber does indeed see in the poet's words "only a vague hint of a suspicion . . . that he [Unferth] is fomenting dissensions within the Scylding dynasty";[27] but there is no escape from the author's deliberate collocation of the statement that Hrothgar and Hrothulf trusted him in spite of his treachery to his kin with the intimation of Hrothulf's

[22] *Ibid.*, p. 20.
[23] *Danmarks Heltedigtning,* I (København, 1903), pp. 25 ff.
[24] *Beowulf: An Introduction*, pp. 27–29.
[25] See note 16, *supra.*
[26] *Beowulf and Epic Tradition*, pp. 76–77.
[27] Edition, p. 148.

coming treachery to his kin and bloodshed between the princes whom Unferth served. If anything, the suggestion of Unferth's mischievous complicity in the quarrels of the Shieldings is stronger than the forecast of those quarrels themselves. And the one generous and sportsmanlike act which the poet attributes to Unferth—the loan of his sword to Beowulf—is valueless as evidence against his ultimate treachery; it weighs no more heavily in the scale than than does Benedict Arnold's leg, shattered at the battle of Saratoga.

We have seen that the legendary episodes of Part I are on a chronological level different from that of the career of Beowulf, and belong to heroic antiquity. The poet obviously thought of the Finn episode as anterior to the action of his poem; the same is true of the stories of Heremod, Sigemund, and Hama. The legend of Ingeld, however, cannot be patly assigned to one level or the other: as the stuff of heroic legend, derived from heroic lays, it is on the same footing with the legends of Heremod and Offa; but its personages are Beowulf's own contemporaries, and its action is conceived as taking place not long after Beowulf's exploits in Denmark. We know that lays of Ingeld were popular in the time of Alcuin, and there is every reason to believe that our poet's audience was thoroughly familiar with the story.

There is still controversy over the proper interpretation of the episode, although most scholars are in substantial agreement on all major points; those features concerning which they disagree do not affect the main outlines of the story. Since the betrothal of Hrothgar's daughter Freawaru to Ingeld is known to Beowulf, though the ultimate catastrophe was to occur some time after his departure from Denmark, the poet is able to bring the tale before us in a manner more immediate and dramatic than that which characterizes his telling of any other of the legendary stories in the poem.

The poet puts the story of Ingeld and his relations with the Danes into the mouth of Beowulf, as part of the report which the hero makes to Hygelac on his return home; the occasion for his telling it is his mention of Freawaru, whom he had seen in Heorot. As a basis for discussion, and admitting that the correct translation and interpretation of vital parts of the episode are still open to controversy,

I translate Beowulf's words as I understand them, in substantial agreement with Lawrence and Chambers, and for the most part in agreement with Klaeber,[28] as follows:

'She is betrothed—young, gold-decked—to the gracious son of Froda; the lord of the Shieldings, guardian of the realm, has determined upon this, and deems it good counsel, to settle some portion of deadly feuds [and] conflicts by means of that woman. As a rule it is seldom that the bloody spear is lowered [even] for a little while after the fall of a prince, excellent though the bride may be! It can then displease the prince of the Heaðobards, and each of the thanes of those peoples, when *he, a lordly scion of the Danes,* walks into the hall with the lady, *past the band of veteran retainers;* on *him* shine the heirlooms of the men of old, hard and ring-adorned, treasures of the Heaðobards, so long as they were permitted to wield those weapons, until they led to destruction at the shield-play their dear companions and their own lives. Then over the beer *shall he speak* who *sees the treasure,* an old spear-warrior, he who *remembers* everything, the spear-slaughter of men—his mind *will be* furious within him,—he *will begin* in his grief of spirit to test the resolution of a young warrior through the thoughts of his breast, to awaken war-bale; and he *will utter* these words:

'"Canst thou, my friend, recognize the sword which thy father bore to battle under the visored helmet on his last campaign—the precious iron,—where the Danes slew him, the fierce Shieldings, held possession of the battlefield after Wiðergyld fell, after the fall of heroes? Now here the son of I know not which of those slayers walks into the hall exultant in the war-gear, boasts of murder, and bears that treasure which thou by right shouldst possess!"

'So *will he admonish and remind* on every occasion, with bitter words, until the time comes when the *thane of the maiden,* because of the deeds of his father, sleeps stained with blood in consequence of the bite of the sword, having forfeited his life; that other will escape with his life—he knows the land well. Then will be broken on both sides the oaths of earls; thereafter [or perhaps 'after,' 'when'] slaughterous hate wells up in Ingeld, and his love for his wife grows cooler in consequence of surges of grief. Therefore I do not reckon the good faith of the Heaðobards, any part of their alliance, reliable for the Danes, [or] their friendship firm.'

The poet has here adopted a direct and consecutive manner of narration quite different from that which characterizes most of the legendary episodes of Part I; the contrast with the manner in which

[28] Lawrence, *Beowulf and Epic Tradition,* pp. 80 ff.; Chambers, *Beowulf: An Introduction,* pp. 20–22; Klaeber's edition, pp. xxxiv–xxxvi, 203–204.

he deals with the legend of Finn and Hengest is striking. This is in part because the conflict between Danes and Heaðobards is thought of as taking place contemporaneously with the main action of the poem, as concerning Beowulf's friend and adoptive father Hrothgar, and as a matter of some political interest to Hygelac.

The story is all—or substantially all—there; and it is told forthrightly, not allusively or elliptically except as the details of the earlier fighting between Danes and Heaðobards are taken for granted. Even in this particular we are told all that really matters: that Ingeld's father Froda had been defeated and killed, and that the Heaðobards now have kinsmen to avenge. Such disagreement as still exists regarding the precise meaning of the story told by the poet does not arise out of any omission by him of essential detail, nor out of any lack of clarity in his narrative. It arises almost wholly out of our uncertainty about the exact meanings of certain words and word-groups which must have been quite clear to his hearers. In the translation given above, I have placed in italics those words and phrases the rendering of which is still matter of controversy.

The majority of scholars reconstruct the episode in virtually the same way, with only minor variations. For this majority—which includes Hoops, Klaeber, Chambers, Lawrence, Girvan, and Huppé[29]—Beowulf is predicting those events which will occur to destroy Freawaru's marriage and bring about a bloody renewal of the feud. As Lawrence puts it: "... the poet of *Beowulf,* anxious that his hearers should enjoy the tragic climax, adopted the bold device of making his hero *prophesy* to Hygelac the future course of events. Probability is here sacrificed; Beowulf might have felt that no good would come of the match, but he could hardly have foreseen the course of future events in so detailed and accurate a way. The point is worth noting, as an example of how far the poet was willing to go for the sake of emphasizing the tragedy of history."[30]

[29] J. Hoops, *Kommentar zum Beowulf* (Heidelberg, 1932), pp. 222–223; Klaeber, as cited in the preceding note; Chambers, *Beowulf: An Introduction,* pp. 20–22; Lawrence, as cited in the preceding note; R. Girvan, review of Hoops's *Beowulfstudien* in *Modern Language Review,* XXVIII (1933), pp. 244–246; B. F. Huppé, "A Reconsideration of the Ingeld Passage in *Beowulf,*" *Journal of English and Germanic Philology,* XXXVIII (1939), pp. 217–225.

[30] *Beowulf and Epic Tradition,* p. 80.

Axel Olrik rejected the prophetic interpretation;[31] and Kemp Malone has exposed its weakness in these words: "The advocates of the prophetic interpretation of the whole passage betray thereby their low opinion of the art of the poet. And yet, other prophetic passages may be found in the poem. The messenger of Wiglaf predicts trouble with Franks and Swedes (lines 2910 ff.) and Beowulf himself makes a couple of predictions (lines 1830 ff.). These predictions are solidly based on present information, and require no magic powers or visions from on high. If Beowulf, then, makes predictions to Hygelac about Ingeld and Freawaru, we have a right to expect these predictions, too, to be rationally based. But the information given in our passage is too precise and detailed to have any such basis, except in the mouth of a prophet or a wizard. And, since the poet portrays his hero neither as a prophet nor as a wizard, the prophetic interpretation of the hero's words makes him speak out of character and is therefore to be rejected."[32]

Malone is certainly right. In the entire poem, no single person ever speaks or acts out of character; the speeches of the hero are all completely in character, consistent both with one another and with all that the poet tells us about him. As Malone has shown, the only actually prophetic elements in Beowulf's report to Hygelac are those contained in lines 2058–66; and these "may be accepted as within the bounds of reason . . ."[33]

Malone's contributions to the clarification of the Ingeld episode have been many and weighty. They have of course encountered opposition from advocates of the prophetic interpretation;[34] but I have seen no defense of that interpretation which meets the argument brought against it by Malone on artistic grounds. I hasten to say that, for all the future tenses in the translation I have given above, I do not regard Beowulf's report of the events as prophecy. Since the poet's hearers were certainly familiar with the tragic climax and the course of events

[31] *Danmarks Heltedigtning*, I (translated by Lee M. Hollander under the title *The Heroic Legends of Denmark*, New York, 1919), pp. 15 ff.

[32] Kemp Malone, "Time and Place in the Ingeld Episode of *Beowulf*," *Journal of English and Germanic Philology*, XXXIX (1940), pp. 84–85.

[33] *Ibid.*, p. 85.

[34] Most notably from Huppé (*op. cit.*, note 29, *supra*).

which led to it, their enjoyment of the story was not dependent upon the fiction of a prophecy placed in the hero's mouth. Indeed, the true climax is not contained in Beowulf's report: we know of it only through lines 45 ff. of *Widsið* and a brief allusion in *Beowulf* 83b–85. The hero's report concerns only the prelude to that climax, and assumes the audience's familiarity with the bloody denouement at Heorot.

Malone has long taken lines 2032–58a as reporting not what lay in the future, but "things that had already happened"[35] during Beowulf's visit to Heorot, and which he could therefore report to Hygelac. From line 2032 on, all the verbs in the passage except those which look back to the earlier conflict between Danes and Heaðobards are in the present tense. Since, in Old English, future time is commonly expressed by the present, these verbs can be, and by most scholars are, taken as indicating future action. Malone maintained, however, that all these present verbs from the beginning of the episode through line 2057 are consuetudinal presents, and state not a course of events predicted for the future, but one which had been going on during Beowulf's visit to Hrothgar's court, which was still going on when he left Denmark, and which was presumably continuing even as he made his report to Hygelac.[36] This view of the time-relations would compel us to conceive the scene of action as not Ingeld's court, but the Danish court; otherwise Beowulf could have known nothing of them. Ingeld, Malone believes, was, during Beowulf's stay in Denmark, "on a visit to the Danish court, presumably in connexion with the betrothal" or for the marriage; and the substance of Beowulf's report is this: During this visit Ingeld "goes to the hall every day, and what he sees there displeases him. This daily displeasure is quite naturally and properly given linguistic expression by *mæg ofþyncan* ... the use of a present tense-form serves to bring out the dailiness of Ingeld's displeasure.... But what displeases him? The insulting conduct of the Danes, who make a habit of wearing, in the presence of the Heaðobards, heirlooms which once belonged to the Heaðobards and which the Danes had taken from them in battle. That this insulting recep-

[35] Malone, "Ingeld," *Modern Philology,* XXVII (1930), pp. 258 ff.

[36] Malone, "Time and Place," p. 79.

tion of the Heaðobards happens many times is clearly implied in the *mæla gehwylce* of line 2057.... The Danes make a point of strutting about, wearing plunder taken from the bodies of Heaðobards.... Then (when they strut) an old spearman of the Heaðobards has a way of speaking up. In particular, every time a certain young Dane flaunts Wiðergyld's old sword in the faces of the Heaðobards (he got it from his father, Wiðergyld's bane), the old spearman whets Wiðergyld's son to vengeance. He keeps up the whetting day after day, and I [Beowulf] predict that the time will come when Wiðergyld's son will kill the young Dane. The slayer will get away alive,... he knows the country well."[37]

Malone justly feels that "the great advantage of this interpretation over the usual one (which makes the whole passage prophetic) lies in the fact that it gives to Beowulf a rational basis for the prediction which he does make at the end."[38] This is true; but in my opinion it provides that rational basis at the cost of a serious violation of consistency and artistic truth—more serious even than the attribution to Beowulf of prophetic powers would have been. However we interpret the episode, the elements of time and place must accord with the data given in the text; since the verbs may denote either futurity or continued present action, the element of time is of first importance, and that of place depends, in large part, on that of time. If what Beowulf reported to Hygelac had taken place during his visit to Heorot, then obviously that action must have occurred in Heorot; and to this, in my opinion, there are grave objections.

Malone's argument for Heorot as the scene of the offense given the Heaðobards, of the old spearman's whetting, and of the killing of a young Dane is very strong: in the first place, there is his fundamental point that to take the episode as prophetic is to ascribe to the poet a serious artistic fault such as he nowhere else commits; and that the only apparent alternative—to take lines 2032–57 as an account of what Beowulf knew at first hand—requires us to take the scene as laid in Heorot. Beyond this is the fact that the related story of the killing of Agnarr, Ingeld's son, at his own wedding-feast, as told in the second

[37] *Ibid.*, pp. 79, 84.
[38] *Ibid.*, p. 84.

book of Saxo's *Gesta Danorum,* has the Danish court as its scene; and that Ingeld's vengeance upon the sons of Swerting at the instigation of the old spearman Starcatherus is accomplished at the Danish court, as told in Saxo's sixth book. The first point can be met if we can find a third possible interpretation of the episode which neither assumes prophetic powers on Beowulf's part nor explains his words as narrating what had already taken place; the second seems to me of small importance. That Agnarr's wedding feast should be held at the Danish court is an inevitable consequence of Saxo's misconception of Agnarr as himself a Dane and a retainer of the Danish king Hrólf. And if, in Saxo's sixth book, the scene of the whetting and of Ingeld's vengeance is laid at the Danish court, that is the consequence of the confusion, in Scandinavian tradition, of the relations between the Shielding princes and the line of Froda, who are themselves conceived, in Scandinavia, as Danish princes and Shieldings. The significant fact is that in Saxo's sixth book the scene of action is *Ingeld's* court,[39] and that this lends support to the view that the poet of *Beowulf* thought of the action as at Ingeld's court.

If we look at the text of *Beowulf* we find the situation presented in terms sufficiently precise, if we could only be sure of their meaning. In line 2035a there occurs the term *dryhtbearn Dena,* which most scholars take as a plural. If it is plural, then *he,* in line 2034a, cannot refer proleptically to *dryhtbearn,* and must refer back to *ðeodne* in line 2032b—that is, to Ingeld; and *him,* in 2036a, must refer to *dryhtbearn,* and, like it, be plural. This would leave us with the identical situation postulated by Malone: Ingeld is displeased at the behavior of the Danes (*dryhtbearn Dena*), on whom shine (*on him gladiað*) heirlooms pillaged from slain Heaðobards. This would imply that the action takes place at the Danish court; since, if the scene were laid at the Heaðobard court, the Danes present there would not be in sufficient numbers to behave so insultingly to their hosts.—Of course, even if *dryhtbearn* be plural, the lines in question need not be taken as meaning that the Danes *deliberately* taunt the Heaðobards by wearing spoils taken in the earlier fighting; but of that more presently.

Malone's argument for the plurality of *dryhtbearn* is impressive:

[39] This was pointed out by Huppé, *op. cit.* (note 29, *supra*), p. 222.

"*dryhtbearn Dena*... is no isolated concoction of the *Beowulf* poet's, but has a number of parallels, although it is not without special features of its own. It is to be associated with half-lines made up of the word *bearn* and a tribal- or group-name in the genitive plural." Citing several such verses (e.g., *Israela bearn, bearn Israela, Eotena bearn, Geata bearn, ylda bearn*), in all of which the meaning is not literally 'sons of,' but rather 'descendants of' or 'people of,' he makes the effective point that such combinations are always plural; in them *bearn* is plural. "The *Beowulf* poet, wishing to use the Danish name with *bearn* in a half-line of the type under discussion, found himself faced with a metrical difficulty: *bearn Deniga* can hardly be made to scan without straining the rules, and its alternatives, *bearn Dena, Deniga bearn* and *Dena bearn,* are even less attractive. The poet solved his problem by compounding *bearn* with *dryht*... Since in half-lines of this type *bearn* is uniformly a plural, we must interpret the *dryhtbearn* of *Beow*. 2035 as a plural. The antecedent of *hē* 2034, therefore, cannot be doubtful: the pronoun refers to *ðeoden* 2032, that is, to Ingeld."[40]

Now it is quite true that, in combination with tribal or group-names in the genitive plural, *bearn* is generally plural; there is some reason to question that it is "uniformly" plural. In *Beowulf* 1408 (*Ofereode þa æþelinga bearn steap stanhliðo*) the verb is singular, which would imply that the subject, *æþelinga bearn,* is singular, referring to Hrothgar or to Beowulf; and its singular number is borne out by the parallel statement in the next clause: *he feara sum beforan gengde*. Klaeber takes this *æþelinga bearn* as "probably... plural, as in 3170";[41] but the context seems to imply that Hrothgar or Beowulf traversed the slopes ahead of the major part of his followers. If the poet meant *æþelinga bearn* here as plural, then the verb *ofereode* must be a scribal error for *ofereodon*. But if so, the scribe—a better judge than we—took the subject as singular, which is fair enough evidence that a use of *bearn* plus group-name in genitive plural to express a singular referent was not sufficiently unique or unconventional to shock him.

[40] Malone, in *Anglia*, LXIII (1939), p. 107.
[41] Klaeber's edition, p. 184.

The fact that such combinations are generally plural does not rule out the possibility that *dryhtbearn* in line 2035 is singular. Malone's belief that the poet's problem was metrical—that, meaning to say 'scions of the Danes' (that is, 'young Danes'), he prefixed *dryht-* to *bearn* to make a regular verse, is not necessarily correct. The question is rather, what *was* it that the poet meant to say? Suppose that he wished to say 'a noble young Dane': how would he express this concept? He could do it only by saying 'a young man of the Danes'—by using a word for 'young man' with the genitive plural of the tribe name; since the *i*-stem *Dene* has no singular, and the adjective *Denisc* is used substantivally only in the plural. *Bearn* is the common term for 'young man' in poetry: to express 'a noble young man' the natural thing to do would be to compound *bearn* with *dryht-*. 'A young Danish noble' would be expressed either by *dryhtbearn Dena* or *dryhtbearn Scyldinga.* Wrenn, though he takes the combination in line 2035 as plural, admits that it "could, grammatically, be singular, agreeing with *hē* in the previous line."[42]

The only thing that is certain is that the poet meant either 'noble young Danes' or 'a noble young Dane.' The base-word *bearn* can be either singular or plural in its uninflected form. It seems to me unreasonable to deny that a word-form which, either as simplex or as base-word of a compound, can be either singular or plural, is necessarily limited by poetic convention to plural use when followed by a group-name in genitive plural. As Malone observes in another context, "After all, a poet may be expected to depart from convention now and then."[43] I agree with Girvan, who takes *dryhtbearn* as singular, and regards *hē* (line 2034) as used in anticipatory reference to *dryhtbearn,* and *him* (2036) as singular.[44]

Another, and a related, difficulty is presented by *duguða biwenede* (line 2035b). If we keep the MS reading, and reject (as I think we must) the view of Kock and Malone that these words are the object of the same *on gæð* which governs *flett,*[45] then either the whole line

[42] Wrenn's edition of *Beowulf* (London: Harrap, 1953), p. 217.

[43] "Time and Place," p. 78.

[44] Review of Hoops's *Beowulfstudien,* in *Modern Language Review,* XXVIII, p. 246.

[45] E. A. Kock, "Interpretations and Emendations of Early English Texts," *Anglia,* XLVI (1922), pp. 173–174; Malone, "Ealhhild," *Anglia,* LV (1931), p. 270.

or its second verse must be taken as standing in a very unusual construction. Hoops and Klaeber[46] regard *dryhtbearn* as plural, and take the line as "a loosely joined elliptic clause indicating the cause of the king's displeasure," meaning 'the noble scions of the Danes [are] excellently entertained.' There are two objections to this: first, such elliptic clauses with the substantive verb omitted are rare; secondly, although the dative plural *duguðum* is, very occasionally, used with adverbial force, the genitive plural *duguða* is not so used anywhere else. Von Schaubert's translation of *duguða biwenede* as "wenn die (beiden) Gefolgsscharen bewirtet werden"[47] assumes a kind of ellipsis for which I can find no parallel. Both of these interpretations reflect an almost desperate desire to avoid emendation.

Grein emended *biwenede* to *bi werede;*[48] and Chambers, approving the emendation, pointed out that it "is exceedingly slight, since the difference between *n* and *r* in O.E. script is often imperceptible, and may well have been so here in the original from which our *Beowulf* Ms. was copied; cf. *urder* for *under,* l. 2755."[49] I follow Chambers in taking *dryhtbearn* as singular, *hē* in 2034 as referring proleptically to *dryhtbearn Dena,* and *biwenede* as a scribal misreading of an original *bi werede.* Lawrence seems to hold the same opinion. If this is correct, then any evidence that more than one Dane offends the Heaðobards by wearing spoils taken in the earlier fighting disappears; and with it disappears all textual evidence in favor of taking the scene as laid in Heorot.

"The escape of the Heaðobardish bane," says Malone, "is the final proof that Denmark was the scene of the episode."[50] "The conduct of the fæmnanþegn must have been as offensive to Ingeld as it was to the son of Wiðergyld, and the slaying, we may be sure, gave great satisfaction to the Heaðobardish king.... Both kings in the circumstances would do the diplomatic thing. The killing would be pro-

[46] J. Hoops, *Beowulfstudien,* p. 73; Klaeber's edition, p. 203.

[47] "Zur Gestaltung und Erklärung des Beowulftextes," *Anglia,* LXII (1938), p. 182. I can find nowhere in Anglo-Saxon a parenthetical participial absolute used in place of a temporal clause.

[48] *Bibliothek der angelsächsischen Poesie,* I (Kassel, 1883), p. 225.

[49] Wyatt-Chambers edition of *Beowulf,* p. 101, note to line 2035.

[50] "Notes on *Beowulf,*" *Anglia,* LXIII (1939), p. 111.

claimed a strictly private matter, without political significance.... If need be, Ingeld, the lord of the bane, would see to it that a proper wergeld was paid. But the kinsmen of the dead man could not be expected to take so calm a view of things. Under Germanic law it was their duty to wreak vengeance, and we have every reason to think that the bane was fleeing from them ... But neither flight nor pursuit would have taken place in the land of the Heaðobards. There the Danish avengers obviously could have done nothing, except enter into negotiations for the payment of a wergeld. In Denmark, on the contrary, one would expect just such a flight and pursuit as we find recorded in our text. We conclude therefore with certainty that the slaying of the fæmnanþegn took place in Denmark."[51]

This is a broad, and in my opinion a rather illogical, interpretation of the meager information given in the text; Beowulf's words are:

'. . . . . . . him se oðer þonan
losað (li)figende, con him land geare.' (2061b–62)

Nothing is told us concerning the feelings or the actions of Ingeld or of Hrothgar immediately after the slaying, concerning the payment of wergeld, or the identity of those who pursued the slayer. Almost immediately *after* these lines, however, we are told of the consequences of the killing:

'Þonne bioð (ab)rocene on ba healfe
aðsweord eorla; (syð)ðan Ingelde
weallað wælniðas, ond him wiflufan
æfter cearwælmum colran weorðað.' (2063–66)

It is clear that the slaying of the young Dane has as its almost immediate consequence (*þonne*) the violation of oaths on both sides—that is, the breach of the compact of peace; hate wells up in Ingeld, and his love for his wife cools. Yet, though the killing of the *fæmnan þegn* may have given great *secret* satisfaction to Ingeld, he was at the moment of the slaying still bound by the compact, and in love with Freawaru; for lines 2065–66 imply that his love for her had not cooled at the time of the slaying. He must therefore have resented a killing which both violated his pledged word and endangered his marriage.

[51] "Time and Place," p. 90.

His word had been set at naught by one of his own retainers; the Danes would have been quick to demand redress, and his honor required him to take some action against the slayer. The text affirms that the latter escaped because he knew the country well. Now it is much more likely that a young Heaðobard would know his own land well than that he should have known the Danish countryside. It is idle to presume that, as a soldier, he had found means to acquire a thorough knowledge of Denmark; he was too young to have taken part in the earlier campaigning against the Danes, and so could have had little opportunity to 'know well' a country potentially hostile. If, after killing a Dane, he sought to escape from Denmark, Danish forces would have been hard on his heels and every man's hand would have been against him. But he did know his own country well and, as Huppé pointed out, there "friendly hands unquestionably help him escape."[52] There, among friends, he could easily lie *perdu* until Ingeld's "love for his wife cooled," and the renewal of hostilities should make it safe for him to reappear. In reality, then, the flight of the slayer in territory familiar to him is evidence that the action takes place in the land of the Heaðobards, and that the slaying occurred at Ingeld's court.

The poet of *Beowulf* gives no motivation at all for the conduct of the *fæmnan þegn* which precipitates his death; he tells us only that the young man wears, in the presence of Ingeld and his following, a sword which his father had taken from a slain Heaðobard, and that an old spear-warrior eggs on the son of the sword's former owner to take vengeance. He neither says nor implies that the *fæmnan þegn* "enlisted confederates among the Danes, . . . and they worked hard to prevent the marriage by constantly insulting Ingeld and his men."[53] Indeed, the assumption that more than this one Dane offered insult to the Heaðobards rests upon the supposed plurality of *dryhtbearn,* and upon Malone's interpretation of *gomelra lafe* (line 2036) as comprising a greater weight of spoils than one man could carry.[54] I have attempted to show that *dryhtbearn* can properly be taken as singular.

[52] *Op. cit.* (note 29, *supra*), p. 221.
[53] Malone, "Time and Place," p. 88.
[54] *Ibid.,* p. 80, n. 11.

It is significant that the embittered spear-warrior does not accuse any of the Danes except the *fæmnan þegn* of wearing spoils taken from the Heaðobards; it is only this one young man whom he denounces. This may, of course, be explained on the ground that he needed only to arouse one Heaðobard to action, and therefore adverts only to the conduct of the one Dane who can be regarded as insulting that particular Heaðobard. Yet, if a group of Danes insulted the Heaðobards in general, we should expect the grim veteran to make something of it. Not at all; he expends his wrath upon the single Dane.

Moreover the poet tells us, not that the young Dane was slain for any deliberately provocative conduct of his own, but that he was killed *fore fæder dædum*. This comes close to an exoneration of deliberate offense. It was natural enough that he should wear a sword which he had inherited from his father; he may have been ignorant of its provenience, or, at worst, he may have worn it in careless forgetfulness. Certainly the son of that Heaðobard who originally owned it shows no knowledge that it had once been his father's, until the old spear-warrior brings the fact to his attention. The reason for the young Dane's death is not simply that he wears the sword of a slain Heaðobard; it is that his father had slain that Heaðobard, and that killing calls for killing. But the killing would not have occurred if a vengeance-hungry veteran had not been present to point out to the son of the slain Heaðobard that splendid weapon which should have been his inheritance but is now being worn in his presence by the son of his father's slayer.

We need not assume more than the text tells us: we need not take for granted that the *fæmnan þegn,* or any group of Danes, meant to offer insult, to boast or strut. The boasting and strutting reside not in his or their actions, but in the interpretation which the old spearman places on those actions. It is he, not the poet, who imputes their actions to malice. He is hungry for vengeance; he is eager to whip up his young comrade's spirit to the killing-point. Naturally he imputes evil motives to the young Dane. How else could he make sure that the Dane is killed than by convincing his comrade that the wearing of the sword is an intended insult, a conscious, boastful provocation?

Nor need we think of the plunder mentioned in the text as constituting a great weight for one Dane to bear. The terms used are *gomelra lafe . . . Heaðobeardna gestreon . . . ðæm wæpnum.* The last of these three terms makes it plain that only weapons are being spoken of; and since the poet on occasion uses a plural for a single person or thing (e.g., *bearnum ond broðrum,* meaning 'a son and a brother,' line 1074a), the three terms just quoted can easily refer to a single object. That they do refer to one object—the sword—seems indicated by the terms used by the old spear-warrior in his speech: having spoken of one article of plunder worn by the *fæmnan þegn,* and identified it as a sword (*mece . . . dyre iren,* lines 2047b, 2050a), he then refers to it—and to it alone—by the plural *frætwum* (2054a), and in the next line he calls it *þone maðþum,* using a word which can be either a strict singular or a collective. In short, the plurals *lafe, wæpnum,* and the collective *gestreon,* in lines 2036–38, may very well refer to that single thing, the sword, which the old spearman calls by the plural *frætwum.* There is no need to take *dryhtbearn* as plural to account for the carrying of the object or objects referred to.

This view is strongly fortified by the adjectives which the poet uses to modify *Heaða-Bear(d)na gestreon*—a term which itself only varies *gomelra lafe.* Those adjectives are *heard* and *hringmæl. Heard* is an epithet appropriate to weapons, but not to other forms of articles of value; *hringmæl* is used of weapons—usually of swords—only. It is an adjective here; in lines 1521 and 1564 it is a noun, and clearly means 'sword.' In *Genesis* 1992 we find the combination *hringmæled sweord.* In all these instances, though they are few, the word *hringmæl* (or *hringmæled*) is used only of swords. In line 2047 the 'plunder' worn by the young Dane is specifically described as a sword. Accordingly, since the action turns on the wearing of a sword by this young Dane, and the only specific terms used in describing the 'plunder' mean 'sword,' the evidence seems to favor singular number for *dryhtbearn* and for the pronoun *him* in line 2036; one young Dane wears a Heaðobard sword, and it is his conduct which offends the Heaðobards.

Now if we look back to lines 2032 ff., and accept Grein's emendation of *biwenede* to *bi werede,* then, with *dryhtbearn* understood as singular, the passage becomes strikingly dramatic and wholly logical:

'It can then offend the king of the Heaðobards, and each of the thanes of that people,[55] when he, a lordly scion of the Danes, comes into the hall with the maiden, *past the ranks of the* [Heaðobard] *veterans;* on him shine the heirlooms of the men of old, hard and ring-adorned, the treasure of the Heaðobards, so long as they were permitted to wield those weapons ...' As the young Danish escort of the princess leads her to the king, past the veteran warriors of the Heaðobards, Ingeld and his warriors recognize the sword as one which had belonged to a slain Heaðobard; and this offends them. So far as the text permits us to judge, if any other Danes are present they take no part in any conduct insulting to their Heaðobard hosts.

Malone's strongest—indeed, his irrefutable—argument against the prophetic interpretation is the argument on artistic grounds. But that argument can be used with still greater force against the historical interpretation. Consider the situation: Hrothgar has determined to betroth his daughter to Ingeld, in order to end an ancient and bloody feud. If we accept the historical view of Beowulf's report, Ingeld comes with a following to Heorot, for the betrothal or for the marriage. Throughout his visit, young Danes (the *fæmnan þegn* and his associates) parade before the Heaðobards wearing precious objects plundered from slain Heaðobards; they do this day after day, giving wanton offense to their guests. Such behavior is, in the first place, most inadequately motivated: if either party were looking for trouble, it should be the Heaðobards. They had lost the last battle; their casualties had been heavy, and their king had been slain. They had cause to desire revenge; the Danes had not. The Danes could afford to let bygones be bygones; yet the historical view of the episode assumes that it is they who desire to provoke a renewal of the feud.

In the second place, the conduct which Malone's interpretation imputes to the Danes is in gross violation of the Germanic code, which held hospitality a sacred duty. The behavior of the Gepidae when Alboin the Lombard visited their court affords a striking contrast, and offers a standard by which that view of Danish conduct may

[55] The text uses the plural: *þara leoda.* This is certainly an instance of plural for singular, since whatever action is referred to in these lines can be offensive only to the Heaðobards, not to the Danes.

be judged.[56] Alboin had defeated the Gepidae and slain the son of their king Thurisind; yet, when Alboin boldly enters his enemy's hall, Thurisind receives him graciously and places him in the seat of that son whom Alboin had slain. When the king's second son mocks Alboin and his men, and one of the Lombards retorts with a savage allusion to that battle in which the Gepids and their king's son had fallen, Thurisind restrains his men's wrath, gives Alboin the arms of his dead son, and sends him home with honor. Similarly Hrólf, in *Hrólfssaga* cap. 23, refuses to let his followers kill Bjarki, who has slain one of them, rebukes his men for their evil custom of throwing bones, and takes Bjarki into his service. Yet the historical interpretation of the Ingeld episode represents Hrothgar as looking on weakly and helplessly, while his men treat their guests with shocking discourtesy.

In situations like those presented by Alboin's daring entry into Thurisind's hall, by Bjarki's killing of a Dane in the hall of Hrólf, or by the assumed presence of Heaðobards in Heorot, it is only to be expected that the monarch who receives hostile guests should keep his men in order, as Thurisind and Hrólf did. It is entirely out of harmony with all that the poet tells us of the noble society of Heorot and the excellence of King Hrothgar that so great a monarch should neither exert nor possess control over his men. Old as Hrothgar is, he is consistently represented as a courteous and gracious king; and—until the revolt of Hrothulf—as in firm control of his thanes. It is inconceivable that the poet, having presented Hrothgar as an almost ideal ruler, should suddenly let him lapse from the character so painstakingly given him. To have done so would have been a much greater artistic blemish than to permit Beowulf to prophesy, in detail, events of the proximate future.

Moreover, neither the time-scheme nor the focus of the main narrative has room for such a dramatic interlude as a visit by Ingeld to the Danish court, nor for daily scenes of provocation by the Danes and resentment by the Heaðobards. The poet has accounted for every hour of Danish activity, every hour of Hrothgar's time and attention;

[56] Paulus Diaconus, *Historia Langobardorum,* ed. L. Bethmann and G. Waitz (*Monumenta Germaniae Historica,* Script. Rer. Germ., XXXIV, Hannover, 1878), I, p. 24.

the king and all his men are absorbed in Beowulf's combats with the two trolls, and with the proper rewarding and entertainment of the hero. Not only is there no indication that these all-absorbing matters were interrupted by, or were concurrent with, any other and disturbing action which could challenge them for attention; the whole narrative is occupied by the deeds and the entertainment of Beowulf—so much so that anything beyond them can hardly be imagined as taking place in Heorot until Beowulf has departed.

If we conceive this scene of violent tension between Danes and Heaðobards as concurrent with the seemly conversation of Beowulf and Hrothgar, with the gracious gift-giving, the songs of the scop to which the warriors listen with rapt attention, then the whole tone of the narrative becomes jangled and false; for the poet has pictured the Danish court as dignified, serene, and harmonious. The author was surely too great an artist to violate this harmony, or to let the epic grandeur of the first part of his work be invaded by an action of sheer sensationalism.

So it comes to this: if the present tenses between line 2032 and 2058 are consuetudinal, setting forth what had gone on day by day in Heorot during Beowulf's visit, then what they report is inconsistent with all that we are otherwise told about the Danish king and the Danish court, improbable in itself, and impossible to reconcile either with the content or with the tone of the main narrative. Therefore we must reject the view that these presents are consuetudinal, and that they relate what had taken place during Beowulf's visit to Heorot and continued for some time thereafter. Accordingly we are forced to find another interpretation of the episode—and it must not be the prophetic interpretation, for Malone has effectively disposed of that.

Those lines which frame the episode, lines 2029b–31 and 2067–69a, express Beowulf's grave doubts that the projected marriage between Hrothgar's daughter and Froda's son will end the feud. Lines 2029b ff. affirm that royal marriages contracted in the hope of settling a feud in which a prince has fallen seldom succeed in averting bloodshed and renewed war. Lines 2067–69a state that, in Beowulf's opinion (*Þy ic . . . ne telge*), the Danes cannot count on the good faith and friendship of the Heaðobards. All that lies between this frame of general axiom and specific though cautious conclusion, then, sets forth Beowulf's reasons for doubting that the marriage of Freawaru to Ingeld will end the sanguinary strife between the two peoples. Reasons for *doubting;* not reasons for *knowing:* Beowulf does not pretend to *know* that the feud will break out again. He merely gives it as his opinion that the faith and friendship of the Heaðobards toward the Danes will be broken. Even allowing for litotes, this is not prediction; it is reasonable conjecture. The very caution with which Beowulf's view is expressed points, I believe, to the proper interpretation of the 'episode,' all of which is used to account for Beowulf's doubts of the success of Hrothgar's policy.

Comparison of the version of the Ingeld story in *Beowulf* with that in the sixth book of Saxo's *Gesta Danorum* will give another clue to the meaning and the purpose of the episode. By Saxo's time, the political realities of the relations between Danes and Heaðobards—indeed, the Heaðobards themselves—had been forgotten, so that Ingeld and his father appear, in Scandinavian story, as Danish kings; and in Saxo the enemies of Frotho and Ingellus are not Danes, but Saxons. Saxo represents Ingeld's bride as daughter of the Saxon king Swerting, who had slain Ingeld's father Frotho; as in *Beowulf* she was daughter of Hrothgar, who (as Hróarr) was one of Froði's slayers in *Hrólfssaga.* In both Saxo and *Beowulf* Ingeld is persuaded by her kindred (in *Beowulf* by her father, in Saxo by her brothers) to take her in marriage, since in both versions the bride's relatives wish to end the feud. In *Beowulf* an embittered veteran present at the feast stirs up the feud anew by egging a young Heaðobard to kill a young Dane; in Saxo the ferocious veteran Starkad, who had been Ingeld's guardian and Frotho's devoted follower, appears at the feast and stirs up Ingeld himself to avenge his father Frotho by killing the sons of Frotho's slayer.

Saxo does not specifically tell us that the feast at which Starkad incites Ingeld to avenge is in celebration of Ingeld's marriage; but the fact that the bride's brothers are present as honored guests, and the magnificence of their entertainment, strongly suggests that it is the wedding feast. In Saxo, Starkad's whetting speech is not repeated, as is the whetting of the old warrior in *Beowulf;* but its intent is the same—revenge. In Saxo, the slaying of the two Saxon princes successfully accomplishes that revenge; in *Beowulf,* the slaying of the young Dane merely makes war certain and Heaðobard vengeance possible. That possibility is not realized; for, as *Widsið* tells us, the Heaðobard invasion was crushed at Heorot.

In spite of their divergences, the two versions are very close to each other. The greatest difference between them resides in the person incited by the bitter veteran to take vengeance for his father. Whereas, in *Beowulf,* the veteran's egging is directed to a nameless young Heaðobard, whom it incites to kill the son of his father's slayer, in Saxo it is Ingeld himself whom Starkad incites, and who kills his bride's brothers and thus avenges his father.

In its representation of the political situation, *Beowulf* is closer to historic reality than Saxo's story: naturally, since it is centuries older. Nevertheless, in the matter of the person incited, the person who slays and thus avenges his father's death, Saxo's account seems to me much closer to what must have been the original form of the Ingeld legend. In both versions we are dealing with legend; there can hardly be any doubt that the source of the episode in *Beowulf* was a heroic lay. We know that such lays of Ingeld were current in England: Alcuin's letter to the Bishop of Lindisfarne "testifies eloquently to the popularity of the Ingeld story, and further evidence is possibly afforded by the fact that few heroes of story seem to have had so many namesakes in Eighth Century England."[57]

Moreover, the pattern of the story in Saxo's version is that which Lawrence has defined so clearly, and which we recognize in other heroic legends: a hero, caught between conflicting obligations, or between duty and self-interest, is for some time unable to resolve his dilemma. At last, often—as in this instance—through the intervention of another person who is a strong partisan, he is stirred to make his decision, and acts in the manner required by the heroic code.[58] The heroes of Germanic legend are princes or notable champions; only such personages could fitly exemplify the Germanic code.

But, strangely, in *Beowulf* the person incited to avenge his father's

[57] Chambers, *Beowulf: An Introduction,* p. 22.

[58] See my "Design and Motive in the Finn Episode," pp. 21–23.

death, the person who, by slaying the son of his father's bane, precipitates the renewal of the feud, is not a personage of any eminence at all. He is a nameless young Heaðobard; his Danish victim is equally nameless; Ingeld remains in the background, taking no action until the killing of the *fæmnan þegn* forces his hand. All the major participants are nameless: a young Dane, an old spearman, a young avenger. This is not at all the manner of heroic legend, and it should excite our surprise. If, in the lays known in eighth-century England, the person who avenged his slain father and brought about the renewal of the feud had been any other than Ingeld himself, there would have been no legend of Ingeld: the hero of such lays would have been the actual slayer, and he would have had a personality and a name. Germanic lays know no nameless heroes. Chambers is certainly right in maintaining that the Danish version of the story as told by Saxo "preserves much more of the original character of the story, for it remains the tale of a young prince who, willing to marry into the house of his ancestral foes and to forgive and forget the old feud, is stirred by his more unrelenting henchman into taking vengeance for his father."[59]

In this respect Saxo's version is in closer accord with the character of the feud as reported in *Hrólfssaga* and in *Widsið:* in both, the participants are named. Prince slays prince; vengeance is always taken by the royal victim's kin: Fróði kills Halfdan, and the latter is avenged by his sons Hróarr and Helgi; Ingeld is crushed at Heorot by Hrothgar and Hrothwulf. In Saxo, Ingellus himself avenges his slain father, in harmony with this pattern. There is therefore every reason to believe that, in the lays known to the poet of *Beowulf,* it was Ingeld himself who, incited by a bitter veteran, slew some Danish noble—quite probably a member of the Shielding house—at the marriage-feast.

Saxo's Starcatherus reviles Ingeld as degenerate and unworthy of his ancestors; Ingellus has to refute the charge by striking down his father's slayers. How much more degenerate and unworthy Ingeld would have seemed to any Germanic audience if he had left to a nameless subordinate the duty which rested upon himself! In any

[59] *Beowulf: An Introduction,* p. 24.

legend of Ingeld, Ingeld must have been the avenger, as he is in Saxo's version; and so it must have been in any lay of Ingeld known to the poet of *Beowulf* and his contemporaries.

It follows that our poet chose to obscure the acting personages of the story as he and his audience knew it, and that he did so for a specific artistic purpose. In doing so, he could count on recognition by his hearers of the nature and the purpose of his procedure: familiar as they were with the traditional course of action, they would perceive his alterations, and understand the reason for them.

But he did more than blur the identity of the acting personages. That feature of the story on which Saxo's version and the episode in *Beowulf* most closely agree is the killing of a kinsman or attendant of Ingeld's wife in consequence of the incitations of an embittered veteran. But the two accounts do not agree upon the occasion for the incitation. In Saxo, Starcatherus is indignant that Ingeld, instead of avenging his father's death upon the sons of Swerting, has accepted their sister's hand in marriage, and shows them marked friendship and favor. In *Beowulf,* on the other hand, the veteran is angered, not by Ingeld's acceptance of peace with the Danes and marriage to the daughter of his father's slayer—which, to the Germanic mind, is really the point at issue,—but by the sight of a nameless Dane wearing arms taken from a Heaðobard slain in the earlier fighting—which is entirely incidental to the main issue.

The poet, then, departed from the typical pattern of Germanic legend both in respect of the person who avenges and in the motivation of the old warrior's egging speech and of the slaying which is its consequence. This is the problem with which the episode confronts us: why has the author of *Beowulf* not told the legend of Ingeld precisely as he and his hearers knew it; why has he furnished the tragic resolution with an unnamed protagonist, and the inciter to bloodshed with a new motive?

He was concerned primarily not with Ingeld, but with Beowulf; he does not tell the story directly, as author, but lets Beowulf tell it. Beowulf can tell only what he knows; though he can put his own construction on what he knows. Beowulf has seen Freawaru at Heorot, and has been told of her betrothal to Ingeld. This is news of political interest to Hygelac. Since Beowulf has pledged Geatish aid to Hrothgar against any foe (lines 1826–35), the success or failure of Hrothgar's design to end the feud with the Heaðobards is a matter of consequence to the Geats; if the Danes should be faced with renewed war, the Geats might find themselves involved in it. Therefore Beowulf honestly tells his uncle that he expects no good results from Hrothgar's policy: in the last previous stage of the feud Froda has been killed, and there will be those among the Heaðobards who will neither forget nor forgive his slaying. And at the conclusion of the episode he observes, somewhat more specifically, that he rather expects the peace to be broken. These opening and closing statements are so phrased as to make it clear that Beowulf is not predicting, but merely expressing his opinion of the probable outcome. Accordingly all that lies between the general observation that peace-weaving marriages seldom end feuds in which a prince has fallen and the concluding statement of a probable outcome must be, not prophecy of what *will* happen to reawaken the feud, but Beowulf's conjecture about the kind of mischance which *may* easily arise to provoke an act of violence. Once that act is committed, the consequence of an uneasy peace will inevitably be catastrophic.

The poet was not concerned to tell the story of Ingeld as it was known already to his hearers; he wished to *use* it to illustrate Beowulf's wisdom and political insight. Accordingly he represents his hero, not as predicting what the audience knew had happened between Danes and Heaðobards, but as seeing clearly the nature of the dangers which must threaten Hrothgar's hazardous policy, and as suggesting how unforeseen contingencies might bring disaster.

This is the implication of the verb *mæg* in line 2032: Beowulf means, not that 'it will,' or that 'it does,' offend the king of the Heaðobards and his men; but that it *can* offend Ingeld and his thanes if a young Dane accompanying the princess to Ingeld's court should enter the hall wearing arms taken by his father from a slain Heaðobard. The poet lets Beowulf put the matter with dramatic force: '... when he, a lordly young Dane, comes into the hall with the maiden past the ranks of the veterans.' So the princess' escort would do: in entering Ingeld's presence he would naturally pass by the

Heaðobard warriors, and each of them would recognize the looted sword, and be angered. Among those veterans there would inevitably be some bitter old warrior (and here, of course, the poet is drawing directly from his lay source) who ardently desires revenge, and who will whet the son of the sword's original owner to avenge his father's death. This act will take the situation out of Ingeld's hands, since the slaying of a Dane at the wedding feast will violate the oaths sworn on both sides to keep the peace, and constitute a *casus belli*. Beowulf says, in effect: "Suppose some young Danish noble, coming into the hall with the princess past the Heaðobard veterans, wears the sword of a slain Heaðobard: that can be a cause of offense to Ingeld and his men." If such a thing happens, some unreconciled veteran will mark it, and will whet the son of the sword's first owner to take vengeance.

Here is the reason for the namelessness of the acting personages: in the lay or lays known to the poet and his hearers, the characters were not nameless; but since Beowulf is conjecturing the sort of thing that *may* happen to break the peace, he cannot *know* the identity of the old spearman, or of the slayer, or of the slain. The present-tense forms carry future sense, because whatever may happen at the wedding feast still lies in the future. Once such a contingency suggested as possible in lines 2032–40 arises, the consequences will be inevitable. Beowulf can foresee the probable outcome once the contingency occurs; he is only conjecturing the possible nature of the contingency itself.

The poet's audience, knowing that it was actually Ingeld who was incited to vengeance for his father Froda, would understand and find pleasure in the dexterous exploitation of the story to illustrate Beowulf's wisdom, which both the poet and Hrothgar had already asserted. They would recognize that Beowulf could not know precisely what, from his point of view, was yet to happen, or through whom it would happen; but they would be impressed by the hero's power to sense the kind of danger to which Hrothgar's policy was liable under the ticklish circumstances, and to see through how slight a mischance the participants might stumble into war. There could be no better demonstration of Beowulf's deep, perceptive wisdom than this dramatic expression of his judgment upon the most serious of Hrothgar's ventures into foreign policy: he reaches, through thoughtful reflection upon the historical background of the royal marriage, upon the sensitive pride of the Heaðobards, and the chance of a single accident of human folly, a conclusion not identical with, but sufficiently similar to, that which the audience knew to have been the actual outcome.

With sound judgment the poet retained the central feature of the legend without substantial change: the bitter resentment of an old soldier who had never forgiven the Danes, and his egging speeches. Almost any unhappy accident could offer such a man an opportunity to set mischief afoot. The poet merely altered the occasion of the veteran's wrath from the royal marriage and Ingeld's acceptance of peace with his father's slayers to the careless or reckless act of Freawaru's escort, and substituted for Ingeld a nameless young Heaðobard as the avenger whose act brought catastrophe in its train.

A poet of slighter skill might have introduced the figure of Freawaru, and told her unhappy story, directly, in the course of his narrative of the feast at Heorot. But our author knew that the scenes in the royal hall are sufficiently loaded with the intimations of tragedy in store for the Shieldings; to have added, at that point, the tragedy of Freawaru to those of Wealhtheow and Hrethric would have been to overload the matter of the subplot to the detriment of the main action. The concluding scene of Part I, in which Beowulf makes his report to Hygelac, is exactly the right place for the story of Freawaru and Ingeld; and Beowulf, rather than the poet himself, is the proper narrator. In this whole scene the admirable qualities of Beowulf are directly and dramatically presented: first through his own words to Hygelac, and through his demonstration of his love and loyalty in his gift to Hygelac of the rewards received from Hrothgar; then through the poet's eulogy of his conduct and character (lines 2177 ff.). Immediately after the conclusion of this scene comes the opening of Part II, in which Beowulf appears as king. The scene in Hygelac's court is obviously intended to show forth those qualities which make Beowulf worthy of the crown. It is most just, therefore, that in this scene he should appear both as loyal and devoted kinsman and as wise and perceptive statesman.

◇ ◇ ◇

NOTE: While I have been occupied with this chapter, I have been in correspondence with Professor Malone, and have discussed my views with him by letter. He now writes to me: "I have been thinking about the Ingeld story a great deal since our last exchange of letters, and have concluded that you *must* be right in your interpretation of *mæg* (Beowulf 2032). Neither the historical nor the prophetic interpretation is free of serious difficulties; your brilliant solution seems inescapable. But I am still convinced that the action of the episode took place at the Danish court and that *dryhtbearn Dena* is simply a poetic way of saying *Dene* (plural)."

This very generous acceptance of my interpretation of the meaning and use of the episode is only one of many great kindnesses which Professor Malone has shown me. If we still differ with respect to the scene of action in the episode and the number of *dryhtbearn,* it is a matter of the greatest pleasure and satisfaction to me to have the assent of so distinguished a scholar to my general interpretation of the Ingeld story.

VII

CHRISTIAN AND PAGAN IN BEOWULF

The late Sir Hector Monro Chadwick believed that the poem of *Beowulf* "has come down from heathen times and acquired its Christian character gradually and piecemeal from a succession of minstrels."[1] In his view the original poem had undergone a succession of interpolations which transformed it from a pagan work into one superficially Christian. Similar opinions had been expressed by Blackburn, Henry Bradley, and others: Bradley attributed the Christian passages to a late redactor, and regarded them as "poetically of no value."[2] Klaeber, on the other hand, regards the Christian elements as "almost without exception so deeply ingrained in the very fabric of the poem that they cannot be explained away as the work of a reviser or later interpolator . . . the main story has been thoroughly imbued with the spirit of Christianity."[3] Klaeber's argument has been

[1] "Early National Poetry," in *Cambridge History of English Literature,* I (1907), pp. 30 ff.; *The Heroic Age* (Cambridge University Press, 1912), pp. 49 ff.

[2] F. A. Blackburn, "The Christian Coloring in the *Beowulf,*" *PMLA,* XII (1897), pp. 205–225; Henry Bradley, article "Beowulf" in *Encyclopædia Britannica,* 11th ed., Vol. III, p. 760.

[3] Edition, p. l. See Klaeber's very important papers collectively entitled "Die christlichen Elemente im *Beowulf,*" *Anglia,* XXXV (1911), pp. 111–136, 249–270, 453–482, XXXVI (1912), pp. 169–199.

powerfully and convincingly sustained by Kemp Malone.[4] Their work, reinforcing that of Brandl and Chambers,[5] has effectively settled the question. The original traditional material of the story was pagan; the poet who composed the *Beowulf* we know was a Christian, and the poem as it has come to us *is Beowulf,* and fully reflects its author's mind and spirit. "It shows us a picture of a period in which the virtues of the heathen 'Heroic Age' were tempered by the gentleness of the new belief; an age warlike, yet Christian: devout, yet tolerant."[6] Although much of the pagan Germanic spirit, together with motifs and situations descending from pagan times, remains discernible, the refashioning of ancient pagan stuff has been so complete that the extant poem is essentially a Christian epic.

I am unable, however, to share Klaeber's conviction that in the figure of the hero the poet "was almost inevitably reminded of the person of the Savior, the self-sacrificing King, the prototype of supreme perfection"; or that "we might even feel inclined to recognize features of the Christian Savior in the destroyer of hellish fiends, the warrior brave and gentle, blameless in thought and deed . . ."[7] Blameless and sacrificial as the hero's life is, he is at bottom a Germanic warrior, whose spirit is touched and refined by the Christianity of the poet. In the figure of Beowulf the heroic ideals of Germanic paganism and of Anglo-Saxon Christendom have been reconciled and fused, so that the hero exemplifies the best of both. This has been admirably shown by Schücking, who has pointed out the distinctively pagan and the clearly Christian elements in the fusion, and shown that some of the finest elements in the character of the hero, and in the ethos of the poet, are common to both ideals.[8]

The pagan and the Christian elements that combine in the person

[4] In a paper read before the Modern Language Association of America, which I have not been able to find in print.

[5] Brandl in Paul's *Grundriss,* 2d ed., II, 1, p. 1003: "Wer die unheidnischen Elemente aus dem Beowulfepos vollständig entfernen will, muss es umdichten." See Chambers, *Beowulf: An Introduction,* pp. 121–128.

[6] Chambers, *Beowulf: An Introduction,* p. 128.

[7] Edition, pp. cxxi, li.

[8] L. Schücking, "Das Königsideal im *Beowulf,*" *Bulletin of the Modern Humanities Research Association,* III (1929), pp. 143–154, and *Englische Studien,* LXVII (1932), pp. 1–14.

of Beowulf complement, rather than oppose, one another. Beowulf's readiness to avenge his slain uncle and cousin, and his counsel to Hrothgar that "it is better for every man to avenge his friend than to mourn him greatly" (lines 1384b–85), are by no means the expression of a spirit purely pagan: throughout the Christian Middle Ages revenge for one's kin or for one's lord continued to be regarded as the duty of a warrior. It is the *moral* virtues of Beowulf which are particularly Christian, although Germanic society in pagan times would have valued them in a prince who was also preëminent as warrior and protector of his people. His *social* virtues are historically pagan; that is, they descend from the traditional code of the *comitatus*. But they are also such as would have won a prince the love of his people in any Christian kingdom. As Chambers reminds us, the age in which *Beowulf* was composed could not wholly cast aside its Germanic inheritance in cherishing the new faith and embracing its teachings.[9] In the poem as in its hero, old and new, pagan and Christian, combine in a heroic synthesis, in which Christianity gives new meaning, new beauty, to the concepts of fortitude and personal fidelity inherited from pagan times.

Blackburn observed that the Scriptural allusions in the poem are to the Old rather than the New Testament; that they include no "reference to Christ, to the cross, to the virgin or the saints, to any doctrine of the church."[10] But this is in perfect harmony with the theme and the purpose of the work: the poet did not set out to compose a *Genesis* or a *Crist;* he had to compose a poem the hero of which moved and acted among men, as warrior and king, in an age which the poet knew to have been heathen. Yet he composed for a Christian public—a public which knew and loved the old pagan legends, but which also knew that salvation could be found only in the Church of Christ. Accordingly he had the task—not an easy one, certainly—of reconciling his hearers not to the story, but to his personages. His audience was, of course, prepared to accept heroes of pagan antiquity as protagonists in a heroic action; but they must also be induced to accept the nobler characters—Beowulf and Hroth-

[9] *Beowulf: An Introduction,* pp. 324, 326.
[10] *Op. cit.* (note 2, *supra*), p. 216.

gar above all—as exemplars of an ideal and a course of conduct in harmony with both the best traditions of antiquity and the highest ideal of Christian Englishmen.

The poet's situation was very different from that of the author of the *Chanson de Roland.* The *Roland,* as we know it, was the product of an age in which, at home, the struggle between Christianity and paganism had long been decided, but in which paganism was an external, yet a living, menacing foe; the Saxon had been converted, but the Saracen constituted an ever-growing threat. *Beowulf,* composed in an effectively converted England, which was as yet not threatened by pagans from without, reconciles the heroic spirit of the pagan past with Christian heroism; the *Roland* opposes to Moslem "heathenism" the unrelenting hostility of the Knights of the Cross:

'"Paien ont tort, et Chrestien ont dreit!"'

The poet of *Beowulf* had no need to polemize or to indoctrinate. His reconciliation of Germanic past with Christian present is so nearly perfect because his story confronted him with nothing that could seriously hamper the reconciliation. Allowing for inevitable social and political change, the ideal which his hero illustrates is admirable in any enlightened age. Loyalty to kindred and to state (however the state be conceived), scrupulous observance of one's word, steadfast fortitude in any situation, readiness to stake one's life in a good cause, trust in God and submission to His will—these are the qualities of the hero, and the virtues emphasized by the poet. Of these, only the last is exclusively Christian; the others are the ingredients of a noble character in any age and culture.

The "Christian coloring" of *Beowulf* does not reveal itself in the action of the poem, except as that action is the expression of character. It appears in the words and the conduct of those personages whom the poet, drawing on older story, conceived as noble, and whom he was concerned to represent as acting nobly by the standards of his own Christian age.

Certain scholars have thought to find, in the most visibly Christian passages of *Beowulf,* evidence of interpolation and expansion by hands later than those of the author, and would excise these supposed additions as unoriginal or inconsistent. It is remarkable how much more fastidious in the matter of consistency critics are than authors. There *are* inconsistencies in *Beowulf* (though not so many or so grave as some believe); and the easiest way to deal with inconsistencies in a work of art is to blame them on an interpolator or a *remanieur*. But the easiest way is not always the best: complete consistency in a long narrative is so difficult to attain that we hardly have a right to demand it. The greatest poet may suffer a lapse of memory; or, in seeking for specific effects at different times, he may fall into discrepancies which, even if discovered, might not have troubled him or his public. Brandl has pointed out that inconsistencies as striking as those in *Beowulf* may be found in the plays of Shakespeare.[11]

Beowulf, like the Homeric epics, was composed for the enjoyment of a society which had not yet produced professional critics. The Anglo-Saxon audience might well have held the poet accountable for defects of diction, style, or meter, and might be critical of his handling of traditional story. But the kind of critical interest which carps at occasional minor lapses in a long narrative poem did not develop until an age posterior to that in which native heroic poetry was created—an age which had witnessed the growth of a tradition of written history and scholarship. The *reading* public for *Beowulf,* in the Old English period, must have been quite small; the work was surely known primarily through oral recitation. So long as there was no large reading public to demand scrupulosity in small matters, a poet could hardly have been expected to concern himself with it.

If, in virtue of these considerations, and in the light of Brandl's discussion, nearly all the inconsistencies of *Beowulf* can be disregarded as irrelevant to a judgment of its artistic quality, one remains which cannot be ignored: the sharp incongruity between the poet's representation of the Danish court in generally Christian terms, together with his attribution to Hrothgar of sentiments monotheistic if not specifically Christian; and his characterization, in lines 175–188, of the Danes as pagans, who offer sacrifice to heathen idols for deliverance from Grendel. Hoops justly refers to this contrast as

[11] In Paul's *Grundriss,* 2d ed., II, 1, pp. 1005–1006.

"diese unleugbare Inkonsequenz";[12] it has plagued generations of scholars.

Tolkien, who has done so much to illumine the meaning of the poem, has failed to clarify this particular problem; indeed, he has complicated the primary inconsistency with a contrast of his own making between the hero and the Danish king. Although he, like Klaeber, sees in the monsters slain by Beowulf the enemies of God, symbolizing "(and ultimately to become identified with) the powers of evil...,"[13] he does not agree with Klaeber that, in the portrayal of Beowulf, the poet had in mind "the person of the Savior,... the prototype of supreme perfection." For Tolkien, the symbolic struggle between good and evil has, in our poem, distinctly pagan Germanic antecedents: "The undoubtedly scriptural Cain is connected with *eotenas* and *ylfe,* which are the *jötnar* and *álfar* of Norse. But this is not due to mere confusion—it is rather an indication of the precise point at which an imagination, pondering old and new, was kindled. At this point new Scripture and old tradition touched and ignited. It is for this reason that these elements of Scripture alone appear in *a poem dealing of design with the noble pagan of old days.*"[14] Tolkien sees behind the struggle of monsters against a God aided by a human hero the poet's inspired remembrance of the myth of Ragnarök, the struggle of the old gods, aided by the *einherjar,* against Surt and Loki, Midgard Serpent, Fenris-Wolf, and their allies. He believes that the author deliberately set the action of his work in days that he knew to be "heathen, noble, and hopeless,"[15] and that the hero is, as it were, transplanted from the ranks of Odin's champions.

In accordance with this view of the fusion of the old pagan with the new Christian ideal, Tolkien draws his distinction between Hrothgar and Beowulf: "It would seem that, in his attempt to depict ancient pre-Christian days, intending to emphasize their nobility and the desire of the good for truth, [the poet] turned naturally when delineating the great King of Heorot to the Old Testament.

[12] *Kommentar zum Beowulf,* p. 39.

[13] Tolkien, "Beowulf: The Monsters and the Critics," *Proceedings of the British Academy,* XXII (1936), pp. 261–262, 269; cf. Klaeber's edition, p. l.

[14] Tolkien, *op. cit.,* p. 269. Italics mine.

[15] *Ibid.,* p. 264.

In the *folces hyrde* of the Danes we have much of the shepherd patriarchs and kings of Israel, servants of the one God, who attribute to His mercy all the good things that come to them in this life. We have in fact a Christian English conception of the noble chief before Christianity, who could lapse (as could Israel) in times of temptation into idolatry."[16] The character of Beowulf, he thinks, is "in some respects much closer to the actual heathen *hæleþ*."[17]

This partly explains the *Inkonsequenz;* but at heavy and needless cost. There is really no parallel at all between the combat of gods and *einherjar* with monsters on the field of Ragnarök and Beowulf's fights with two trolls and a dragon. In the Norse myth, the gods cannot defend themselves without the help of the heroes; that is why, in *Eiríksmál,* Odin explains to Sigmund why it has been necessary for him to deprive Eirík of life. In *Beowulf* the situation is reversed: Beowulf can conquer Grendel and his dam only through the help of God (lines 1270 ff., 1657b–58). The imagery of the pagan myth would hardly bear the same meaning to a pagan as to a Christian poet of the Age of Bede: to the latter, the old gods themselves were devils (note the poet's use of the term *gastbona* in line 177). Moreover it is doubtful that the myth of Ragnarök was known to eighth-centry Englishmen. In the form in which it has come down to us in the Eddas, that myth is to a considerable degree the invention of skalds rather than a genuine and widely accepted belief. The figures on the Gosworth Cross do indeed attest that the struggle of Ragnarök was known in Northumbria at a later time; but the artist who created those figures was quite certainly a Scandinavian. Again, Tolkien seems to believe that the conflict between the ancient gods and the host of Surt ended in the defeat of the gods; but this is a misapprehension. If Odin, Thor, and Frey were slain by their terrible adversaries, these also perished in the fight; and the destruction of the old universe was conceived as followed by the emergence of a new and better world.

Neither the dragon in *Beowulf* nor the race of Grendel represents the types of monster which engaged in that last struggle with the

[16] *Ibid.*, p. 270.
[17] *Ibid.*

gods of Asgard. Fenris-Wolf and the Midgard Serpent are cosmic monsters, quite unlike the gold-guarding dragons slain by Sigemund and Beowulf; Loki, Surt, and their allies, however gigantic, are the foes of gods, but not devourers of men. Grendel and his dam are not themselves engaged in direct conflict with God: they are His enemies only in virtue of their descent from Cain and because they prey upon mankind. They are *trolls:* their hate is directed against mortals. They are creatures of the same sort as the trolls killed by Grettir at Sandhaugar. No Englishman of pagan times—much less a Christian poet—would have associated such man-eating trolls with the much more portentous monsters that stormed Asgard.

It is scarcely just, then, to see in our poet's insistence upon the descent of the race of Grendel from Cain—a conception otherwise well attested in medieval Christian belief—"an indication of the precise point at which an imagination, pondering new and old, was kindled." The linkage of Grendel and his kind with the race of Cain—twice made specifically, and reinforced by the implication in lines 1688 ff. that the 'writing' on the magic sword of God's victory over the giants is a kind of symbol of Beowulf's victories,—means only that Beowulf is conceived as the champion chosen, and helped, by God against the monstrous foes that harry mankind in this world.

In the opposition between Klaeber and Tolkien more than the character of the hero is involved: if the poet regarded his story as one "of ancient pre-Christian days," and his hero as a noble pagan, that is one thing; if, as Klaeber believes, "the whole life was felt to be dominated by Christian ideas,"[18] that is something quite different, and the difference affects our interpretation of the entire poem. Since both opinions are founded upon the same evidence, the evidence needs to be reconsidered. First we must examine the relative frequency and force of those Christian sentiments expressed by Hrothgar, by Beowulf, and by the poet as commentator; leaving until the last those two conflicting passages which confront us with the *unleugbare Inkonsequenz.* For those two throw little light upon all the other expressions of piety in the poem, but are rather illumined by them.

[18] Edition, p. xlix.

The "Christian passages" in the poem are numerous: without counting as separate instances those which occur in clusters within a few lines of one another, approximately twenty-seven are the utterances of the poet himself. These range from such brief and relatively unimpressive expressions as 'such as God had given him' (line 72), or the commonplace that 'mighty God ruled the race of men universally' (lines 701–702), to such longer and more striking passages as the two accounts of the descent of Grendel and his dam from Cain, and the first of the massive controversial passages which we are for the moment passing over (lines 168–188). The author's allusions to God crop up so frequently, and often so casually, as to exclude the possibility of regarding them as later additions to an originally pagan poem. Their pervasiveness, and the warmth and vigor of a number of them, show that the poet was a man of deep Christian conviction.

Hrothgar speaks with the piety of a Christian king. Although religious sentiment is expressed in only five of his speeches, one speech alone, uttered when he sees Grendel's arm hung up over the gable of Heorot, contains no fewer than five exclamations of thanks to God and recognitions of God's power and mercy (lines 928–956). His long moralizing address to Beowulf (lines 1709–84) is the most significant and outspoken Christian passage in the poem. The frequency of Hrothgar's utterances of this sort is all the more notable because they occur within 1,507 lines (lines 381–1887), at the end of which he has no further part in the action.

Beowulf is a very close second to Hrothgar in the number of his allusions to God, to God's mercy, or to God's power or judgment. These appear in nine of his speeches—more correctly in eight, since his long monologue in Part II is broken only momentarily at line 2510. One of his speeches contains two recognitions of God's mercy in close succession (lines 1657b–58; 1661 ff.).

Tolkien does less than justice to the Christian character of the hero's words. Hrothgar, he says, "refers all things to the favour of God, and never omits explicit thanks for mercies. Beowulf refers sparingly to God, except as the arbiter of critical events, and then principally as *Metod,* in which the idea of God approaches nearest to the old Fate. We have in Beowulf's language little differentiation of God and Fate.... Beowulf only twice explicitly thanks God or acknowledges His help... Usually he makes no such references. He ascribes his conquest of the nicors to luck... Beowulf knows, of course, of hell and judgement: he speaks of it to Unferth; he declares that Grendel shall abide *miclan domes* and the judgement of *scir metod;* and finally in his last examination of conscience he says that *Waldend fira* cannot accuse him of *morþorbealo maga.* But the crimes which he claims to have avoided are closely paralleled in the heathen *Völuspá*... Other references he makes are casual and formal, such as *beorht beacen Godes,* of the sun (571). An exceptional case is *Godes leoht geceas* 2469, describing the death of Hrethel... Both these expressions have, as it were, inadvertently escaped from Christian poetry.... Where Beowulf's thoughts are revealed by the poet we can observe that his real trust was in *his own might.*"[19] Tolkien even maintains that Beowulf's fear that he has offended God, and that the dragon's ravages are visited upon him in punishment (lines 2327a–32), "is a heathen and unchristian fear—of an inscrutable power, a *Metod* that can be offended inadvertently: indeed the sorrow of a man who, though he knew of God, and was eager for justice, was yet far estranged, and 'had hell in his heart.' "[20]

All this is sadly mistaken. Hrothgar acknowledges God's mercy and power in terms no closer to those of Christian devotion—and no less close—than those used by Beowulf. The king observes that *Halig God* in His mercy has sent Beowulf to deliver the Danes from Grendel (lines 381b ff.); that God can easily dispose of Grendel (478b–79); that God has power to work wonder upon wonder (930b–31); that Beowulf has conquered Grendel *þurh Drihtnes miht* (940); that Beowulf's mother can say the Ancient of Days (*Ealdmetod*) was gracious to her in her childbearing (945 ff.); he thanks God for the sight of Grendel's arm (928 ff.); he prays that the All-Ruler (*Alwalda*) may continue to reward Beowulf (955 ff.). There are four references to God in Hrothgar's long address to Beowulf (1700–

[19] "Beowulf: The Monsters and the Critics," pp. 285–287.
[20] *Ibid.,* p. 287.

84), and one in his last words to the hero (1841). He uses the word *God* six times, the word *Metod* (or, once, *Ealdmetod*) twice.

Beowulf three times "refers to God ... as the arbiter of critical events" (lines 440b–441; 685b–687; 967–979)—as often as Hrothgar. The hero acknowledges God's help, or gives thanks to God, *not* twice, but three times, twice in a single speech:

1) '. . . . . .   ætrihte wæs
guð getwæfed,   nymðe mec God scylde.'   (1657b–58)
2) 'ac me geuðe   ylda Waldend,
þæt ic on wage geseah   wlitig hangian
ealdsweord eacen   —oftost wisode
winigea leasum—   (1661 ff.)
3) 'Ic ðara frætwa   Frean ealles ðanc,
Wuldurcyninge   wordum secge,
ecum Dryhtne,   þe ic her on starie
þæs ðe ic moste   minum leodum
ær swyltdæge   swylc gestrynan.'   (2794 ff.)

In addition, he attributes his inability to prevent Grendel's escape from the hall to the fact that *Metod* did not will it; and in lines 977b–979 he couples his mention of the Last Judgment with the term *scir Metod*.

In the three passages just quoted Beowulf expresses a gratitude to God, and a recognition of His protection and goodness, fully as deep and strong as any of the pious expressions of Hrothgar. The second, moreover, contains an explicit recognition of God's special favor to the friendless—a sentiment which no pagan would have been moved to utter in praise of Fate. The third passage, in its threefold designation of God as Lord of All, King of Glory, and Eternal Lord, is fully as Christian as anything spoken by Hrothgar.

Tolkien's dismissal of Beowulf's examination of conscience on the ground that "the crimes which he claims to have avoided" are also reprobated in *Völuspá* is beside the point. Murder of kin and the breaking of oaths are abhorrent to any decent society; the point of importance is that Beowulf disclaims having offended God by such crimes. The term he here applies to God, *Waldend fira,* is identical in meaning with *ylda Waldend* in his decidedly Christian speech which includes lines 1657–64.

The characterization of Beowulf's fear that he has offended God as "a heathen and unchristian fear," and the assertion that the hero "was yet far estranged, and 'had hell in his heart,'" are rejected by the two Catholic theologians whom I have had the privilege of consulting. Beowulf's state of mind here is not attrition, but readiness for contrition: in his last speech (lines 2794 ff.) he manifests "a lively sense of the infinite goodness of God." It is only right and proper that a man visited by affliction should search his heart for evidence of sin, lest he incur the peril of questioning God's justice.

It is not true that Beowulf "refers sparingly to God, . . . and then principally as *Metod*." He refers to God three times as *Drihten* (lines 441, 686, 2796); four times as *God* (570a, 685b, 1658, 2469b); once as *ylda Waldend* (1661); once as *Waldend fira* (2741); once as *Frea ealles* (2794); once as *Wuldorcyning* (2795); and only twice as *Metod* (967, 979). The poet himself—a thoroughly good Christian—repeatedly refers to God under the title *Metod*. Indeed, far from being a term close in sense to the heathen Fate, *Metod* is one of the commoner terms for God in the purely Christian religious poetry of Anglo-Saxon England.—Tolkien makes much of Beowulf's use of *Metod* in line 2527, where *metod manna gehwæs* is apparently a variation of *wyrd;* but this is the only instance of the word in *Beowulf* in which the referent is not God.

Hrothgar refers to God in five of his seven speeches; such references occur in seven out of Beowulf's fourteen. Most of Hrothgar's expressions of piety are concentrated in two speeches (lines 928–956; 1716–79). Hrothgar's 'Christian' sentiments are more concentrated; Beowulf's, more widely distributed and fully as fervent. Obviously, in composing every utterance of each person, the poet considered the relevance of the words to the speaker and to the occasion of the speech. In Part I, Hrothgar is an old man, to whom long experience of life, the persecutions of Grendel, and the mounting infirmities of age have brought home the dependence of man on the power and mercy of God. Beowulf, on the other hand, is, during this part of the action, young and strong; he has known no affliction, and has excellent reason to be confident in his own might. If anything should surprise us, it is that, so circumstanced, he so readily and frequently acknowledges the power of God, and so warmly expresses his indebtedness to God for his victory over Grendel's dam. In Part II, when Beowulf is himself old, and has suffered the loss of his kinsmen and seen the decline of his nation's strength, he acknowledges God in each of his three speeches.[21] If his mention of God is brief and apparently casual in the long monologue (line 2469b), it is longer and full of piety in lines 2741 ff., 2794 ff. In rendering fervent thanks to God for permitting him to buy the dragon's treasure for his people at the price of his own life, Beowulf expresses a feeling fully as pious and as unselfish as the gratitude of Hrothgar for the deliverance of the Danes from Grendel.

I see little justice in Tolkien's distinction between the value of Beowulf's direct testimony about his own state of mind and that of the poet's statements concerning it. Surely we should not expect the two to differ? Who should know better than the author what went on in the minds of his characters? Tolkien tells us: "Where Beowulf's thoughts are revealed by the poet we can observe that his real trust was in *his own might.* That the possession of this might was a 'favour of God' is actually a comment of the poet's . . . Thus in line 665 we have *georne truwode modgan mægenes, metodes hyldo.* No *and* is possible metrically in the original; none should appear in translation: the favour of God *was* the possession of *mægen.* Compare 1272–3: *gemunde mægenes strenge, gimfæste gife þe him God sealde.*"[22] But Tolkien has ignored a piece of evidence which destroys his argument, and shows us plainly what the poet had in mind. The lines last quoted (1270–71 in most editions) are immediately followed by

> ond him to Anwaldan are gelyfde,
> frofre ond fultum . . .

Here is a parallel to Tolkien's first quotation (actually lines 669–670): in both passages, the poet affirms that Beowulf was confident in his own might but looked to God for favor and help. This combination

[21] I count his entire monologue as one long speech, since the breaks at lines 2510–11a and 2516–18a are only momentary.

[22] "Beowulf: The Monsters and the Critics," p. 287.

of faith in oneself and trust in God is what one expects in a hero; later echoes of it sound in "Trust in God and keep your powder dry," and in "Praise the Lord and pass the ammunition."

It is to be observed that other personages of the poem, directly associated with Beowulf, express Christian sentiments. The Captain of the Shore, once assured of Beowulf's friendly purpose, prays that the All-Ruling Father (*'Fæder Alwalda,'* 316 ff.) will preserve him. Hygelac thanks God that he is permitted to see Beowulf safe (*'Gode ic þanc secge . . . ,'* lines 1997b–98). Wiglaf twice uses the name of God (2650b ff.; 2874b–75). The poet twice assures us (227–228; 1626b ff.) that the Geats who accompanied Beowulf to Denmark gave thanks to God for benefits received.

Only two of Beowulf's utterances—and nothing else in the poem—afford even negative support to Tolkien's supposition that the poet thought of his hero as in any sense a heathen *hæleþ*. The first instance is the opening of Beowulf's reply to Hrothgar's appeal for help against Grendel's dam. Beowulf's commendation of the act of avenging a slain friend, and his assertion that the achievement of glory 'is best for a man of valor afterward, when he is no longer living,' may sound pagan to the modern ear; but it did not sound so to the Anglo-Saxon. Leofsunu and Dunhere, who were indubitably Christians, speak in precisely the same terms in *Maldon* (lines 258–259, 246–248).

The second of the two speeches in question is uttered just before the dragon-fight begins, and contains the lines on which Tolkien relies most heavily:

'. . . . . .　　Nelle ic beorges weard
oferfleon fotes trem,　　ac unc [furður] sceal
weorðan æt wealle,　　swa unc wyrd geteoð,
Metod manna gehwæs. . . .'　(2524b–27a)

This may mean 'as Fate appoints, as the Lord of each of men ordains'; if, however, *Metod* is a variation of *Wyrd,* then Beowulf refers, not to God, but to Fate, as the 'measurer' of life for every man. But even if the second translation is correct, there is no reason to suppose that he is thinking as a pagan, or that he has in mind a heathen Fate uncontrolled by God. Hrothgar, the "noble monotheist," declares that

Wyrd has swept away his thanes (line 477); the poet tells us that *Wyrd* took away Hygelac in Frisia, and forecasts his hero's death by saying that, in the fight with the dragon, "*Wyrd* had not ordained for him triumph in battle' (lines 2574–75a). Yet Tolkien would not admit that Hrothgar was thought of as heathen, or that the poet was pagan.

Line 1056 affords us some insight into what the poet meant by *Wyrd:*

> nefne him witig God   wyrd forstode
> ond ðæs mannes mod.

The poet evidently conceived *Wyrd*—except when he uses the word in the sense of a fate befalling a man—as a force determining a man's life subject to the authority and will of God. This is very close to the Boethian conception of *Fortuna.* The poet could properly permit his hero to speak of *Wyrd,* as the agent of God, as the *metod* of every man. In the Alfredian *Boethius, Wyrd* is used in just this sense:

Ðæt ðætte we hataþ Godes foreþonc and his foresceawung,... siððan hit fullfremed bið, ðonne hataþ we hit wyrd... Sio wyrd dælþ eallum gesceaftum andwlitan and stowa and tida and gemetgunga. Ac sio wyrd cymð of ðam foreþonce Godes...[23]

It would be most unfair to assume that, in Beowulf's speeches alone, *Metod* is used in a pagan sense. In the many lines in which it is used by the poet as narrator or commentator it plainly and invariably means 'God'; the words used as variations for it demonstrate this: *vide* lines 106–110; 180b–181; 1056–57; 1609–11.

Tolkien's distinction between Hrothgar the "noble monotheist" and Beowulf the noble "heathen *hæleþ*" is, then, to be rejected. The hero is as much a Christian as Hrothgar—and no more. The question is: did the poet really conceive either of them as a Christian? Both speak as believers in the One God quite consistently; both act as Christian Englishmen of the eighth century might, at their best, be expected to act. More we cannot say until we have explored more deeply.

And first we must consider the *unleugbare Inkonsequenz.* If lines

[23] Bertha S. Phillpotts, "Wyrd and Providence in Anglo-Saxon Thought," *Essays and Studies by Members of the English Association,* XIII (1928), pp. 17–27, does not consider this.

175 ff. are genuine, then it is necessary to reconcile the poet's direct statement that the Danes seek deliverance from Grendel by offering sacrifices to heathen gods with the Danish king's frequent expressions of thanks to God and acknowledgment of God's mercies—and particularly with the patently Christian sentiments of Hrothgar's long address to Beowulf after the overthrow of Grendel's dam. Lines 175 ff. (the so-called Christian Excursus) also conflict with the attribution to Hrothgar's scop of a lay of the Creation, only 77 lines earlier.

The simplest way of resolving the inconsistency would be to throw out as interpolated all of the Christian Excursus; but few would go so far. The more generally favored course is to reject its more troublesome lines, and to exclude also those portions of Hrothgar's long speech (1700–84) which are most difficult to reconcile with whatever parts of the Excursus one wishes to retain. This is questionable procedure, and it will not solve the problem; it is still necessary to interpret whatever of the Excursus one retains in a manner which the text scarcely admits.

Tolkien rejects lines 168–169 and 181–188; and from Hrothgar's sermon he excludes as interpolated lines 1724–60[24]—the most genuinely Christian passage in the poem. This would soften, but would not remove the inconsistency. Klaeber, more conservatively, finds the sermon "open to the charge of having been interpolated by a man versed and interested in theology . . . ," and observes that "one might suspect an inept interpolation [in lines 168 ff.]." This passage, he feels, "appears singularly awkward."[25]

If we delete as unoriginal all that Tolkien wishes to exclude, the way then appears to lie open to the solution which he offers: in what remains, "the poet must have intended a distinction between the wise Hrothgar, who certainly knew of and often thanked God, and a certain party of the pagan Danes—heathen priests, for instance, and those that had recourse to them under the temptation of calamity."[26] But this is open to serious objection: it is incredible that the poet could have thought of the Danish society of Heorot as divided into a thoroughly pagan priesthood and a laity which, normally worshipers

[24] "Beowulf: The Monsters and the Critics," n. 34, p. 284; pp. 287–288.

[25] Edition, pp. 190, 135.

[26] "Beowulf: The Monsters and the Critics," p. 287.

of the true God, could relapse into paganism. His argument is inconsistent in itself: at one point he includes even Hrothgar among the relapsing Danes;[27] and his view of the Danes as in large part normally worshipers of God is in conflict with his belief that the poet "knew clearly" that "those days were heathen."[28]

Even if we regard as interpolated all the lines which Tolkien wishes to delete, there is still no possible support for the view that the idol-worship of the Danes was a temporary relapse into paganism under the impact of Grendel's persecution. Tolkien himself does not reject lines 171b–180:

. . . . . . Monig oft gesæt
rice to rune; ræd eahtedon,
hwæt swiðferhðum selest wære
wið færgryrum to gefremmanne.
Hwilum hie geheton æt *hæ*rgtrafum
wigweorþunga, wordum bædon,
þæt him gastbona geoce gefremede
wið þeodþreaum. Swylc wæs þeaw hyra,
hæþenra hyht; helle gemundon
in modsefan, Metod hie ne cuþon . . .

This clearly describes a general and undivided appeal by the great men of the Danes to their pagan gods, not the apostasy of a mere faction led by heathen priests. The poet makes no distinction between a party of monotheists and a party of pagans. The influential men among the Danes, after solemn deliberation over all imaginable means of meeting the national peril, offered sacrifice at the fanes of their idols. This could not have been done without the active participation of the king; there is not the slightest evidence that the poet meant to except Hrothgar.

Nor can the idol-worship of the Danes be explained as a relapse; the poet is quite clear on that point:

. . . . . . Swylc wæs þeaw hyra,
hæþenra hyht . . . . . .
. . . . . . Metod hie ne cuþon . . .

[27] *Ibid.*, p. 270.
[28] *Ibid.*, p. 264.

Both Tolkien and Klaeber admit these lines as genuine. The poet tells us in the plainest terms that the Danes—all of them—were heathen; that their sacrifices to their heathen gods were 'their custom, their hope,' and that they 'did not know the Lord.'

We are, then, compelled to the conclusion that the poet knew the Danes were, and always had been, pagan. Klaeber, after considering the possibility that their idol-worship "might . . . indicate that in time of distress they returned to their former ways—as was done repeatedly in England . . . ," says justly that "it is at least equally possible that the author, having in mind the conditions existing among the Danes of the sixth century, . . . failed to live up to his own modernized representation of them."[29]

Nothing can justify a critic either in ignoring the plain language of a text, or in excising all those lines of an ancient poem which fail to accord with his preconceptions or to please his taste. The charge that a passage has been altered or added by a hand later than the poet's can be maintained only by concrete and convincing evidence: evidence of style, grammar, meter, or diction too clear to be ignored; not evidence of content alone, unless the content conflicts with its context in ways that admit of no reasonable explanation. To find such evidence is not easy: Schücking, great as his authority is, has not been able to convince the majority of scholars that certain passages of *Beowulf* show grammatical, syntactic, or metrical divergences sufficient to warrant their exclusion.[30]

Tolkien's rejection of lines 181–188 is supported by no such evidence; he simply feels that, "unless my ear and judgement are wholly at fault, they have a ring and measure unlike their context, and indeed unlike that of the poem as a whole."[31] This is too vague and subjective to constitute valid criticism. One may agree with him that "the place is one that offers . . . special temptation to enlargement or alteration," and still doubt that it offers "special facilities for doing either without grave dislocation."[32] And how do the lines which he believes interpo-

[29] Edition, p. 135.

[30] Schücking's views are criticized effectively by Chambers (*Beowulf: An Introduction*, pp. 117–120).

[31] "Beowulf: The Monsters and the Critics," p. 288.

[32] *Ibid.*

lated affect the situation? They merely expand and emphasize, without altering, the sense of those lines (171–180) which he admits as genuine.

Klaeber and Tolkien object to lines 168 ff. on different grounds. Tolkien, deeply impressed with the piety and the consonance with Christian belief of almost all the utterances of Hrothgar, rejects these lines because they may be so interpreted as to raise a question of the king's monotheism. Klaeber, rather unhappily accepting this portion of the text as it stands, feels that the only grammatically justified interpretation of the lines is "singularly awkward" and "inept."[33] The major difficulty lies in the pronoun *hē,* in line 168:

> no he þone gifstol gretan moste,
> maþðum for Metod, ne his myne wisse.
> Þæt wæs wræc micel wine Scyldinga,
> modes brecða.

There are minor difficulties in almost all these seven verses; but the major problem is the reference of *hē*. The pronoun is generally taken as referring to Grendel: Klaeber puts the case thus: "The possibility of identifying *hē* with the king is too remote to be seriously considered," since Grendel has been the subject for the preceding 15 lines,[34] and Hrothgar has not been mentioned since line 152a. If *hē* refers to Grendel, then lines 168 ff. must be understood in one of the following ways:

1) Grendel was not permitted to approach the throne of God; that is, because of the monster's evil nature and God's hostility to him, he had no hope of heaven; or

2) Grendel was not permitted to approach Hrothgar's throne on account of the Lord, nor did he know God's favor (or: 'nor did God take thought of him').

The second of these interpretations is itself capable of two meanings: (*a*) Though Grendel haunted Heorot every night, and killed many thanes, he was not allowed to attack the king personally, because of the interposition of God, who had no love for the monster;

[33] Edition, p. 135.
[34] *Ibid.*, p. 134.

or (*b*) Grendel was not allowed, because he was prevented by the Lord, to approach the royal throne; i.e., though making his home in the hall at night, he was unlike a faithful retainer, who can approach the throne to receive gifts from his lord.[35] "This explanation," Klaeber remarks, "is sufficiently strange, but, perhaps, less far-fetched than the one resting on the interpretation of this noun [*gifstol*] as the throne of God."[36]

In and of itself, the first interpretation of the second rendering given above (2, *a*) is entirely reasonable: God intervened to exempt Hrothgar's person from Grendel's attacks, though no other Dane was safe. The second interpretation of this translation (2, *b*), based upon the poet's ironical characterization, in line 142, of Grendel as *heal-þegn,* would carry irony to the point of absurdity; moreover, if *hē* cannot refer to Hrothgar because the king has not been mentioned since line 152a, it is unlikely that the ironic *healþegn* in line 142 can be felt as carrying over to lines 168 ff. The rendering of *gifstol* as the throne of God is indeed far-fetched; the poet would hardly trouble to insist upon Grendel's damnation in this context. But Klaeber, by insisting that *hē* must refer to Grendel, has compelled himself to choose among interpretations none of which satisfies him, or to admit that "one might suspect an inept interpolation here."[37]

Moreover, all these interpretations which assume that *hē* refers to Grendel are abruptly rendered ridiculous by the lines immediately following (170–171a): 'That was a great distress to the lord of the Shieldings, a torment of spirit.' It should be obvious that Hrothgar would not be in the least distressed by God's intervention to prevent Grendel from 'approaching his throne' to kill the king, or by the knowledge that Grendel, the 'hall-thane,' could not expect gifts from him.

Klaeber, conscious of this incongruity, attempts to resolve it by setting off lines 168–169 with dashes, so that it becomes a parenthesis, and that lines 170–171a may be taken as referring to the content of lines 164–167: 'Thus many terrible deeds the foe of mankind, the cruel walker in solitude, often performed, cruel humiliations; he in-

[35] *Ibid.,* pp. 134–135.
[36] *Ibid.,* p. 135.
[37] *Ibid.*

habited Heorot, the treasure-bright hall, on dark nights—he was not permitted to approach the throne, that precious thing, because of the Lord—that was a great distress to the lord of the Shieldings, a torment of spirit.' This does not help matters much. If we imagine the poet as declaiming these lines to his audience, we recognize that to indicate with any clarity the parenthetical nature of lines 168–169 would be difficult. Logically they should not be parenthetical: the emphatic expression of Hrothgar's distress (lines 170–171a) ought to follow directly upon the exposition of its cause. Moreover, this great grief and affliction stressed here looks like something other than the grief ascribed to Hrothgar in lines 129 ff. and 147–166a; this is not his long-endured sorrow at Grendel's depredations, but a particular sorrow, emphasized by the demonstrative *þæt* in line 170a, a sorrow which should arise from a very specific cause. So long as we refer *hē* in line 168 to Grendel, lines 170–171a appear to imply that Hrothgar was distressed at his own exemption from attack, or at Grendel's damnation; for the demonstrative *þæt* should refer to the statement immediately preceding.

The problems posed by these lines can be solved, at once and completely, by taking *hē* as referring to Hrothgar—and in no other way. It was so taken by Holtzmann, who was not disturbed by the fact that Grendel had been the subject for the last seventeen lines: "Solche plötzliche Übergänge sind in der angelsächsischen Poesie bekanntlich nicht selten. *Weil* Grendel Heorot bewohnte, konnte er, Hrodgar, den Gabenstuhl nicht grüssen, d.h. den Thron nicht besteigen, und das war ihm ein grosser Kummer."[38] Trautmann also took *hē* as refering to Hrothgar, and translated lines 168 ff. thus: "Er [Hroðgar] durfte den gabenstuhl, den kostbaren, wegen Gottes nicht berühren, und er kannte nicht die absicht des schepfers. Das war dem Hroðgar ein grosses elend, ein herzeleid."[39] Trautmann, like Klaeber, was indeed disquieted that *hē* stands so far from the name *Hroðgar,* and supposed that a line or more had been lost just before line 168. But such an assumption is quite unnecessary.

[38] A. Holtzmann, "Zu *Beowulf,*" Pfeiffer's *Germania,* VIII (1863), pp. 489–490.

[39] M. Trautmann, "Berichtigungen, Vermutungen und Erklärungen zum *Beowulf,*" *Bonner Beiträge zur Anglistik,* II (1899), p. 135.

George Lyman Kittredge, in oral comment to his students, also took *hē* as referring to Hrothgar, and as used in anticipation of *wine Scyldinga* in line 170b. He regarded *wine* as nominative, and read the lines thus:

no he þone gifstol   gretan moste,
maþðum for Metode,   ne his myne wisse,
(þæt wæs wræc micel)   wine Scyldinga
(modes brecða).

Use of the personal pronoun (especially the third-personal pronoun) in anticipation of a noun which explains the reference is very common in Old English poetry: Klaeber mentions among the stylistic traits of *Beowulf* the "following up of a pronoun by a complementary descriptive phrase—in the manner of a variation,—as in *hi . . . swæse gesiðas* 28 f., *þæt . . . Grendles dæda* 194 ff. . . ."[40] There are many instances in the poem: *he . . . sigerof cyning,* 618b–619b; *hie . . . Denigea leode,* 694b–696a (involving a change of reference from Geats to Danes); *him . . . Wedera leodum,* 696b–697a (with change of reference); *he . . . mæg Higelaces,* 913b–914a; *he . . . rice þeoden,* 1207b–09a; *he . . . mancynnes feond,* 1274b–76a, etc. Lines 913b–914a offer a parallel of particular force, since in this instance—as in 168–170b—the pronoun refers to one person, though a different person has been the subject throughout the preceding twelve lines; all that is required to make the reference clear is the "complementary descriptive phrase" *mæg Higelaces.*

Nevertheless I cannot regard *þæt wæs wræc Micel* and *modes brecða* as parenthetical; I prefer to take *wine* as dative, and to find support for the reference of *hē* to Hrothgar in the many instances in the poem of wide separation of the pronoun from the last previous name or designation of the referent. Old English authors were not at all troubled by looseness of reference. In the *Anglo-Saxon Chron-*

[40] The same point is made by Brandl, in Paul's *Grundriss,* 2d ed., II, 1, p. 1014: "Vorgesandte Pronomina künden wichtige Begriffe an . . . ," and by Paetzel, *Die Variationen* (see note 2 to chapter ii, *supra*), p. 2: "Ein neuer Begriff wird oft vom Dichter nicht gleich mit dem eigentlichen Wort genannt, sondern wie ein bekannter durch ein Pronomen eingeführt . . . wer gemeint ist." Paetzel cites an instance from the *Heliand: he . . . lofsalig man* (lines 174 ff.). The sentence quoted from Klaeber appears on p. lxv of his edition of *Beowulf.*

icle (*sub anno* 897) the account of Alfred's naval engagement with the Danes uses the plural of the third-personal pronoun in the most ambiguous manner. The references in *Beowulf* 2614–19 are equally loose. It is important to observe, however, that very often—though by no means invariably—the express use of the third-personal pronoun suffices to mark a change of subject, as in lines 1087, 1093, 1263, 1270. In line 2619, after Onela has been the subject for three lines, *hē* refers to Weohstan. To the modern reader this last passage seems ambiguous; to the Anglo-Saxon it was clear: *him* in 2616 changes the referent from Onela to Weohstan; *his* in 2617 changes it back to Onela; *hē* in 2619 changes it back to Weohstan.

But the most remarkable illustration of the use of the third-personal pronoun in reference to a person who has not been mentioned for many lines is that of *him* in line 2490: it refers to Hygelac, though Hygelac has not been mentioned in the preceding 56 lines, and several other men have been mentioned by name in those lines.

Accordingly it is entirely reasonable, and in harmony with Old English poetic practice, to take *hē* in line 168 as referring to Hrothgar; the reference is made quite clear by the explanatory *wine Scyldinga* in line 170b. Once we identify *hē* with Hrothgar, all difficulties vanish, and the whole passage becomes clear and logical. As Holtzmann rendered it: *because* Grendel haunted Heorot every night, Hrothgar could not approach his own throne—on account of the Lord, whose love (or favor) Hrothgar did not know; this was a great affliction to Hrothgar. This interpretation permits a close and lucid integration of lines 168–171a with what precedes and follows: lines 159–167 describe the systematic nightly haunting of Heorot, so ruthless that the king could not enter his own hall after dark (line 168); line 169 gives the reason for this: Hrothgar was a pagan, who did not know God's love, and the Lord was punishing him. Lines 170–171a describe Hrothgar's grief at his nightly exclusion from his hall; lines 171b–183a set forth the sin of the Danes in appealing for help to their false gods, and explain that sin on its natural ground—their inherited custom and belief, and their complete ignorance of the true God. Indeed, lines 178b–183a attempt to excuse them so far as, to a Christian mind, excuse was possible: they did *not* commit the more grievous sin of relapse from Christianity to paganism; they prayed to false gods only because 'such was their custom, the hope of the heathen; they did not know the Lord, ... they had no knowledge of the Lord God, nor indeed did they understand how to praise the Protector of Heaven, the Ruler in Glory.' Thus the poet attempts, so far as he can, to defend the Danes as sinners not from intent, but from inherited ignorance. Lines 183b–188 at once set forth true Christian doctrine and express the poet's feeling that it is a great pity that good men, with the best intentions, can through sheer ignorance of the One God plunge their own souls into damnation.

This is exactly what we should expect from the author of *Beowulf*. As he makes us feel the tragic irony of Wealhtheow's appeal to Hrothulf's loyalty, of Beowulf's well-intentioned but ultimately fruitless promise of help to Hrothgar and Hrethric, of the covenant between Finn and Hengest, and of Beowulf's sacrifice of life to save a people whom his death dooms to destruction; so here he expresses movingly the tragic irony of the situation of the Danes before God mercifully sends Beowulf to them: since they are pagan, king and people, Grendel is permitted to afflict them. Against his furious ravages—which make the hall untenable at night for Hrothgar as well as for his thanes—they take counsel together; but the only recourse which can occur to pagans is prayer and sacrifice to their false deities; they know not God. But this recourse only brings more affliction upon them: Grendel's persecutions continue, and their own souls are placed in peril of hell-fire.

We must admit the inconsistency of the poet's recognition ot their paganism with Hrothgar's almost constant readiness to acknowledge God's mercy, and with his explicitly Christian 'sermon' on the sin of arrogance. But before we examine the inconsistency, we should be sure that we apprehend the nature of the Christian sentiments in *Beowulf*—those uttered by the poet and his personages alike. Some very pertinent things have been said on this point by Chambers: "... to a devout, but not theologically-minded poet, writing battle poetry, references to God as the Lord of Hosts or the Giver of Victory came naturally—references to the Trinity or the Atonement did not ... it may be that in *Beowulf* the poet has consciously avoided dogmatic references, because he realized that the characters in his story were not Christians. That, at the same time, he allows those characters with whom he sympathizes to speak in a Christian spirit is only what we should expect. Just so Chaucer allows his pagans—Theseus for instance—to use Christian expressions about God or the soul, whilst avoiding anything strikingly doctrinal."[41]

In *Troilus and Criseyde* Chaucer puts definitely Christian phrases and sentiments into the mouths of his three chief characters: see, for example, Book I, lines 554–560, 1002–08; Book II, lines 381, 1638; Book III, lines 260, 372–373, 925–926, 1501. On a smaller scale, moreover, Chaucer mixes the elements of Christianity and paganism in a manner completely foreign to the poet of *Beowulf:*

'For love of God; and Venus, I the herye' (III, 951)

The author of *Beowulf* was in a potentially difficult situation, and he faced it as a medieval Christian had to do. Having conceived Hrothgar and Beowulf as good and noble men, he must of necessity represent them as speaking and acting as his hearers would expect good and noble men to do. He could not let them express thanks to pagan gods, which, to him and his contemporaries, were devils—as the word *gastbona* (line 177) attests. Accordingly they must either acknowledge no power superior to themselves, and express no gratitude for mercies and help; or they must acknowledge God and give thanks to Him. The second was the only possible course; the poet could not have exposed Hrothgar and Beowulf to the charge of godlessness and pride. Moreover, a medieval Christian could hardly manage a narrative in which such personages figure without attributing Christian sentiments to them, since such sentiments were part of his own thinking and feeling.

Religious or quasi-religious sentiments in the speeches of the characters in *Troilus and Criseyde* take, in the fashion of the time, three different forms: that which, making use of Christian imagery, has every appearance of genuine Christian utterance, like the speeches of Pandarus in Book I, lines 554–560 and 1002–08; that which, like the Prologue to the *Legend of Good Women,* applies the terms of

[41] *Beowulf: An Introduction,* pp. 126–127.

Christian imagery and doctrine to the convention of Courtly Love; and that which deals frankly with, or directly addresses, pagan gods. Here, if one will, is real inconsistency. Not so with *Beowulf:* in it, the only passage inconsistent with the attribution to its characters of Christian thought and feeling is the Christian Excursus.

In my opinion that passage is wholly genuine, and most deliberate. I believe the poet wished to put on record, once for all, the fact that Hrothgar and his Danes were pagans, and were punished for their idolatry; this was an almost necessary concession to his own place and age. Even so, he could not permit himself to pronounce this judgment without reminding his hearers plainly that the paganism of this good king and his people was their misfortune, not their fault. He could hardly have avoided the admission of Danish heathenism, since his audience surely knew that both Danes and Geats were heathen. The chief personages of his story were Danes and Geats; Beowulf must illustrate the heroic ideal, and Hrothgar must be shown as a great and good king. Therefore, he wisely admitted, early in the poem, the paganism of the Danes, explained it as their unfortunate heritage, and made the most of the tragic irony of the situation. Thereafter he was free to let them speak in those terms of gratitude and reverence for God which, by the standard of his own time and country, good men use. As Chambers has pointed out, the poet's avoidance of more strictly doctrinal terms, of reference to Christ or the saints, is to be explained on the ground that he knew the Danes and Geats *were* pagans.

It may not be inappropriate to point out that Chaucer also stressed, in the much-debated Epilogue to *Troilus and Criseyde,* the tragic consequences of the worship of heathen gods, as the author of *Beowulf* did in the Christian Excursus. The necessity of this procedure should be apparent.

Our poet's intentions have, I think, been somewhat obscured by interpretation of the phrase *þurh sliðne nið* (line 184a) as equivalent to a simple adverbial phrase of manner: Klaeber translates it "in dire distressful wise."[42] This translation finds support in such phrases as *þurh egesan* 'terribly' (line 276), *þurh hæstne had* 'violently' (line

[42] Edition, p. 136.

1335). Such *þurh* phrases are indeed often equivalent in sense to simple adverbs; but they are not always so used. They are not restricted to the expression of manner; many of them express means, instrument, or cause: e.g., *þurh rumne sefan* (line 278); *þurh sidne sefan* (1726); *þurh Drihtnes miht* (940); *þurh wæteres wylm* (1693); *þurh hreðra gehygd* (2045). The context of line 184 favors taking *þurh sliðne nið* in a causal or an instrumental sense, since the poet's comment is a generalization from the situation in which the Danes find themselves in consequence of Grendel's persecution: 'Woe to him who is compelled, *through cruel persecution,* to thrust his soul into the embrace of fire, to hope for no solace . . . !' It was the cruel ravages of Grendel which imperiled both the bodies and the souls of the Danes. Thus understood, the conclusion of the Excursus is in complete harmony with all that goes before; the Excursus begins, not with line 175, but with line 168; and it is a consistent and logical whole, needing neither emendation nor defense.

Hrothgar's address to Beowulf after the hero's return from the mere has been held to have suffered more or less extensive interpolation; and it has been severely criticized as prolix and unduly moralistic.

Now that Müllenhoff's views of the composition of *Beowulf*[43] are discarded, the charge of interpolation rests most heavily upon the shoulders of Cynewulf.[44] Hrothgar's speech does indeed contain both ideas and turns of phrase which recur in *Crist.* Nevertheless, since the passages of *Crist* which find parallels in the 'sermon' are widely scattered in that poem, and since *Beowulf* is earlier than *Crist,* the most reasonable explanation of the resemblances is that the later poet was influenced by *Beowulf.* We should be justified in assuming that any portion of Hrothgar's speech was interpolated by the author

[43] R. C. Boer "continued to the last to believe that, though Müllenhoff and ten Brink might have applied their methods wrongly, it was still possible to divide up our extant epic of *Beowulf* into the different lays and interpolations out of which it was compounded" (Chambers, *Beowulf: An Introduction,* p. 397). Chambers has refuted Boer's views in his paper, "Beowulf's Fight with Grendel, and Its Scandinavian Parallels," *English Studies* (Amsterdam), XI (1929), pp. 81–100.

[44] G. Sarrazin, "Die Abfassungszeit des Beowulfliedes," *Anglia,* XIV (1892), pp. 399–415, and "Zur Chronologie und Verfasserfrage angelsächsischer Dichtungen," *Englische Studien,* XXXVIII (1907), pp. 145–195.

of *Crist* only if the common matter were more effectively used, and more in harmony with its context, in *Crist* than in *Beowulf*. This is not the case.

It has been persuasively argued by Thomas that our poet derived from the *Daniel* much of the thought and language of the 'sermon,' and the sentiment of the Christian Excursus.[45] Coincidence between two poems in widely separated contexts is much more impressive than coincidence in a single context. If our poet knew *Daniel,* he may have adopted, consciously or unconsciously, thoughts and phrases impressively used in the older poem.

Certainly both the thought and the diction of the portions of Hrothgar's speech that resemble *Daniel* are as effective artistically in the one poem as in the other. The parallelism seems superficial to me, however: the theme, in the passages in question, is the same in both poems; but mood and purpose are quite different. Both poets were concerned with the causes and effects of arrogance in a ruler; but that which, in *Beowulf,* is concentrated in a single speech is scattered, in *Daniel,* over nearly five hundred lines. Moreover, if the poet of *Beowulf* did derive ideas or language from *Daniel,* he has subdued them beautifully to his own purposes.

Klaeber seems to favor Thomas' view of the relation between the two poems: "That Hrothgar should caution Beowulf against the sin of pride, and that the poet should go out of his way to denounce the supposed heathen worship among the Danes, will not appear quite so far-fetched, if the author was guided by reminiscences of *Daniel* which he adapted—not entirely successfully—to the subject in hand."[46] This sentence contains several judgments of value, with all of which I disagree. The poet does *not* "go out of his way" in his comment on the pagan practices of the Danes; he does *not* denounce their heathen worship, but pities them for it and for its consequences; I see nothing far-fetched in either the Excursus or the 'sermon'; and the poet seems to me to have been, in both passages, entirely successful.

Cook's suggestion that the poet of *Beowulf* drew his material for

[45] P. G. Thomas, "'Beowulf' and 'Daniel A,'" *Modern Language Review,* VIII (1913), pp. 537–539.

[46] Klaeber's edition, p. cxi.

Hrothgar's sermon directly from Gregory, rather than through any Old English intermediary, is an excellent one.[47] Marie Padgett Hamilton has shown how deeply the thought of Gregory and of St. Augustine has permeated our poem.[48] She makes an illuminating comment which bears directly upon lines 168–188: "The orthodox Christian belief that the Divine mercies never have been reserved exclusively for the faithful would have left a poet free to represent the Creator as conferring grace on Scandinavian men of good will . . ."[49] We remember that 'God sent' Scyld's son 'as a comfort' to the heathen Danes; and Hrothgar is certain that 'Holy God has sent him [Beowulf] to us out of His mercy.'

It is possible that the poet derived the thought of his sermon from St. Augustine directly rather than through Gregory: the former constantly emphasized the moral danger of pride. Yet we must remember that determination of a poet's sources is of importance only historically, and for our knowledge of his intellectual background; it has no relevance to the artistic quality of his work.

I have said that the poet does not blame the Danes for their inherited paganism. When he regarded them objectively, as a Christian, he necessarily regarded their sufferings as brought upon themselves. But since in his eyes they were good men in all respects save in their unhappy ignorance of God, he was sorry for them; the Christian Excursus makes that plain. He was able to rise above religious difference to explore the tragedy of good men to whom fate had denied knowledge of the true faith. In their ignorance they could not see that, through their very acts of piety, directed toward the only gods they knew, they were the more surely bringing down upon themselves the destruction which they sought to avert through their misdirected prayers. Their tragedy was of the sort that most strongly excited his sympathy: the tragedy that is only exacerbated by the

[47] A. S. Cook, "Cynewulf's Part in Our *Beowulf*," *Transactions of the Connecticut Academy of Arts and Sciences*, XXVII (1925), pp. 385–406.

[48] "The Religious Principle in *Beowulf*," *PMLA*, LXI (1946), pp. 309–330.

[49] *Ibid.*, p. 314.—I incline to seek the source of the poet's thought in Augustine rather than in Gregory: Augustine was constantly preoccupied with *superbia* as the fountainhead of sin, as William M. Green has pointed out ("Initium Omnis Peccati Superbia: Augustine on Pride as the First Sin," *University of California Publications in Classical Philology*, XIII, No. 13, 1949, pp. 407–431).

best-intentioned attempts to avert it. It is only an act of grace—God's inspiring of Beowulf to deliver them—that frees them from affliction in this world.

One consideration which impels me to follow Miss Hamilton in seeking in Gregory or Augustine, rather than in the Old English *Daniel,* the underlying thought of the Excursus and—more particularly—of the sermon is that, in *Beowulf,* Hrothgar and the Danes are the objects of the poet's sympathy; whereas in *Daniel* the worshipers of idols, and the proud king whose arrogance must be humbled, are persecutors of the righteous, for whom, while their idol-worship and pride continue, the poet feels no pity. Moreover, in *Beowulf* the very king whose paganism is made clear in the Excursus is the eloquent speaker against the sin of pride.

Yet the poet's views on the subject of arrogance might well have been the same if he had not known the Fathers. They are views such as any intelligent and well-instructed Christian of his age might have held: *superbia* is a deadly sin. The manner in which his ideas are developed emerges naturally enough from the opening lines of Hrothgar's speech. The whole monologue is well conceived and sustained: unified, eloquent, in harmony with the circumstances and the setting. Klaeber once held this view of it: his analysis of it, and his estimate of the poet's skill in the management of its parts, and of the "weise zurückhaltung des dichters in der ausführung der christlichen motive," betray an enthusiasm not to be found in the comments in his edition: "Jetzt wird dasselbe [the Heremod legend] voll und ganz ausgenutzt und zur grundlage einer direkten predigt gestaltet, welche der lebenserfahrene, friedenliebende könig zur warnung an den auf der gefährlichen höhe des ruhmes stehenden jungen freund richtet.... Und zwar steht die moral der mahnrede in vollem einklang mit dem ton der ganzen dichtung: weises masshalten, gesittung, milde steht dem dichter höher als wilde, rücksichtslose kraft."[50]

Klaeber has here quite justly stressed the occasion which evoked the speech. After long and fearful affliction, Hrothgar has at last

[50] Klaeber, "Die christlichen Elemente im *Beowulf,*" *Anglia,* XXXV (1911–12), pp. 479, 480.

before his eyes the evidence of his complete deliverance. He looks on the severed head of Grendel, and holds in his hand the hilt of the sword with which Grendel's dam has been slain. Before him stands the champion who has saved him and his people, and upon whom he looks as a son. Examining the hilt, with its graven story of God's destruction of that race of giants who had defied Him, the king meditates upon the overthrow by Beowulf of the gigantic Grendel and his mother, descended from Cain, as were those whom God slew through the flood. Thus the hilt assumes the character of a symbol of God's justice on His and on Hrothgar's demonic foes. Surveying it, Hrothgar bursts into praise of the young hero through whom God has delivered him: 'Lo, whosoever furthers truth and justice among the people, who remembers all that is past, the ancient protector of the realm, can truly say that this hero was better born! Thy renown, my friend Beowulf, is exalted throughout the far-lying ways, over all nations!' (Lines 1700–05a.)

But his praise is tempered with gentle admonition; his next words strike the keynote of the sermon that is to follow: 'Thou wilt hold it all—strength together with wisdom of spirit—with steadfast patience' (lines 1705b–06a). This is the indirect statement of the 'text' of the sermon, the text strongly and directly stated in line 1760b: 'Give not thy mind over to arrogance!' Even as Wealhtheow had tactfully assumed Hrothulf's loyalty, so Hrothgar—with better cause—assumes that Beowulf will carry his might and wisdom temperately. Yet, knowing that the greatest heroes are especially susceptible to the sin of pride—as the tragic instance of Heremod attests,—Hrothgar cites that instance, and points its moral. His account of Heremod's sins and their calamitous consequence ends with a direct application of their lesson: 'Do thou take example of him; perceive what is the true virtue of a man! Out of the wisdom of my many winters *I have wrought these words for thy instruction!*' (Lines 1707b–24a.)

Twice—once with complimentary assumption, once by dread example, Hrothgar has warned Beowulf against that sin of *superbia* to which the very gifts that God has lavished upon the young hero make the young and brave most vulnerable; and he leaves no room for doubt that he has spoken for Beowulf's good.

The 'sermon' proper follows immediately. It is not of "excessive length";[51] it extends only from line 1724 to line 1757. It is not the loquacious eloquence of a senile sage: Hrothgar, though old, was by no means lacking in mental or in physical vigor, as Ingeld was yet to learn to his sorrow. Neither is it merely an expression of that love for moralizing with which the poet has been charged. It is straightforward, pertinent counsel from the heart of a wise and experienced ruler to guide the mind and spirit of the young hero whom he loves as a son.

It is excellently designed. Hrothgar has cited the example of Heremod, a prince so richly endowed that his youthful glory could bear comparison with Sigemund's (lines 898 ff.), but who became a bloody tyrant and suffered a miserable end. The very thought of Heremod could not but arouse in Hrothgar's mind wonder at the manner in which 'mighty God, in His great wisdom, dispenses to men understanding, land, and lordship ...' (lines 1724b–27a). Strange also, he reflects, how men so blest may, in their folly, fail to recognize either the divine source or the impermanence of these blessings. Excess of power and fortune induces in them arrogance and greed, till conscience sleeps, and the unwary soul becomes a mark for the arrows of the Devil's temptations. Such a man lays up for himself treasure on earth, and forgets the life to come, because God has given him honors greater than his spirit can bear. In the end he dies; his heirs, without care or compunction, squander his long-accumulated wealth (lines 1728–57).

Here the 'sermon' ends; what follows is its direct application, pointedly addressed to Beowulf: 'Guard thyself, beloved Beowulf, against this fatal sin, O best of men; choose for thyself the better course, eternal counsels; *give not thy mind over to arrogance*.... Now, for a while, the glory of thy strength endures; in time it will come to pass that sickness or the edge shall part thee from thy might—or the clutch of fire, or the surge of flood, or the bite of the sword, or the flight of the spear, or cruel old age; or the brightness of thine eyes

[51] Klaeber, in his edition, p. 190, speaks of the "excessive length" of the moralizing passage.

will diminish and darken:—presently it must be that death, O lordly man, shall conquer even thee!' (Lines 1758–68.)

Here Hrothgar speaks with deep personal feeling: he has felt the cruel power of age, and helplessness under affliction. And so he says at once, pointing his advice with his own experience: 'So I ruled the Ring-Danes for fifty years 'neath the heavens, and with warlike might I fended them in safety from many peoples throughout this earth, ... so that I came to reckon no man under heaven my rival. Lo, a change from all this came upon me in my own realm, misery after mirth, when Grendel, that ancient adversary, became my invader. Great distress of spirit I bore continually from that affliction!' (Lines 1769–78a.)

This is a confession well calculated to impress sharply on Beowulf's mind the lesson which Hrothgar has been reading him. Though Hrothgar had never been arrogant or avaricious like Heremod, yet he himself, in the invincible strength of his youth, and in his resolve to build such a royal hall as men had never known, had sinned the sin of pride; and God had punished him. Recognizing within himself the source of his past wretchedness, the king gives thanks to God that he has lived to look upon the bloody head of that monster through whom his punishment had come upon him. He sends Beowulf to his seat, with the promise of ample gifts in the morning.

It is not the poet, but the king, who speaks: warning, with intense earnestness, one who has become very dear to him to arm himself against that fatal sin which can turn a mighty hero into a grasping, bloody tyrant; or which at best must subject him—as it had done Hrothgar himself—to God's chastisement. In this speech the old king is at his best, wise and great-hearted, passionately concerned that his 'beloved Beowulf' fulfill his youthful promise in a blameless and honored life. The speech is perfectly framed; every sentence is calculated, and nobly phrased, and reminiscent of the Psalms. Only forty-five of the eighty-four lines have any appearance of conventional morality; and these are general only as truth is general—the whole is unmistakably marked as aimed at Beowulf, and animated by paternal love for him.

Very recently Wrenn has revived the charge that the speech is too prolix.[52] It is certainly one of the longest speeches in the poem, exceeded only by Beowulf's long monologue in Part II (lines 2426–2537), and by the melancholy prediction of the Messenger (lines 2900–3027). But it is not at all verbose; it says what it has to say fully, but sharply and plainly. Its occasion, and its motivation, justify it dramatically; in its warm expression of Hrothgar's love for the hero it affords the fullest and most explicit characterization of Hrothgar himself. Without it, that characterization would be incomplete. Klaeber describes the Danish king as "the grand and kindly ruler, full of years, wisdom, and eloquence";[53] but it is in this speech that his kindliness, wisdom, and eloquence most clearly appear. And it is in this, and in his last speech (lines 1841–65), that the poet reveals with greatest beauty the generous affection that had arisen between Beowulf and Hrothgar. The long address, with its 'sermon,' serves to make the final dialogue between them convincing and moving. If the audience's knowledge that the two were never to meet again, and the poet's intimations that Hrothgar and Hrethric have not long to live, lend pathos to the parting scene, it is our recognition of the nobility and wisdom of Hrothgar, and of the depth of his love for the hero, which make the parting tragically beautiful. Without the fullness and warmth of the king's long speech, these qualities would have been imperfectly disclosed.

In spite of the lines with which the Christian Excursus concludes, we can hardly imagine that the poet or his public seriously thought of Hrothgar as doomed to damnation. They knew that Danes and Geats were pagan; but in the character of Beowulf the Geat the poet has given us the very pattern of nobility, the exemplar of *caritas* beyond the measure of any other hero of medieval secular narrative. He surely knew that neither his hero nor the Danish king was in fact a monotheist—for this we have the evidence of the Excursus in the case of Hrothgar. But in the eighth century Englishmen had not yet had cause to think of heathen Danes as their descendants were to think of them; the Danes were not yet, like the King of Spain in

[52] C. L. Wrenn's edition of *Beowulf* (London, Harrap, 1953), p. 90. Yet Wrenn defends the 'sermon' as "entirely satisfying and appropriate in its context and in the ears of the assumed audience" (*ibid.*, p. 213).

[53] Klaeber's edition, p. lxii.

the ballad, "heathen hounds." To the poet's contemporaries, Hrothgar was a heroic figure, a noble personage of ancient legend. Alcuin might insist that Ingeld was damned; but to the generality of laymen in the Age of Bede the characters of heroic legend could hardly have seemed deserving of eternal torment. They had been the models of heroic behavior for centuries; their deeds were still the favorite themes of heroic lays; the heroic code is still reflected in songs as late as that on the battle of Maldon.

It has often been pointed out that an English poet living in the ninth century could not have treated Danes sympathetically. Once England had begun to suffer devastation and slaughter at Danish hands, the paganism of the Danes would have been one more count—and a bitter one—against them. But in the Age of Bede, Englishmen had no reason to regard Danes with hostility; Danish paganism would have been felt as the poet of *Beowulf* feels it: as a natural misfortune for which they could not be blamed. A good Christian, our poet could not ignore their ignorance of the true God; it was a real issue, and he must face it. And so, in the Excursus, he does face it, and reminds us that it is a woeful thing for good men to be compelled, through cruel persecution, to thrust their souls into the eternal fire, and to have no hope of solace or of conversion. If these lines had been interpolated by a later poet, they would have been, not tinged with pity, but informed with hate.

Once he had placed the fact of Danish paganism upon the record, the poet presents Hrothgar in the character of a wise and noble king, and so frames his words and acts as to reflect that character. In the poet's own land and age, such a man would recognize the power and goodness of God; the poet therefore—most fittingly—puts in the good king's mouth such recognitions of God's sovereignty and grace as, to him and his hearers, good men must make. Beowulf, historically a pagan, acts as the instrument of God for the deliverance of the Danes; it is therefore appropriate that he should be treated as possessing the Christian virtues. His life is as noble as that of any English lay Christian of the poet's day; he is in all his words and actions the perfect Christian warrior. The author must have intended his hearers to think of both Hrothgar and Beowulf as not beyond the saving grace of God: so much is explicit in lines 2819–20. Klaeber rightly says that the poet has raised Beowulf "to the rank of a singularly spotless hero, . . . a truly ideal character . . . the warrior brave and gentle, blameless in thought and deed, the king that dies for his people."[54] Beowulf and Hrothgar are the fairest reflection of the poet's ideal: they speak for him to our age as to his own.

And this is why there is no real inconsistency between the Christian Excursus and the poet's attribution of Christian sentiments to his chief characters. They were in fact pagans; and so he tells us frankly in the beginning. But in spirit, as their words and acts reveal them, they are essentially Christian. Having confessed the fact, he thereafter lets them show themselves as deserving God's grace; and that God's grace was vouchsafed to the hero at least the poet attests, in the lines

. . . .   him of hræðre gewat
sawol secean   soðfæstra dom.

Over against the heathenism of the Danes, the poet recognizes a deeper, darker heathenism, for which there is no forgiveness nor grace: that of the race of Grendel. They are *hæþen,* not only in their monstrous nature and actions, but in their descent from Cain; and on all these counts they are damned. Tolkien has shown us how these monsters are "essential, fundamentally allied to the underlying ideas of the poem, which give it its lofty tone and high seriousness."[55] Grendel and his dam represent the forces of darkness and evil as no human enemies could: this is apparent in the terms which the poet applies to them; and we are twice assured that the kin of Grendel are of Cain's race and inherit his curse. They are associated with the giants that contended against God and suffered the due reward for their presumption; they are linked with demons and devils. Such foes are far more formidable than men; in conquering them, Beowulf performs mightier and more glorious deeds than in facing any merely human power. As defender of men against these monsters, he is the champion of God.

But, as we have seen, the dragon, unlike the kin of Grendel, is

[54] Edition, p. li.
[55] "Beowulf: The Monsters and the Critics," p. 261.

not of Cain's brood. Monstrous in shape and strength and fury, he is nonetheless one of God's creatures, neither by definition nor by descent an enemy of God. In fighting him, Beowulf acts as champion of his people, but not as God's champion; and since it is within the foreknowledge of God that Beowulf's people must perish, Beowulf cannot survive his combat with the dragon. This much the poet has made clear: God does not 'avert fate' to save Beowulf's life in his last adventure, as He had done in the hero's earlier struggles. Indeed, we are told specifically (lines 2855–59) that the hero's fall is the judgment of God. Beowulf himself tells us, however, in his last words, that God had permitted him to win the treasure for his people. These two passages together imply plainly that God has willed both Beowulf's victory over the dragon and his death. In both, *Wyrd* has acted as God's agent. *Wyrd,* then, as the poet conceives this force, is not the pagan goddess, and retains no trace of the heathen Norn; the poet's conception of *Wyrd* is purely Boethian.

Since Beowulf's last adversary is not of the brood of Cain, and in consequence his last fight is not against an enemy of God, the hero dies, not as a martyr, but simply as defender of his people. Nevertheless his death is a supreme act of self-sacrifice, a very imitation of Christ; and it is the crowning act of a sacrificial life. Therefore the poet affirms that 'his soul departed to seek the judgment of the righteous'; and the judgment accorded the righteous is a share in the joys of Heaven.

We are given no such assurance with respect to the destiny of Hrothgar's soul. If we are to form a judgment on the basis of what the author tells us, we must balance against the Danish king's noble life and pious recognition of God's mercies the poet's plain statement of the pagan worship of the Danes, in which we must assume Hrothgar's participation. It is entirely possible, however, that the poet thought of Hrothgar, as a good man who lived by such light as was vouchsafed him, as entitled to God's mercy. The only one of the human personages of the poem who is clearly said to be destined to suffer in hell is Unferth, who, in his responsibility for the death of his brothers, had committed the sin of Cain.

We should not forget that the poet of *Beowulf* derived his story from traditional sources. However that story had developed before him, its materials were originally pagan. The persons and the peoples with whom it deals were themselves pagan; and the poet reveals his awareness of their heathenism in the Christian Excursus. It is probable that, during the generations between the conversion of the Anglian kingdoms to Christianity and the poet's lifetime, much that had been essentially pagan had been purged from the story: we can hardly believe that the cult of the old Germanic gods had survived in it, for example. Nevertheless the story of Beowulf had its roots in pagan times and in pagan thought, as did the stories of Finn and of Ingeld; and much of the manners of those times must have been preserved down to the poet's day. As a good Christian, the poet found himself faced with the task of treating this originally pagan material in a manner acceptable to a Christian audience. Yet, though it is hardly likely that he consciously attempted to archaize, he was fully aware that the times with which he dealt were "heathen and hopeless." He could not consistently represent them so; the Christianity of his own time forbade; but he could admit their paganism—as he does in lines 168–188,—and from then on he could, by ignoring all that was pagan in his story, present his personages as if they had been Christian. But in doing so it was necessary for him to exclude any specifically dogmatic expressions; necessary to present both Danes and Geats as Abraham and his descendants were presented in the Old Testament. It was essential that they retain the sympathy of his hearers; therefore, once the early admission of their paganism had been made, they must speak and act as Abraham or Isaac might have done. Grendel and his dam bear the full onus of all that is blackest in heathenism, in which indeed they had their roots; Hrothgar must appear as "the noble monotheist." The true Christianity of the poem is represented by the figure of Beowulf alone.

VIII

ANTICIPATION, CONTRAST, AND IRONY

I have tried to show, in the preceding chapters, how the author of *Beowulf,* composing a heroic poem on traditional themes, and fully accepting those conventional modes of expression which he had inherited from generations of scops, nevertheless discovered new ways of organizing, constructing, and telling his story, and new forms and uses for the primary traditional devices of rhetoric. His poetic vocabulary is unique in its range and in its precision and force; it deviates from the traditional not in its essential character, but in its richness and in its capacity for projecting vivid and impressive images. "In the handling of the delicate instrument of verse," as Klaeber says, "the poet shows a strict adherence to regularity and a surprisingly keen appreciation of subtle distinctions which make *Beowulf* the standard of Anglo-Saxon metrical art."[1] In these two respects, the individuality of his diction within accepted limits, and the restraint and flexibility of his verse, the poet reveals himself as in the fullest sense a trained professional, actively aware of all that could be done within the

[1] Edition, p. lxix.

bounds of the conventional poetic art; his familiarity with that art enabled him to experiment, to make innovations, to create a diction and a style which, much as it owes to his unknown predecessors, yet transcends anything that other Old English poets accomplished.

It has also become apparent that the scope and sweep of his vocabulary owes much to his extensive use of variation; and that in his variations he is neither overlavish nor undiscriminating: if, in his work, variation seems occasionally a mere ornament of style, it is most frequently an instrument which he uses with conscious art. Apart from its employment in formal speeches, for effects of stateliness and dignity, and its use at points of major transition, variation in *Beowulf* serves to communicate dramatically significant emotion. Since it is in the emotions of the principal personages that the springs of action lie, variation becomes an important narrative device. It is through the repeated or sustained emphasis upon these impelling emotions—emphasis conveyed primarily through the variations—that the poem acquires a close dramatic texture. Even in those passages of vigorous action which narrate the major exploits of the hero, excitement is communicated not through the details of what happens, but through variation in the statement of the emotions of the participants. Indeed, in the account of the combat with Grendel it is through the vivid communication of the feelings of the combatants and of the Danes and Geats that the very course of action is chiefly set forth; and these feelings are expressed in variations.

The poet was aware, moreover, as no other Old English poet ever became aware, of the potentialities of variation extending through, or recurring over, larger narrative sequences. On the one hand it could give unity to a scene, even to a sequence of scenes; on the other, transferred from phrasal to structural use, it could establish a structural unity through the poem as a whole. For this is precisely what we have in the fourfold telling of Hygelac's death: in four situations of different dramatic moment the same story is told, with different emphases; and thereby main plot and subplot are knit together; the balance between the hero as retainer and as king, between heroic youth and heroic old age, is underlined, and the unity of the entire poem effectively established.

To perceive these potentialities, resident, but hitherto undeveloped, within the figure of variation, required an imaginative genius of a high order; to use them as tellingly as our poet has done demanded a discriminating taste and a highly developed dramatic sense. These qualities are also vividly displayed in the author's careful and deliberate envelopment of the fights with Grendel and his dam, each in its own atmosphere of terror—an envelopment so successful that the sensitive modern reader, no less than the contemporary listener, feels the mounting shock of the successive stages of the action. In these accumulations of the effects of terror, variation once more plays its part—its dual part, focusing in the account of the first fight upon the several stages of Grendel's advance, his eruption into the hall, and the slaughter of Hondscio; and in the second fight centering, first, in the descriptions of the approaches to the Mere, and secondly, upon the states of mind of the hero.

In the story of the second fight the primary effects of horror reside in the details of the setting, first as it is described by Hrothgar, then as its terrors impinge upon the imaginations of the Danes and Geats as they march through the uncanny region: this setting is perfectly calculated to accord with the frightful nature of its occupants and their ruthless power. It had been otherwise with the setting for the combat with Grendel: there it is contrast which lends dramatic significance to the setting—contrast between the beauty and wealth of Heorot, and the graciousness of Danish life within it, and humbled Danish pride and fearful bloodshed within its lordly walls through twelve bitter years. Both settings are elaborate; in each scene, by concord or by contrast, the setting serves admirably to enhance the terror and the significance of the action.

It is, as we have seen, quite otherwise in the story of Beowulf's last exploit. There, terror resides in the hero's antagonist itself; setting is bare and stark. Not terror, but the imminence of tragedy, is communicated through the poet's use of anticipation. We know—and the poet will not let us forget—that Fate, and God's foreknowledge, will bring death to Beowulf as well as to the dragon. And through the magnificent monologue of the Messenger after the hero's fall, our concern is transferred from Beowulf to his doomed people, who cannot long survive him. The circumstances which account for the impending destruction of the Geats are carefully imparted to us—chiefly in the words of Beowulf and the Messenger, but also in direct statement by the poet—through the skillful communication of historical tradition. These traditions are the essential stuff of the subplot in Part II; they are intrinsic to the very matter of the poem. The legendary episodes which enrich Part I, on the other hand, are illustrative, or are used to impart a kind of characterization, or—as for example the Finn Episode and the allusion to Hama and the necklace of the Brosings—for purposes of dramatic analogy. But all are important; none, not even the story of Thryð, is superfluous; and all are told with power and charm. Between the two contrasting types, heroic legend and historical tradition, stands the legend of Ingeld, itself doubly valuable as relating to the stuff of the subplot and in its value as characterization of Beowulf, the wise prince who can perceive the perils resident in a well-intentioned but dubious policy. All this matter, episodic and historical, enriches the story and deepens the emotional current of the narrative; every instance of its use is fine in itself, and pertinent to the context into which it is introduced.

Both types are frequently introduced in passages of anticipation or of contrast. These are qualities of the manner and tone of the poem; like the elements of diction and style, they show the poet a man of his age, yet greater than his age: a poet deriving much from tradition, and using traditional elements with a perceptiveness and sensitiveness unequaled in Anglo-Saxon England.

The elements of repetition, anticipation, and contrast were traditional in Old English poetry. I shall say little of the first of these: it has been universally recognized and widely misapprehended. So far as I am aware, none of the repetitions of incident in the poem is superfluous; each has its specific purpose in its place. Whenever action or situation is retold, it is told with different stress, and its retelling has a function important in each of its contexts. Indeed, these repetitions are really instances of what I have called narrative variation; and each in its turn aids in giving unity and binding strength to the entire work. I cannot think of any repetition in the poem which does not have some structural function. There are, indeed, a number of repetitions of author's comment; these also have their specific purpose.

Adrien Bonjour, in a very significant paper, "The Use of Anticipation in *Beowulf*,"[2] concludes that "the anticipations assume an important function in the architecture of the poem, and, thanks to the deft and subtle hand with which they are used, decidedly contribute to the group of qualities which make the *Beowulf* a work of art."[3] He divides the anticipations into two main groups: anticipations of events which we actually see happening later on in the poem, in accordance with the prediction; and " 'allusive' anticipations . . . i.e. anticipations of events which are supposed to happen in a near or distant future, but are never set forth in the course of the poem; they may refer . . . to facts probably well known to the reader (or the audience) of *Beowulf*, but . . . there is no single confirmation of them anywhere in the poem, apart from further allusions."[4]

This is quite sound; it is also true that the poet "sometimes takes care to tell . . . no less than three or four times in advance" what is going to happen. I cannot agree with Bonjour, however, that "the ultimate object of these anticipations is to suggest the transience of everything in this world"; or that "almost all [the anticipations] are connected specifically with the idea of fate . . ."[5] He qualifies this last statement in a parenthesis: "(or, for that matter, God; but, as Klaeber remarks,[6] the functions of fate and God seem quite parallel)." This qualification itself seems to me quite dubious: the poet is at some pains to distinguish between Fate (*Wyrd*) and God.

The nature and the role of the anticipations of Bonjour's second group are essentially different from those of his first. With the single exception of the fall of Hygelac (which occupies a kind of middle ground between the two groups), those which can be associated with the first are closely restricted in scope, and appear in three principal connections: first, in association with the first incursion of Grendel into Heorot and the later vengeful raid of Grendel's dam; secondly, during the story of Grendel's last invasion and his combat with Beo-

[2] *Review of English Studies*, XVI (1940), pp. 290–299.
[3] *Ibid.*, p. 299.
[4] *Ibid.*, p. 291.
[5] *Ibid.*, pp. 295, 298.
[6] See Klaeber's edition, p. xlix.

wulf; and thirdly, in connection with Beowulf's fight with the dragon. That is to say, they are part of the machinery of the narrative of two of the hero's three great exploits. Bonjour, like Klaeber, errs in seeing any real use of anticipation in the story of the fight with Grendel's dam: in his account of that adventure the poet was so anxious to impress upon his audience the peril of his hero and his close escape from death that his only suggestion of Beowulf's triumph comes at the very moment when Beowulf throws off the monster, gets to his feet, and sees and strikes with the magic sword. All these anticipations of the first group concern the major events of the main action—what happens and what is to happen in the course of the hero's fights with Grendel and with the dragon.

Those of the second group are not anticipations in the same sense: they are rather allusions to coming political events which constitute the matter of the subplot, and impinge upon the career of Beowulf indirectly, though importantly enough. Those in Part I concern, first, the revolt and usurpation of Hrothulf; secondly, the fall of Hygelac; and thirdly, the impending clash between Danes and Heaðobards; those in Part II forecast the overthrow of the Geatish nation after the hero's death.

These allusive forecasts of political catastrophes deal with events which, from the point of view of the poet's audience, were familiar matters of historical tradition; the poet could present them in allusive form because his hearers already knew of them. The poet therefore does not report them in detail, but passes them by with a mere intimation of what is to come. On the other hand, the anticipations of Beowulf's victory in the fight with Grendel, and those of his death in combat with the dragon, are much more detailed and specific—and are thus in line with all that he tells us about his hero.

For if he could take for granted full knowledge of the dynastic quarrels of the Danes and the overthrow of the Geats on the part of his audience, he does not take for granted their familiarity with the adventures of Beowulf. Not only does he report the hero's three great combats in full detail; all that he tells us of his hero is similarly detailed: his youthful exploits, his fostering at Hrethel's court, his vengeance for Hygelac and escape from Frisia, his refusal of the throne and his regency, and the vengeance he took for Heardred. Even his father's feud with the Wylfings, and the relations of the Wægmundings, are reported; so that it appears that the poet did not expect his hearers to know the hero's life and exploits as they did know of the quarrels among the Shieldings and the conquest of the Geats by the Svear.

We have seen in chapter iv what are the primary functions of the anticipations in the narratives of Beowulf's combats with Grendel and with the dragon; these last have a fuller, richer function than any others in the poem. But they are different in character and in purpose from the prophetic allusions of the second group; they are the means by which the dangers and the meaning of the hero's undertakings are enforced upon the reader's or the hearer's consciousness.

Among those of the second group, in Beowulf's comment to Hygelac on the relations between Danes and Heaðobards anticipation is of an order all its own: it is not the poet, but the hero, who anticipates what is to come. He foresees with great wisdom and keen political insight that the feud will break out again, but cannot foresee with accuracy the manner of its breaking out or the person of the avenger who precipitates catastrophe. The anticipation of Hygelac's fall is also managed in an individual way: the poet himself forecasts the fatal raid into Frisia in the course of his account of the feast in Heorot; the other three accounts occur in Part II—not as anticipations, but as report or reminiscence of what had long since taken place.

If we examine carefully what the poet tells us in these anticipatory passages, we shall see that the events which they forecast are by no means all specifically attributed to Fate. The fall of Hygelac is so attributed: *hyne wyrd fornam* (line 1205b) 'Fate took him off' in consequence of his pride and folly (*syþðan he for wlenco wean ahsode*). The revolt of Hrothulf and the bloody strife among the Shieldings, like the renewal of the feud between Danes and Heaðobards, seems to be conceived as the outgrowth of the passions of men. To revert to the anticipations of the first group, the poet's anticipations of Beowulf's victory over Grendel mention *Wyrd* only once (lines 734b–736a), and then apparently not in the sense of 'Fate,' but in that of what is destined; otherwise these anticipations of the outcome attribute Beowulf's impending victory to the overruling will of God, and to His power to set aside Fate (696b–700a; 705b–707). It is the mercy and favor of God which upholds Beowulf's arm: this is specifically asserted in lines 1056 ff.; Beowulf himself attributes his victory to God's help (967, 979), as does Hrothgar (928–931, 940). We see the same situation underlined in the poet's comment on the fight with Grendel's dam: "Holy God determined victory in the fight..."

It is in the second part of the poem that the role of Fate becomes dominant; and here, truly, the poet's repeated anticipations of the outcome of the dragon-fight "assume an important function in the architecture of the poem..."[7] But there is surely little justification for thinking of every matter of major concern in the action as determined by Fate, for insisting, as Bonjour does, that the "gloomy series of Cassandra-like, yet unobtrusive, prophecies... conflagration, renewal of bloody feuds, hate, thirst for revenge, treachery among kinsfolk, extermination of peoples... are the sinister images called forth from an apocalyptic future."[8] This is surely to confuse the substance of the poem with its accidents.

The poet, and his hearers, knew well enough that evil exists; but they knew also that God exists, and that His will prevails; so much the poet tells us. Beowulf must die, and his people perish; the Geats themselves were aware of their impending doom, and were specifically warned of it by the Messenger. Yet, through the final scene, it is not their own approaching misery that occupies their thoughts; it is grief for their lost lord; the dominant note is that of his magnanimity and glory. The poet emphasizes, even in the unrelieved hopelessness of the second part of his work, the conquest won by heroism over death. In dying the hero achieves his greatest grandeur, and his people most deserve our admiration. In the end Fate wins an empty triumph, for Beowulf has gone 'to seek the judgment of the righteous.' In death he is transfigured; in their coming ruin the Geats are glorified by his sacrifice and their love for him.

For the poet and his audience were Christian: for them, evil might

[7] Bonjour, "The Use of Anticipation in *Beowulf*," p. 299.

[8] *Ibid.*, p. 298.

triumph for a time, but must fail in the end. It is not the burning of Heorot, nor the murder of Hrethric nor the fall of Heardred, through which the poet speaks to us. He intimates to us that these things must happen; but that which he brings most vividly and lovingly before us is the graciousness and largeness of heart of Hrothgar, and the flawless courage, the loyalty, the loving self-sacrifice of Beowulf.

It appears to me that the anticipations in the poem have not one single function and aim, but several. Those which forecast Beowulf's victory over Grendel are the mechanism by which the author relieves the mind overburdened by fear sufficiently to prepare it for effects of greater horror, so that the full peril of Beowulf's undertaking is present to our minds. Those which prepare us for Beowulf's inevitable death—and these, more than any others, stress the role of Fate—serve as a necessary justification for the tragic close. Those which forecast allusively the bloody division within a dynasty, and the ultimate doom of the Geats, are the matter of the subplot, although they likewise illustrate those political ends for which the hero vainly strove.

"It is always," Bonjour justly says, "when something looks or is described as splendid, stable, or peaceful, or when friendly people are in the midst of rejoicing, that they [viz., anticipations] take place.... This skilful element of contrast evidently heightens the intended effect."[9] This is certainly true for the first part of the poem; it is less true for Part II. Before we examine the use of contrast in Part I, it is worth while to reflect upon the fact that contrast is commonplace in Old English poetry. We find it powerfully used in *Genesis,* in the treatment of the chained Satan and in that of Adam and Eve after the Fall: in *Andreas,* in the catastrophic humbling of the Mermedonians; in *Daniel,* in the punishment of Nebuchadnezzar. These instances derive from Scripture or religious literature; but their treatment in poetry is thoroughly Old English. Contrast is the central element of *The Wife's Lament;* it is the heart of *The Ruin.* The sharp and immanent sense of contrast is persistent in the thought of Anglo-Saxon poets.

Contrast is, moreover, the essence of tragedy; in the words of Chaucer's Monk:

[9] *Ibid.,* p. 299.

> 'Tragedie is to seyn a certeyn storie,
> As olde bookes maken us memorie,
> Of hym that stood in greet prosperitee,
> And is yfallen out of heigh degree
> Into myserie, and endeth wrecchedly.'

The elegiac poems, and the elegiac passages in Old English narrative poetry, reflect a preoccupation with tragic situation and tragic mood, a fondness for contemplation of the emotions of those who fall from happiness into misery, or of the ruin of the hopes or the mighty works of men; and this inevitably expresses itself in poetic contrast. This is vividly illustrated in what is said of the bereft Hildeburg: 'Not at all without cause did the daughter of Hoc bewail her fate, when morning came, and she could see the murderous slaughter of kinsmen, where she had once possessed the greatest joy in the world!' When a poet projects such contrasts in general terms, thinking not of the griefs of an individual, the emotions of a participant in the action, the result is an elegiac set piece. The ruined city is not the poet's city, but the remains of a Roman town, with their physical evidence of the contrast between past glory and present decay. The Lament of the Last Survivor in *Beowulf* expresses the imaginary grief of a fictive person, nameless, almost without personality. The emotion represented is not real or individual; it is impersonal or typical; the situation described is no more than an illustration of the theme *tout passe, tout casse*.

Such elegiac set pieces in Old English poetry rarely have any narrative vitality; they show an author playing, more or less successfully, with a conventional theme. So it is with the Lament of the Last Survivor, the value of which resides solely in its exceptional melancholy beauty. It has nothing to do with any of the acting personages of the poem; even as an explanation of the presence of the treasure in the barrow it is superfluous. Yet the poet's deep feeling, and his power to project the images of the gems falling from their settings and the fine armor rusting away even as the warriors who once wore it moulder in the grave, make of this passage something too precious to discard.

Again, in the elegiac parable of the old warrior whose son has been hanged, the poet transforms the convention into an expression of individual sorrow. This, too, is essentially a set piece; but it is brought into direct relation with the actual grief of King Hrethel at the loss of his most beloved son; the parable has the specific purpose of accentuating the tragic pathos of Hrethel's bereavement and broken heart. The connection between the imagined instance and the personal suffering of the Geatish king is brought out immediately after the close of the elegiac passage:

'. . . . . . . *Swa* Wedra helm
æfter Herebealde heortan sorge
weallinde wæg; wihte ne meahte
on ðam feorhbonan fæghðe gebetan;
. . .
gumdream ofgeaf, Godes leoht geceas . . .' (2462b ff.)

In both of these elegiac passages, the heart of tragedy lies in a shocking contrast between past joy and present sorrow; and the sense of suffering investing each is deeply moving.

Contrast is not only the essence of tragedy; it also serves to convey the sense of dramatic irony. When the poet suggests to his listeners an impending catastrophe, of which the personages to be involved have neither awareness nor expectation, but which will plunge them from prosperity and power into misery and ruin; when, in their ignorance of what is to come, they continue in their joy and pride, the contrast between their present and future states communicates the tragic irony to the audience. The poet of *Beowulf,* possessing a strong dramatic sense, uses such contrasts frequently and with telling effect. The most obvious and beautiful instance appears in the scene of the feast in Heorot, when the poet's first account of Hygelac's fall (lines 1202 ff.) warns the audience of the futility of Wealhtheow's appeals to Hrothulf to be gracious to her sons, and to Beowulf to protect them. This is reinforced later, when, with the fact of Hygelac's death and Geatish weakness in mind, we become conscious—as neither Beowulf nor his Danish hosts are conscious—that Beowulf will be unable to give effective aid to Hrothgar or protection to

Hrethric. A more monumental, if less subtle, instance appears in Part II: the audience, aware—as Beowulf is not consciously aware—that the hero is to perish in his fight with the dragon, perceives that the cause for which he ventures his life is hopeless, and that his death will involve the ruin of the people whom he dies to protect. In the first of these two situations, the contrast is drawn between the joy and splendor of the feast, with its demonstrations of the present loyalty of the Danish princes to one another, and the faithlessness and murder of kin which are to come; in the second, the poet carefully contrasts the confidence with which Beowulf sets out to meet the dragon with his unavailing struggle to resist its attacks until Wiglaf comes to his support.

There are, of course, many lesser instances: Grendel's first invasion of Heorot comes hard upon the tumultuous joy of the Danes at the feasting and gift-giving in the new-built hall; Grendel's dam slays Æschere just when all the Danes are confident that their woes have ended with the death of Grendel. This contrast the poet emphasizes vigorously by laying great stress upon the excellent armor and the courage and resolution of the Danish warriors in the hall (lines 1242–50). Here, too, the audience is warned of the impending evil of which the Danes have no presentiment: 'They knew not Fate, cruel appointed doom, as it had befallen many an earl when evening came.... Many a feaster, ready for death and doomed, bent to the hall-couch ... one paid sorely for his evening rest.... That became manifest, widely known among men, that an avenger yet lived after the hated foe ..., the mother of Grendel ...' (Lines 1233b–57a.) The tragic irony is heavily underlined; as it is also in those early lines which forecast the destruction of Heorot amidst fire and slaughter, immediately after the poet has described the unique splendor of the hall, and made much of Hrothgar's pride in fulfilling his boast to build the finest hall on earth and distribute treasure within it.

Verbal irony also is often effectively served by contrast. It is present, though lightly, in the statement that Scyld's retainers equipped their dead king, when they placed him in the funeral ship, 'by no means with lesser gifts, treasures of a people, than those had done who had sent him forth at the beginning, a child alone over the waves.' For whoever had first sent him forth had furnished him with no gifts, no treasures at all; the litotes and contrast carry the irony. Irony resides in the implication, through the word *ealuscerwen,* of the bitter contrast between the joy of the Danes in feasting and their terror when the din of struggle between Beowulf and Grendel—a struggle which is to deliver the Danes from the monster—overwhelm them with fear, fear as though at the deprivation of ale! The contrast here is delicately implied; the poet of *Andreas,* perceiving its effectiveness, picked it up and made the contrast explicit:

> myclade mereflod: meoduscerwen wearð
> æfter symbeldæge... (*Andreas* 1526–27a)

Verbal irony is too frequent in *Beowulf* to require much illustration. It appears in Beowulf's taunting reference to the incapacity of the Danes to dispose of Grendel through their own efforts:

> 'ac he hafað onfunden þæt he þa fæhðe ne þearf,
> atole ecgþræce eower leode
> swiðe onsittan, *Sige-Scyldinga*...' (595–597)

It resides often in the poet's comment on situation; after Grendel's second raid the author observes, in ironic understatement:

> Ða wæs eaðfynde þe him elles hwær
> gerumlicor ræste [sohte],
> bed æfter burum, ða him gebeacnod wæs,
> gesægd soðlice sweotolan tacne
> healðegnes hete; heold hyne syðþan
> fyr ond fæstor se þæm feonde ætwand. (138–143)

The litotes itself is ironic; the participial phrase *gesægd soðlice sweotolan tacne* is a bitterly ironic understatement of the bloody nature of the evidence; the term *healðegn* is applied ironically to Grendel—as *renweard* is in line 770, and as *selegyst* is used of Beowulf in the lair of Grendel's dam.

The passage just quoted, in its rather savage report of the almost tumbling eagerness with which the Danish survivors of Grendel's early attacks sought places of safety, suggests that the poet's attitude toward the Danes is itself slightly ironic. This seems to be supported by Beowulf's sharp reflections on Danish prowess in his retort to Unferth, and by the poet's double reference to the terror of the Danes at the very clamor which should have assured them of Beowulf's sure advantage over Grendel. In the second such reference, moreover, the poet contrasts the fearful behavior of the Danes with the desperate courage of Beowulf's Geatish thanes. Such an attitude on the author's part is particularly striking in view of his sympathetic treatment of Hrothgar, and against the background of his glorification of the Danes and their mighty rulers in the prologue. The point must not be pressed too far; but it appears that the poet wished to emphasize the might and valor of the Geats by contrast with the helplessness of the Danes to defend themselves against the monsters: their valor, though great, is less than that of the hero and his men. The key to the meaning of this contrast may perhaps be found in Beowulf's own words; after his savage comment on the incompetence of the Danes he says: 'But I am to make known to him shortly now the might and valor, the warfare, of the Geats!' Conscious of his own great strength, and of the courage of his thanes—who do indeed strive mightily, though vainly, to cut Grendel down while the Danes, at a safe distance, are terror-stricken,—Beowulf means to say, not that the Danes are cowards, but that he and his men are stronger and braver than they. And this is true. The Danes, under their early kings, had proved their military might against mortal foes; but against the demonic Grendel no Dane could oppose the strength of thirty men, and the Geats are worthy of their lord. The contrast is illustrated by the opposition between Unferth and Beowulf: Unferth, who did not dare confront Grendel's dam in her lair, 'lost his glory there, his renown for valor. It was not so with that other, once he had girded himself for battle.' (Lines 1470b–72.)

Contrast is used, without irony, for many minor effects. It is a common means of characterization in general terms: Beowulf, the gallant but magnanimous hero, is twice contrasted by implication with the savage and ruthless Heremod; the gentleness and propriety of Hygd are pointed by contrast with the bloodthirst of the youthful Thryð; the valor of Wiglaf stands out by contrast with the cowardice of his comrades. Yet on one occasion contrast is employed with unhappy effect, to enhance the glory of Beowulf by opposition to the supposed ingloriousness of his early youth. It is well and delicately used near the end of Part I, when, after illustrating the loyalty and love of Beowulf toward his uncle by his transfer to Hygelac of the gifts received from Hrothgar, the poet observes: 'So ought a kinsman to do; not at all should he weave a net of malice for the other with secret cunning, nor prepare death for his close comrade.' These lines directly precede a specific assertion that 'his nephew was very faithful to Hygelac'; the mention of this particular relationship, nephew to uncle, makes me question Chambers' view that the poet here intended a contrast between Beowulf and Heoroweard;[10] for Heoroweard was cousin to the prince whom he betrayed, not his nephew. I think the poet clearly meant to contrast the loyalty of Beowulf to his uncle with the disloyal revolt of Hrothulf against his uncle Hrothgar.

The sharpest case of tragic contrast—and one wholly free from irony—marks the transition between the end of Part I and the opening of Part II. Lines 2177 through 2211 contain, indeed, all the essential elements of that true balance of the poem so admirably described by Tolkien. The closing lines of Part I leave the hero at home in his uncle's court, in the matchless might of his youth and at the height of his glory. Hygelac is yet alive and powerful; his realm is rich and strong. Beowulf stands at his right hand, and the two princes are united by mutual love. The opening lines of Part II confront us, suddenly, with the terrible antithesis: Hygelac has been slain, and his host destroyed; the Svear have invaded, defeated the Geats, and killed Heardred. Beowulf is now king; but he who had been the matchless young champion is now old, and a dragon is about to ravage his realm. The contrast is sufficient in itself, without irony: we sense at once that the existence of the Geatish nation depends upon the life of their hero-king. And his death is at once forecast: 'he had held the broad realm well for fifty winters . . . until one, a dragon, began to tyrannize on dark nights . . .' From that point on, over and over, the poet repeats his dark anticipations of Beowulf's death. God has foreseen the fall of prince and people, and both are in the hands of Fate.

[10] *Beowulf: An Introduction*, pp. 428–429.

In such situations as that presented by the combat with Grendel, anticipation must be so used—as it is—that it does not dissipate suspense; it must be balanced by a degree of force and vividness in narrative detail to compel the interest of reader or listener to fix itself upon the salient features, the meaning, and the value of the action. Such a balance, achieved as it clearly is in the story of the fight in Heorot, actually heightens the impact of each stage of terror in the action, so that the next stage may exert its full effect, and the resolution is eagerly welcomed. In the account of the dragon-fight the repeated use of anticipation serves a different purpose: the listener's mind must, from the first, be made ready to accept the fact that Beowulf is to die in his hour of victory. So anticipation is heaped upon anticipation, with the result that each successive forecast of the inevitable end comes like the iterated tolling of a funeral bell; and their cumulative effect prepares us for the Messenger's prediction of Swedish invasion and the collapse of the Geatish nation. Between these anticipations, the action is so sharply and powerfully reported that it loses nothing of its force and moment through our certainty of the tragic outcome. Anticipation serves, here, to bind together the themes of main plot and subplot, giving to the figure of the heroic Beowulf a greater than personal significance: he is protector and sole prop of a people. This gives value and validity to the ultimate irony of the sacrifice by the Geats of that treasure which Beowulf had bought with his life for them, and of their ruin through his death to save them.

Contrast, anticipation, and the use of elegiac elements to establish a tragic atmosphere are as conventional, as fully traditional, *in themselves,* as are the types of poetic appellation common in Old English poetic diction, or as variation. But just as the poet of *Beowulf* gives his diction freshness and force through new coinages of his own, and uses variation consciously and consistently for specific textural or dramatic effects, so too, in his hands contrast, anticipation, and elegiac passages alike become effective instruments. Just as one can—with wariness and prudence—occasionally venture on an emendation which will bring the text more squarely into line with the typical structures of variation, so, with equal discretion, one may test the genuineness of a passage by the skill with which these other elements are used. Thus it is, above all else, the overwhelming force of the dramatic irony in the Christian Excursus which persuades me that the whole passage is the genuine and deliberate expression of the poet's intent. This is the proper, the inevitable summation of the tragic dilemma in which the Danes find themselves: the pagan Hrothgar is prevented, by God's will, from entering his own hall at night; and the appeal of the heathen Danes to the only gods they know has the most fatal consequence. Their very piety only involves them in greater horror; effective aid can come to them only through the grace of that true God whom they do not know. The frequent acknowledgments by Hrothgar of the power and mercy of God might almost make it appear that the exercise of that grace exerted a kind of reciprocal effect.

◇ ◇ ◇

All that we know of the author of *Beowulf,* or of his procedures as storyteller and poet, lies before us in his work; there is no other evidence. We know that only an educated man would have been familiar with the teachings of Gregory or Augustine; the internal evidence for his familiarity with the *Aeneid,* though not conclusive, is fairly strong. He was a gentle and tolerant Christian; this appears not only in the testimony of his own words and those of his personages, but in direct reference to Scriptural story as well. His knowledge of heroic legend richly reveals itself in the numerous episodes of Part I; his familiarity with historical tradition in the matter of the wars between Geats and Svear is so comprehensive and detailed that his poem is still our chief source of information about that series of conflicts and the participants in them. Like Hrothgar's scop, he was

> guma gilphlæden, gidda gemyndig,
> se ðe ealfela ealdgesegena
> worn gemunde . . .

His wide knowledge of Germanic story and tradition, and his incomparable mastery of meter, afford sufficient evidence that he had been trained as a scop.

But out of all the poetry that has come down to us from the Germanic past—most of it, of course, Old Norse—there is nothing that can be compared with *Beowulf,* except for the late and somewhat romanticized *Nibelungenlied:* nothing like it in scope and complexity, in pace or tone, or in excellence of structure. It is a finished work of art—not flawless, but finely conceived and executed.

We should not expect it to be flawless. Much attention has, indeed, been given to the inconsistencies in the narrative; some, I think, are imagined. Brandl has met the charge of inconsistency effectively; most instances are of no particular importance, and may be matched in the longer works of other great poets. Yet three are real, and deserve attention. The first of these is the disparity between what Beowulf is permitted to tell of his own heroic deeds in youth (lines 419–424a; 532b–581a) and the poet's account of the hero's youth as inactive and inglorious. The second is a serious inaccuracy in Beowulf's report of the feast in Heorot (lines 2105–15). The third is the twofold account of the manner in which the treasure came to be in the dragon's barrow.

The first and third of these illustrate a curious flaw in the author's vision: although, for the most part, he has seen his story whole, and managed it with remarkable unity and consistency, he could, at times, become so fascinated with the moment that, in his desire to achieve a particular effect here and now, he could forget or ignore what he had told us before. The second is a plain confusion of two separate, but somewhat similar, situations. Describing the feast after the killing of Grendel, Beowulf tells us that Hrothgar, 'the ancient Shielding, very wise, recounted long-past things; from time to time ... he touched the joy of the harp, the wood of mirth; at times the great-hearted king recounted strange stories truly; at times, in turn, bound by old age, the ancient warrior began to lament his youth, his strength in battle; his breast welled within when, old in winters, he remembered many things.'

Now this bears no just relation to anything that is directly told, or suggested, in the poet's account of the feast; yet it is precisely in that context that Beowulf's words place it. Indeed, Beowulf's words can refer to nothing other than Hrothgar's long monologue, uttered after the slaying of Grendel's dam. The 'strange stories, ancient things' spoken by Hrothgar are clearly the king's tale of the pride and fall of Heremod, and his example of the ruler who, swollen with pride, forgets his debt to God; Hrothgar's lament for his youth and departed strength form part of the same monologue. In his concern to make clear that Hrothgar's words of wisdom had sunk deep into Beowulf's heart, and to give that fact a place in Beowulf's report to Hygelac, the poet confused two different scenes—scenes similar in that, in each, Hrothgar is moved by gratitude and joy at deliverance from a monster and is moved to speak 'wise words.'

The first inconsistency is equally easy to understand and to pardon: the author's fondness for contrast misled him into attempting to enhance Beowulf's heroism in young manhood by setting it off against an imagined sluggishness in youth. The flaw lies in the total absence of anything outside this single passage to support a tale of the hero's early inactivity. It seems probable that a "male Cinderella" tradition had associated itself with the figure of Beowulf, and that the poet, knowing of it, made the mistake of using it. It is contradicted not only by Beowulf's own reports of his youthful exploits, but also by his direct statement that he was loved and highly regarded in his childhood by King Hrethel.

Klaeber attempts to harmonize the two accounts of the origin of the treasure in an ingenious synthesis: "Supplemented by the account of an earlier stage (3049 ff., 3069 ff.), the history of the hoard is briefly this. Long, long ago . . . the hoard had been placed in the earth by illustrious chieftains (3070). A curse had been laid on it. After a time, it was discovered and seized by certain warriors (2248 ff.), who made good use of it. The last survivor of this race returned the treasures to the earth, placing them in a barrow or cave. There the dragon found them and kept watch over them for three hundred years (2278), until the theft of a cup aroused his anger and brought on the tragic fight, in which both Beowulf and the dragon lost their lives."[11] This would constitute an admirable resolution of the problem, and obviate the necessity of charging the poet with two distinct and mutually inconsistent versions. To me, however, the inconsistency appears to be real, and I believe Lawrence was right in his recogni-

[11] Edition, p. 209.

tion of it.[12] The text tells us, not that illustrious chieftains placed the treasure "in the earth," but that they placed it in the barrow: *biorges weard . . . þeodnas mære, þa ðæt þær dydon;* and in his earlier version the poet tells us that the last survivor placed the treasure in that same barrow: *Beorh eallgearo wunode on wonge . . . þær on innan bær eorlgestreona hringa hyrde hordwyrðne dæl.* (Lines 3066–70; 2241–45.) That the Last Survivor should have hit upon the same barrow in which the treasure had long since been placed by those chieftains who laid the curse upon it appears a perilous coincidence; it is an almost certain indication that, in these two widely separated passages, the poet actually explained the presence of the treasure in the barrow in two different ways. As Lawrence has pointed out, the later version is the more original: the curse laid upon the gold by the "illustrious chieftains" is a characteristic feature, in Germanic dragon-tales, of a dragon-guarded hoard. But the poet was unable to resist his love for so finely typical a situation as that of the depositing of the treasure by the last of a tragically extinguished people; it is the Anglo-Saxon weakness for the elegiac which misled him. The later explanation is not only more characteristic; it is also more logical; it is essential to the tragic feature of the operation of the curse upon Beowulf and his people, which the poet is at some pains to represent (lines 3074–75) as undeserved, but inevitable.

In short, the author's few oversights are exactly that: he saw too much, and occasionally erred in imparting to his listeners an excess of beauty. Moreover, in every instance in which he has gone astray, he has followed the path of convention, pursuing the traditional lure of tragic or of elegiac contrast. Yet we should certainly be grateful to him for the story of the Last Survivor, with its beautiful expression of lyric sorrow for a vanished past; and we may be glad that Beowulf had been touched by Hrothgar's melancholy mood, though he reports it out of its proper context. These represent errors of judgment, not errors of artistic taste; the only error of taste is to be found in the tale of Beowulf's sluggish youth, which is out of harmony with the hero's character and career as these had already been represented. And this much the poet may be forgiven.

[12] *Beowulf and Epic Tradition*, pp. 213–220.

There is, on the other hand, a remarkable consistency in the author's management of the hero's rather complex family and political relationships. Early in the poem Beowulf tells the Captain of the Shore that he is son to Ecgtheow, who had been famous among men for his valor; somewhat later Hrothgar recalls how Ecgtheow had involved himself in a feud among the Wylfings; the Geats had not dared to keep him among them, for fear of retaliation. Hrothgar settled the feud by paying wergeld, and Ecgtheow repaid his obligation by swearing oaths to Hrothgar. Hrothgar's account of these events explains in part Beowulf's readiness to deliver the Danes from Grendel. In Beowulf's long monologue in Part II we are told that Ecgtheow entrusted his son, then seven years old, to his father-in-law Hrethel—presumably at the time when Ecgtheow, unable to find asylum among his wife's people, sought the protection of Hrothgar. As son to Ecgtheow, Beowulf is a Wægmunding; in his last moments he entrusts the care of his people to his Wægmunding kinsman Wiglaf. In appointing Wiglaf as his successor, Beowulf followed the logical and inevitable course: the Hrethling line became extinct with his own death, and Wiglaf was his next of kin; moreover Wiglaf alone, among Beowulf's trusted retainers, had demonstrated such courage as a ruler of the Geats must display in face of certain invasion by the Svear. At no point in his treatment of these relationships does the poet forget what he has told us before. Although Wiglaf does not appear upon the scene until Beowulf is in desperate need of help against the dragon, it would appear that this part of the story had been carefully thought out from the beginning.

We can, moreover, trace in the development of the subplot a clear and statesmanlike view of the political relationships of the Geats, and the policy adopted by Beowulf both as prince and as king. In his dying words the hero tells us that he has sought no quarrels, but has held his own so well that no other monarch has dared attack him. It appears clearly that he had attempted, so far as was possible, to make his people secure by peaceful means. For a nation situated as the Geats were, between Danes and Svear, such a course was difficult. Hrothgar states explicitly (lines 1855 ff.) that there had been strife between Danes and Geats; and the Svear had made war upon the

Geats after Hrethel's death. So placed, the Geats must have found it the part of wisdom to convert enemies, whenever possible, into friends. Accordingly, although Beowulf's motives in undertaking to purge Heorot were quite unselfish, the inevitable consequence of his deliverance of the Danes was an alliance between Danes and Geats: this is the plain meaning of Hrothgar's final words to Beowulf; and they are confirmed by the king's adoption of Beowulf as his son. In short, Beowulf, whose wisdom Hrothgar has praised, wisely secured the support of the Danes for his own people. For this he had offered a *quid pro quo:* aid to Hrothgar against any foe, and protection at need for Hrethric. Had Hygelac not fallen in Frisia, Hrethric would not have been slain by Hrothulf, and a king under deep obligation to the Geats would have succeeded Hrothgar upon the Danish throne. The fatal Frisian raid broke the power of the Geats; Hrothulf's revolt was successful, and the alliance between Danes and Geats was broken. The Geats were once more isolated, with the two most powerful nations of Scandinavia hostile to them, and a boy king on the throne.

Heardred, upon reaching maturity, seems to have tried—without sufficient discretion—to follow the policy of making alliances through intervention in the dynastic affairs of a neighbor. He championed the cause of the rebel princes Eanmund and Eadgils against their uncle Onela; his purpose was evidently to replace a warlike and hostile king of the Svear with a prince who owed his throne to the Geats. The scheme failed: Onela was victorious; Eanmund and Heardred were slain. We are not surprised, therefore, to learn that in due course Beowulf championed the brother of Eanmund, Eadgils, and helped to establish him upon the Swedish throne, thus winning a friend for his people. Apparently Beowulf also took measures to secure the loyalty of his powerful Wægmunding kinsmen, by confirming Wiglaf in possession of the lands and privileges of his father Weohstan, even though the latter had supported Onela in the previous fighting, and had slain Eanmund.

In all this we see the poet following a clear, consistent line. Presumably the stories of the Geato-Swedish wars had come to him from oral tradition; it is doubtful that he was obliged to invent anything of consequence. But he organized his matter according to a preconceived plan, and we may take it for granted that the representation of political policy is his own. At no point do the threads of his story become entangled or confused.

It remains to reconsider the one charge of inconsistency against the poet which has most seriously troubled critics: the contradiction between his unquestionably deliberate statement that the Danes were pagan and knew not God, and his consistent representation of Hrothgar as acknowledging the power and mercy of God. In a very real sense the author *is* inconsistent here: the inconsistency actually is foreshadowed in lines 90b–98, in which Hrothgar's scop is represented as chanting a song of the Creation. Beowulf, moreover, is as ready as Hrothgar to give thanks to God; and a number of minor personages also express themselves like Christians. I have argued, in chapter vii, first, that the poet fully intended his characterization of the Danes as pagan, and explains on this ground the long continuation of their affliction; and secondly, that in placing Christian sentiments in the mouths of his more sympathetic characters he is, in effect, representing them as speaking as he and his contemporaries thought of good men as speaking. The inconsistency between the Christian Excursus and the pious utterances of his personages would not, I think, have been apparent to men of his age as it is to us. But the question involves more than the antithesis between the poet's recognition of the heathenism of the Danes and the attribution to them of piety expressed in Christian terms. It involves also the nature of the poet's conception of his hero's life and acts.

The various undertakings of Beowulf, as the poet reports them, are by no means uniformly successful. In his combats with the trolls of the mere the hero is triumphant; in his fight with the dragon he is victorious, but perishes himself. In his attempts to protect first Hrethric and then his own people from mortal foes, he is defeated. Hygelac's fall is the means by which his policy is frustrated; it leads, first, to his powerlessness to save Hrethric or Heardred, and finally, when he himself has fallen, to the overthrow of the Geatish nation. These considerations bring us to the relative roles of God and of Fate (*Wyrd*) in the outcome of his undertakings.

As we have seen, in the anticipations of the fight with Grendel, the poet attributes Beowulf's impending victory to the might and mercy of God (*Dryhten, mihtig God,* lines 696, 701; *Metod,* 706). This attribution is supported by the characterizations of Grendel as *Godes andsaca* (786) and *he fag wið God* (811b); and by Hrothgar's expression of thanks to God for Grendel's fall (928–931) and Beowulf's own recognition that God had given him victory (967; 977–79). In the fight with Grendel's dam, the poet expressly assures us that the outcome was determined by *halig God, witig Drihten, rodera Rædend* (1553b ff.); and Beowulf attributes his success to the fact that 'God shielded me.'

It is very different with the dragon-fight. Here, in two most explicit statements, Beowulf's impending death is attributed to Fate:

> . . . . . . Him wæs geomor sefa,
> wæfre ond wælfus, *wyrd* ungemete neah,
> se ðone gomelan gretan sceolde,
> secean sawle hord, sundur gedælan
> lif wið lice . . . (2419b–23a);
> ðær he þy fyrste forman dogore
> wealdan moste, swa him *wyrd* ne gescraf
> hreð æt hilde. (2573–75a)

It is Fate that decrees death for Beowulf; Fate that, on this occasion and for the first time, permits him to prevail, but without complete triumph. Klaeber's belief that the functions of God and Fate are quite parallel is effectively denied in line 1056: the poet tells us that Grendel would have slain other men besides Hondscio 'unless wise God and the courage of that man had averted Fate' (*nefne him witig God wyrd forstode ond ðes mannes mod*). As I have indicated in chapter iv, Beowulf, in contending against Grendel and his dam, was God's champion against His foes, the descendants of Cain; God was with him, and averted Fate from the hero and his men. But the dragon was not of the race of Cain; moreover, the Geats had, in fact, been crushed by the Svear, as poet and audience knew; it was necessary that Beowulf perish in the dragon-fight, lest the course of history be denied. Therefore—and for a deeper reason—God does not intervene to save the hero from death in his last fight.

This is, indeed, the tragedy of Beowulf: in all that human strength, courage, and wisdom may achieve, he is victorious; but against God's foreknowledge neither human might nor human wisdom may prevail. This is precisely what the poet tells us, and at a moment of high significance: Beowulf is dead; Wiglaf, unwilling to believe that the end is come, tries vainly to bring him back to consciousness. The poet comments: 'He could not, greatly as he wished it, retain life in the chieftain, nor set aside anything ordained of God; the judgment of God insisted upon governing the deeds of each of men—as He still does!' (Lines 2855–59.) Beowulf's death in victory was the work of Fate, operating as God's agent, to justify God's foreknowledge that the Geats are to be conquered in consequence of the hero's death.

This is not the first time in the poem that we have been reminded of the overruling power of God. It was God's will which had made it impossible for Hrothgar to approach his own throne after nightfall (lines 168–169); Beowulf, in his first speech to Hrothgar, had made the point that whichsoever is defeated in his fight with Grendel 'must trust to the judgment of the Lord.' Hrothgar, in his account of Grendel's ravages, admits the power of God to end them if He would: '*... God eaþe mæg þone dolsceaðan dæda getwæfan!*' The hero, as he goes to bed that night, prays, 'may wise God then assign victory on whichsoever hand seems meet to Him!' Instances might be multiplied; but one other is of special significance: in his grief at the ruin wrought by the dragon, Beowulf thinks that 'he had bitterly offended the Ruler, the eternal Lord, against ancient right.' This can hardly mean that the stainless hero is conscious of some specific grievous sin; it implies that he fears he has somehow set himself against God's will. Taken together with the poet's comment that Wiglaf's efforts to revive Beowulf are hopeless against God's decree, all these mean just one thing: from beginning to end, the poet thinks of the issue of each event in the hero's life in terms of its relation to the will of God. Constantly recognizing the power and goodness of God, Beowulf attempts to regulate his life and deeds in accordance with God's will. In his fights with God's enemies he is God's instrument; this accounts for his victories. In his attempts to ensure the strength and security of his people through military alliances, he unconsciously undertakes that which is at variance, if not with God's will, at least with God's foreknowledge. For this reason he fails in these attempts; whereas, in the main action of Part I, God lends His countenance to the hero's combats and averts Fate, in Part II God suffers Fate to have its way with him. One is tempted to see in all this the influence of Boethius upon the poet's thought; although his attitude toward the problem of evil is not Boethian.[13]

The essential Christianity of the poet's thought resides, then, not merely in the piety of his utterances, or in that expressed by his personages, but in his persistent illustration of this underlying principle, that God's foreknowledge and God's will control all things, and control them for the best. There is no conflict here between God's foreknowledge and man's free will: as Hrothgar tells us in his long monologue, God is all good, and distributes all benefits in accordance with His wisdom; but through pride and covetousness man works evil; only through "eternal counsels" and through temperance may man win to happiness. Beowulf, with full freedom of will, sets out against the dragon with the noble purpose of preserving his people; but God's foreknowledge that the Geats are soon to be destroyed requires the hero's death. Although Beowulf has no clear knowledge that he is to perish, Fate touches him with feyness, a kind of instinctive apprehension of death; and in the face of this he goes, with unshaken fortitude, to his end, foredoomed by divine foreknowledge.

Yet his soul departs 'to seek the judgment of the righteous'—a pretty clear indication that the poet thought of his hero as among the saved. Since he knew that Geats as well as Danes of that day were pagan, this suggests that he thought of salvation as attainable by good men through good works. The poet's sense of the mercy of God is acute and strong. By God's will the heathen Danes suffer Grendel's persecution, and their sacrifices to false gods imperil their souls; but after they have suffered grievously for twelve years God wills that Beowulf shall rescue them. Thus, by an act of special grace, they are delivered. One might almost think of the pious utterances

[13] The possible influence of Boethius on the poet was first suggested by John Earle (*The Deeds of Beowulf*, Oxford, 1892, p. 147). It is excellently discussed by Marie Padgett Hamilton, in her paper "The Religious Principle in *Beowulf*," *PMLA*, LXI (1946), pp. 309–330.

of Hrothgar as a kind of reaction to this act of grace, a recognition, vouchsafed even to a pagan, that only the One God could have sent him such a champion to save him from unendurable affliction. Beowulf, in his expressions of gratitude to God and acknowledgment of God's mercy, speaks as the human agent of God for noble ends. His soul is saved in virtue of those finer qualities in which, as in his strength, he exceeds other men: courage, loyalty, and love, and willing self-sacrifice.

The Christianity of the poem, then, is much more than "coloring." It manifests itself in the constant affirmation and illustration of a principle which underlies all the dealings of God with men. The primary sin of man against God is pride: through pride Heremod is brought low; through pride *(for wlenco)* Hygelac suffers death in Frisia; Hrothgar, in his monologue, attributes the persecutions of Grendel to Hrothgar's own pride, and he warns Beowulf against this sin. This sin motivates the envy of Unferth, and the usurpation and murder of kin of Hrothulf. From it Beowulf is free, and Beowulf is saved. God's will rules all creation; God's foreknowledge determines Beowulf's victories, failures, and death. Well is it with him who after death—like Beowulf—is permitted to seek peace in the embraces of the Father.

In this, as in his management of the details of his hero's life and as in his use of the complicated materials of the subplot, the poet controls the threads of his design admirably, and weaves them into a magnificent whole. As Walter Morris Hart has said, in the conclusion to *Ballad and Epic, Beowulf* "must be regarded as the work of a poet of remarkable taste and technical skill, who flung aside, far more boldly than the poet of the *Roland,* the binding conventions of popular art, and succeeded in impressing far more deeply his own powerful personality upon his work."

APPENDIX A

The Varieties of Poetic Appellation

Old English poetic appellations fall, in general, into the same categories as those of Old Norse poetry. In practice, however, we observe two major differences: (1) the Old English poetic periphrases are much less esoteric and far-fetched than the Norse; and (2) whereas, in Icelandic poetry, the periphrasis, or the traditional poetic simplex, for a given concept, functions most frequently as substitution for the direct, literal term, in Old English substitution is somewhat less common than the use of the poetic appellation as a variation of an *expressed* literal term, or as a variation of a transparent equivalent for the literal word.

I have discussed elsewhere—"The Meaning of Snorri's Categories," *University of California Publications in Modern Philology,* Vol. 36, No. 4 (1952), pp. 129–148—the categories of skaldic appellation listed and illustrated by Snorri Sturluson in his treatise *Skáldskaparmál.* Since all these categories are represented in Old English poetry, it seems logical to use the Icelandic terms—indeed, we have no others—to label each of them, as we have already adopted the term *kenning.*

Snorri called the simplices *ókend heiti,* which may be translated 'unqualified' or 'uncharacterized terms'; they are uncompounded nouns the reference of which is not limited in area of application or in scope, nor characterized by a modifying genitive. The *ókent heiti* is simply an unqualified simplex denoting a person or thing. Thus, in Old English, a ship may be called by the literal term *scip,* or *bat;* or by the more figurative *flota,* or *ceol.*

Compounds, too, may be literal or figurative: a ship may be called *wegflota* or *sæbat.* Similarly a sword may be called, quite literally, *guðsweord;* or—in a striking metaphor—*hildeleoma.*

The Icelandic rhetoricians who described the language of skaldic poetry made no distinction between the poetic compounds and the combinations of basic noun with limiting genitive. The two types are indeed logically equivalent: *yðgewinn* and *yða gewinn* mean precisely the same thing. The first element of a compound limits or characterizes the meaning of the second, or basic, element; just as the genitive in a combinatory appellation limits or characterizes the meaning of the basic noun combined with it. The limiting word most frequently expresses the area, the medium, or the object of the action or function denoted by the base-word. In *hildeleoma,* the sword is conceived as a flame which flashes in battle; in *beaga brytta,* a prince is thought of as one who breaks—i.e., who dispenses—rings.

It would be difficult to determine whether poets felt *beaga brytta* as a more elevated term than *beahgifa,* which expresses the same concept without metonymy. In all probability the choice between two such terms for the same referent, the one a compound and the other a basic noun plus genitive, was determined largely by metrical considerations. The compounds are, on the whole, more numerous; but the proportion of one type to the other varies with the concept to be expressed: *Beowulf* contains but two compounds for 'sea' with *yð-* as first element, as against four combinations with the genitive *yða.*

The poet had wide latitude for substitution in these compounds and combinations: he could substitute for either member an exact or approximate synonym. Thus the concept 'sword' may be expressed by the compounds *guðbill, guðsweord, wigbill, hildebill, hildemece;* or the poet might use any of the simplices for 'sword': *bill, sweord, mece, heoru.* Words sufficiently archaic to have lost something of their original sense, or to have acquired wider connotations, might be used rather loosely as the first or limiting element in compounds. *Heoru* originally meant 'sword'; but *heorowearh* means 'savage outcast'; *heorodreor,* literally 'sword-gore,' means no more than blood shed from mortal wounds; yet, when the poet says that Hygelac died of 'sword-drinks' (*heorodryncum swealt*), the first element of the compound is literal, and the metaphor—almost a personification—resides in the basic noun.

Among the compound or combinatory appellations which may substitute for the literal word for a concept or accompany it in variation, the kenning is the most strained, the farthest from the natural and obvious image. As Heusler observed, Meissner's definition of the kenning as a substitution of two or more members for the literal substantive of prose ignores the distinction between two different types of substantive appellation: that which calls the referent something that it is, and that which calls it something which it actually is not. Under Meissner's definition the appellations 'helm-bearer' for 'warrior,' 'wave-traverser' for 'ship,' 'slayer of Fafnir' for Sigurðr are kennings; so also are 'oak of the enforced ransom of the otter' for 'woman,' and 'snow of the crucible' for 'silver.' But we must observe a fundamental distinction here: a warrior actually *is* a helm-bearer; a ship *is* a wave-traverser; whereas a woman is *not* an oak of any kind; nor is silver snow. We are dealing here with two quite distinct rhetorical devices, structurally analogous but in quality utterly distinct. Periphrastic substitutions of the nature of 'helm-bearer,' 'wave-traverser,' 'slayer of Fafnir' can be found on almost any page of Milton; but nothing comparable with 'oak of the enforced ransom of the otter' exists outside of Old Norse poetry. The one is a simple, immediately intelligible allusion; the other is an elaborate, far-fetched conceit, intelligible only to a special audience. The one is not intended to puzzle the hearer even for a moment, but rather to please him by recalling a familiar story or situation or a useful or pleasant quality of the referent, and to permit him to share in the poetic experience. The other pleases only as a riddle pleases; it also contains an allusion or a comparison, but requires the listener to ferret out its secret through the exercise of his own ingenuity.

The skaldic periphrasis for 'woman' just cited is a complex puzzle, involving allusion, substitution, and a grammatical trick. The limiting element is not a single word, but is itself a substituting periphrasis: 'enforced ransom of the otter' stands for the concept 'gold,' in allusion to the ransom which three of the Æsir were compelled to pay Hreiðmarr for the killing of his son Ottarr, the gold of the ransom having itself been taken by force from Andvari. Woman is conceived as the giver of gold, *selja gulls*. Having periphrased the concept 'gold' (*gull*) by *ótrs nauðgjöld,* the skald then substituted for the word *selja,* 'giver'—which also means 'willow'—the word *eik,* which, like *selja,* is a feminine tree-name. But there is a difference between the character of the puzzle involved in periphrasing 'gold' as 'enforced ransom of the otter' and that presented by 'oak' for 'giver': the first is a mythological allusion, and in the myth gold *was* a ransom demanded and paid under duress—gold is characterized as something which, in a given context, it actually *was*. But a giver is *not* an oak: woman, as giver, is called something which woman is *not*. And here, in the identification of a person or thing with something which it is *not,* except in a very special and artificial sense, lies the nature of the true kenning; a kenning is not merely a metaphor; it is, in Heusler's words, *metapher mit ablenkung*. The base-word identifies the referent with something which it is not, except in a specially conceived relation which the poet imagines between it and the sense of the limiting element. An example which is clearer because it involves no play on words is the skaldic *hliðar þang,* 'tang of the hillside,' for grass or brush, which is not tang, but is called tang because it grows on the hillside as tang grows in the sea. Similarly 'sea of beasts' is a kenning for 'earth': earth is the abiding-place of beasts, as the sea is of fish.

I have used skaldic examples to illustrate the kenning because the extremes to which they carry the principle underlying the figure emphasize the difference between the kenning and other images of similar structure. The Old English kennings are much simpler and more transparent. *Hildenædre,* 'battle-adder,' is a kenning for 'arrow' or 'javelin' (*Elene, Judith*); *garbeam,* 'spear-tree,' is a kenning for 'warrior' (*Exodus*). In these, as in the skaldic kennings, the base-word identifies the referent with something which it is not, except in relation to the concept expressed in the limiting word: an arrow is thought of as stinging those wounded by it in battle, as an adder stings in the field; a warrior stands firm in strife, as a tree stands in the forest; the limiting noun 'spear' substitutes for a noun denoting 'battle,' the sphere in which the warrior functions. In all kennings there is a tension between the concept and the base-word; the limiting word partially resolves the unreality of that relation.

The qualitative difference between these kennings and such compounds and combinations as 'helm-bearer,' 'wave-traverser,' 'heath-stepper,' 'breaker of rings' is obvious. These last, unlike kennings, express the concepts for which they stand through an identification of the referent with something which it actually *is*. In the four metaphorical instances cited by Klaeber, however, we have genuine kennings: 'candle of the sky,' 'gem of heaven' are terms for 'sun' in which the base-word calls the referent something which it is not, except in an imagined relation to the sky or the heavens. The sun is neither a candle nor a gem; but it illumines the sky as a candle illumines a room, and it adorns the heavens with its gleam as a gem adorns and shines upon a garment. The body is not a house; but it may be called *banhus* because it contains the bones as a house contains its occupants. A sword is not a flame; but in the kenning *beadoleoma* it is imagined as giving forth light in battle as a torch or brand gives light in darkness.

The kenning is indeed a metaphor; but it is not a direct or a just metaphor. It depends for its effect not upon the listener's recognition that a given thing is so like that with which it is identified that the identification has immediate poetic truth; it depends upon the hearer's ability and willingness to see likeness within unlikeness, and the unlikeness must seem to be dissipated through the limiting word, which expresses an area, or a condition, within which likeness may be imagined. There are metaphors which are not kennings: for example, *forstes bend* for the ice which 'binds' the water in winter; *wintergewæde* (*Phoenix*) for the snow which covers the earth. A metaphor is a kenning only if it contains an incongruity between the referent and the meaning of the base-word; in the kenning the limiting word is essential to the figure because without it the incongruity would make any identification impossible.

Those periphrases which are not kennings, but which possess the same structure as the kenning, and which identify the referent as something which it *is,* may best be called by the Old Icelandic term *kend heiti.* A *heiti,* in its more precise sense, is a substantive simplex; such a *heiti* becomes *kent,* that is, 'characterized,' in terms of some actual quality or relationship, when it is combined with some limiting word. *Kend heiti* emphasize "a certain quality of a person or thing," as Klaeber says, or one of its aspects or functions. A great many *kend heiti* denoting persons have as base-word a noun of agency: a king is 'breaker of rings'; a warrior is a 'helm-bearer.' Even *kend heiti* denoting some animals or objects may have nouns of agency as base-words: a dragon is an 'air-flyer,' a ship is a 'wave-traverser.'

One special variety of *kent heiti,* very common in both Icelandic and Old English poetry, is called by the Icelanders *viðkenning.* This is one of two varieties of appellation which Snorri groups together as *fornöfn*—that is, as substitutions not for concepts, but for the *names* of persons. The *viðkenning* has the structure base-noun combined with limiting genitive; but its base-word is always a term of ownership or of personal relationship (e.g., 'owner,' 'father,' 'brother,' 'son,' 'friend,' 'enemy,' 'slayer,' etc.); and its limiting word is the *name* of the person or the owned object with whom, or with which, the specified relationship exists, or a recognizable substitute therefor. In skaldic poetry Thor is called 'Lord of Bilskirnir'; Njörðr is 'father of Freyr'; Freyr is 'foe' or 'slayer of Beli'; King Olaf I of Norway is 'son of Tryggvi.' In Old English poetry Beowulf is *sunu Ecgðeowes, bearn Ecgðeowes,* etc.; Hrothgar is *Healfdenes hildewisa;* Hygelac is *bona Ongenþeoes.*

The *viðkenning* is NOT a variety of kenning, nor does its name imply that it partakes of the nature of the kenning. The word means, simply and literally, 'a characterization in terms of' a specific person or named thing; it is derived from the verb *kenna,* which in rhetoric meant 'to make a characterizing periphrasis.' Snorri, in his initial classification of the skaldic poetic appellations, carefully excluded the *fornöfn* from the category of the kenning. The word *fornafn* is regularly used in the Icelandic grammatical treatises to translate *prænomen;* and indeed the *viðkenning* is pronominal in function: it stands for a *name.* Other types of *kend heiti,* and all kennings, stand not for names, but for concepts. As *fornafn,* a *viðkenning* always stands for the name of one specific individual, and distinguishes him from all others; whereas other kinds of *kend heiti,* and kennings, describe the referent typically. Thus *eodor Scyldinga,* 'protector of the Shieldings,' is a *kent heiti* applied to Hrothgar, but it could be applied with equal propriety to any Danish king; but the *viðkenning sunu Healfdenes,* used of Hrothgar after the death of his brothers, could mean no one but Hrothgar. The *viðkenning* identifies a specific individual, and stands for him alone. It stands lower than any other type of appellation in its poetic quality, which resides entirely in its allusiveness; in its direct and unmistakable identification it is poles apart from the kenning.

In the use of the *viðkenning* for the name of any person, there is no intent to mystify, to compel the listener to supply the answer to an unasked question. The scop's audience was thoroughly familiar with royal genealogy and with heroic legend, and recognized instantly the person referred to. The *viðkenning* at once lost its character as a rhetorical device when it was used with, instead of as a substitution for, the name of the referent. *Mago Healfdenes, sunu Frodan,* used instead of the name, had the same poetic quality that attaches to any simple literary allusion; but this was instantly lost when the *viðkenning* stood in close juxtaposition to the name. Thus, in the well-known formula *Beowulf maþelode, bearn Ecgðeowes,* the combination *bearn Ecgðeowes* is not a *viðkenning,* but a mere patronymic.

And therein lies a most important distinction between the *viðkenning* on the one hand and other varieties of *kend heiti* and the kenning on the other: whereas the *viðkenning* loses all poetic quality, and its very existence as an allusion, in combination with the name of the referent, other kinds of *kend heiti,* and kennings, are used freely in Old English poetry either as substitutions for, or side by side with, the literal word for the referent, without losing, in either case, any of their poetic effect. Too much emphasis has been placed upon substitution as an essential character of the kenning: it is most commonly a substitution in Old Norse, but not in Old English. Most frequently, in Old English poetry, we find kennings and *kend heiti* used as variations of the direct and literal word for the referent, or as variations of one another. Old English poets did not share the fondness of the skalds for mystification; and they carried variation to lengths undreamed of by Norse poets. In *Elene* 117–120 we find the kenning *hildenædran* used as a variation for the specific term for the referent, *flana scuras, garas;* and in *Judith* 221–222:

leton forð fleogan flana scuras,
hildenædran of hornbogan.

In *Beowulf* 1965b–66a the kenning *woruldcandel* is explained in the next line by the variation *sigel,* an *ókent heiti* (i.e., a poetic simplex) for the referent, the sun. Indeed, it is one of the characteristic traits of Old English poetic style that kenning and *heiti* are most often used in variations: the variation, rather than kenning or *heiti,* is, for the poet, the prime consideration; the poetic simplex or periphrasis is the material out of which the variation is made.

The essence of the kenning is the incongruity between its referent and that which it is called in the base-word, and an artificial resolution of the incongruity through the choice of limiting word. When a ship is called 'wain of the roller,' it is conceived as moving forward on the rollers which permit it to be thrust down to the water as a wain moves forward on its wheels. The identification is unreal; the very resolution is imperfect, since a wain moves forward not on rollers, but on wheels. Creation and apprehension of such a strained metaphor require an act of intellectual exercise not unlike that required by a riddle. The *kent heiti,* possessing the same structure as the kenning, embodies not a strained image, not an identification of the referent with something which it is not, but a just metaphor or metonymy; it involves no incongruity, and may be apprehended at once. Its base-word may be a noun denoting the material of which the referent is made, or one of its parts, or one of its functions or qualities; the limiting word expresses the medium or area in which the function is performed, or the object upon which it is performed, or some characterizing attribute (as in *fetelhilt, wundenstefna*) or some quality which gives the thing its value (*mægenwudu, ellenweorc*).

In the formation of kennings and *kend heiti* substitution plays a most important part. Once a poetic appellation has been formed and has become an accepted part of the language of poetry, new compounds and combinations may be formed to express the same concept, by the substitution for either one, or for both, of its parts of an exact or approximate synonym. This is, indeed, the primary manner in which the poetic vocabulary was expanded. A spear may be called *mægenwudu;* for the first element its approximate synonym *þrec-* may be substituted. Since *hild* and *beado* are synonyms, a sword may be called either *hildeleoma* or *beadoleoma.* A warrior may be called *guðwiga, guðfreca, guðbeorn;* or *hilderinc, hildemecg, hildfreca.* This is a procedure less artificial than it may appear: it is almost inevitable that the poetic vocabulary should develop largely in this manner in a compounding language.

APPENDIX B

Check-list of Compounds Formed on the Same Base-words in Beowulf and in Other Poems

The following analysis of compounds formed on the same base-words in *Beowulf* on the one hand, and in the whole corpus of other Old English poems on the other, will throw some light on Old English poetic diction in general, and will indicate a number of significant characteristics of the vocabulary of *Beowulf*. I have selected for study fifty-seven different base-words, the compounds of which seem especially illuminating.

1. *-ærn* compounds: As simplex, *ærn* means simply 'house,' 'habitation,' 'structure'—a sense which appears clearly in *winærn* (*Glosses*), 'a store-house for wine' or 'a tavern.' In religious poetry *-ærn,* as base-word in compounds, usually retains this meaning: *holmærn* (*Noah's Ark, Genesis*) is, in a rather special sense, a 'sea-house' for its occupants; *eorðærn, foldærn* (*Höllenfahrt Christi, Guðlac*), 'earth-house,' is the grave; *carcærn* (?) is a prison; *blacærn,* a 'house of light,' is a lamp (*Psalms*). There are five *-ærn* compounds in *Beowulf* (*heal-, medo-, þryð- hord-, win-*): none of these is found elsewhere in poetry; in all, the meaning is 'hall,' 'royal residence,' except in *hordærn,* which is applied to the dragon's barrow, with its treasure. *Hordærn* also occurs in prose, with the meaning 'treasury' or

'storehouse.' Except for this one compound, the *-ærn* words in *Beowulf* have a more elevated sense than elsewhere in poetry or in prose. *Gystærn* in *Judith,* however, approaches closely to this sense.

2. *-bana* (*-bona*) compounds: Of the five in *Beowulf,* four are not found elsewhere: *ecg-, hand-, gast-, muþ-; feorhbana* is common to *Beowulf* and *Genesis.* Compounds in other poems are: *ord-* (*Genesis*); *susl-* (*Christ and Satan*); *ealdor-* (*Genesis*); *broðor-* (*Genesis*). In these compounds the first element denotes (a) the instrument of killing: *ecg-, hand-, muþ-, ord-*; (b) the character of the slayer: *susl-*; (c) the person or thing slain: *gast-, feorh-, ealdor-, broðor-. Gastbona,* peculiar to *Beowulf,* means the Devil. The most vigorous and imaginative of all these compounds is *muþbona,* also peculiar to *Beowulf.*

3. *-bend* compounds: Of the six in *Beowulf,* five (*ancor-, fyr-, hyge-, searo-, wæl-*) do not appear elsewhere; *irenbend* is used also in *Genesis.* Three others appear elsewhere: *leoðu-* (*Andreas* and *Genesis*); *orþanc-* (*Riddles*); *wite-* (*Andreas*). In all these the base-word is used quite literally; the only figurative compound is *hygebend* ('bonds of melancholy thought'), peculiar to *Beowulf.*

4. *-byrðen* compounds: Three are known, each peculiar to a single poem: *mægen-* (*Beowulf*); *syn-* (*Crist*); *sorg-* (*Andreas*). Only *mægenbyrðen* is literal; yet this Beowulfian compound is most effectively used: the hero 'rejoiced in his sea-spoil, the mighty burden of those things which he had with him'—that is, Grendel's head and the hilt of the magic sword, the trophies which attest the peril and glory of his exploit. It took four men to carry the 'mighty burden' of Grendel's head.

5. *-candel* compounds: These are almost always kennings for 'sun,' 'moon,' 'sun and moon,' or 'stars.' One, *woruld-,* is peculiar to *Beowulf;* one each to *Genesis* (*frið-*), *Phoenix* (*swegl-*), *Guðlac* (*wyn-*), *Metra* (*mere-*). *Dæg-* is common to *Riddles* and *Andreas;* (*weder-*) to *Andreas* and *Phoenix. Heofoncandel* appears in several poems, with surprising diversity of meaning: in *Andreas* it is the sun, in *Crist* sun and moon, in *Wonders of Creation* the stars, and in *Exodus* it denotes the pillar of fire. The wide distribution of these compounds, the almost total restriction of their application to sun or moon, and the easy use of the base-word with genitive (*Godes condel, Brunanburh* and *Phoenix*) indicate the great age and traditional character of these kennings.

6. *-cearu* compounds: Of the four in *Beowulf* (*aldor-, guð- mæl-, mod-*), only *mod-* is found in other poems. Outside *Beowulf* we find *breost-* (*Seafarer, Wife's Lament*); *lif-* (*Andreas, Genesis*); *sorg-* (*Guðlac*). *Sorgcearu* is a tautological compound; except for it and the Beowulfian *guð*—which denotes grief resulting from strife,—the compounds have as limiting words nouns denoting the duration of grief or the seat of grief. *Guð-* alone indi-

cates in its first element the *cause* of grief (the persecution of the Danes by Grendel).

7. *-clif* compounds: These are descriptive, usually topographical; four of the six which I find are peculiar to *Beowulf: brim-, ecg-, holm-, weal-; stan-* occurs in *Beowulf* and in four other poems; *heah-* is peculiar to *Crist.* The distribution suggests that these compounds are not traditional.

8. *-cofa* compounds: There is but one in *Beowulf, bancofa*—a very common word in poetry. Other poems have many *-cofa* compounds, mostly figurative, and, like *bancofa,* nearly all kennings. The most poetic are *hordcofa* (*Wanderer*) and *þeostorcofa* (*Guðlac, Elene*). *Hordcofa* literally means a 'receptacle for treasure,' a 'treasure-chamber'; but in the recorded instances the meaning has either faded (in *Blickling Homilies* 143, 34 *on hire hordcofan* translates *in cubiculo suo*) or become metaphorical: in *Wanderer* 14 it means 'one's mind, one's secret thought,' and is thus synonymous with *breosthord.* The limiting element, *hord-,* thus appears to have taken over the function of a base-word—a rather rare phenomenon. *Þeostorcofa* means 'grave.'

9. *-cræft* compounds: The meanings of the base-word make it useful for the formation of compounds denoting any kind of strength, power, dexterity, or special ability. The five compounds in *Beowulf* mean 'strength in war' (*guð-, wig-*); physical strength (*mægen-*); manual dexterity (*leoðo-*); magical power (*nearo-*); of these, only *leoðo-* occurs elsewhere (*Be manna cræftum* 29, where it has lost the force of its first element, and means 'skills'). Twenty-four compounds occur in other poems, denoting military prowess; magical power; the power of evil or of hell (*firen-, Juliana; hell-, Andreas*); skill in song (*sang-, Phoenix; woð-, Phoenix, Whale*); learning or wisdom (*lar-, snytru-*); worldly wisdom (*woruld-*). Apparently *-cræft* compounds have a long history in poetic tradition.

10. *-cwalu* compounds: These have one of two senses: 'death, destruction to life,' and 'the tortures of hell.' The sole instance in *Beowulf, deaðcwalu,* there means 'death'; but in *Elene* 765 it has the other sense. *Feorhcwalu* (*Juliana, Whale*) and *swyltcwalu* (*Guðlac, Phoenix*) mean physical death; *hel-* (*Crist*), *nið-* (*Crist*), *gast-* (*Guðlac*), and *lig-* (*Elene*) all denote the tortures of hell. *Feorhcwalu, swyltcwalu,* and *deaðcwalu* in *Beowulf* evidently retain the older, nonreligious sense; in religious poetry the shift in meaning to spiritual death was easy. *Cwalu* appears only rarely as simplex, and is never used as first element in compounds.

11. *-cwealm* compounds: There are three in *Beowulf* (*bealo-, deað-, gar-*), all peculiar to our poem: they denote either death suffered (*bealo-*), or death inflicted upon others (*deað-*). *Gar-* appears to mean the former. In *Andreas* 1702 *beadocwealm,* which, like *garcwealm,* should mean death suffered in battle, is used inappropriately of the martyrdom of St. Andrew.

Broðorcwealm (*Genesis*) refers to the killing of Abel; *niðcwealm* (*Psalms* 77, 50) denotes 'pestilence.' *Cwealm,* unlike *cwalu,* is often used as simplex, and serves as first element in four compounds, two (*cwealmbealu, -cuma*) peculiar to *Beowulf,* two (*-dreor, -þrea*) to *Genesis.*

12. *-cyning* compounds: There are eleven in *Beowulf,* three of which (*leod-, beorn-, sæ-*) occur nowhere else. Nine of the eleven are used of the king of a people, and are obviously traditional; two (*Wuldor-, Soð-*) are appellations for God; these two occur in religious poems. *Eorð- þeod-, worold-, guð-, folc-,* and *heah-* are common to *Beowulf* and to other poems. Twelve compounds not in *Beowulf* appear in other poems; eight of these denote 'God.' The old simplex *cyning* was inevitably taken over by religious poets as base-word in compounds for the King of kings.

13. *-deað* compounds: These are not numerous; every one is peculiar to a single poem. Three (*guð-, wæl-, wundor-*) occur only in *Beowulf; ende-* is peculiar to *Crist, swylt-* (tautological) to *Psalms, ær-* and *mere-* to *Exodus.* Distaste for naming death (tabu) may account for the rarity of these compounds, which do not appear to be traditional.

14. *-dream* compounds: The five in *Beowulf* all denote, either specifically (*gleo-, medu-, sele-*) or abstractly (*gum-, mon-*) earthly joys, with particular reference to those experienced in the royal hall. *Gleo-* and *gum-* are peculiar to *Beowulf; medu-, seledream* occur in other poems, and are too specific to shift their meanings to religious use; *eðeldream* (*Genesis*) also is used in a secular sense. But in religious poetry all other *-dream* compounds denote the joys of heaven: *god-* (*Guðlac*), *sin-* (*Elene, Phoenix, Guðlac*), *swegl-* (*Andreas, Guðlac, Crist*), *heofon-* (*Psalms, Azarias, Soul to Body*), *wuldor-* (*Hymns and Prayers*). The cleavage between the old, traditional compounds and the purely Christian, religious ones is thus absolute.

15. *-drync* compounds: These, curiously enough, are few: I find four, each in a different poem. *Meodo-* (*Seafarer*), *win-* (*Psalms*), and *mán-* (*Riddles*) all appear literal; but *mán-* is used in a metaphorical sense: not poison drunk, but poison absorbed by a wound; the metaphor is actually contained not in the word, but in its context. *Hioro-* (*Beowulf*) is a pure metaphor: Hygelac 'died of sword-drinks.' If one may judge from their distribution, these compounds do not appear to be traditional.

16. *-fæt* compounds: Of the five in *Beowulf,* four (*drync-, maðþum-, wundor-, sinc-*) are quite literal, denoting actual cups or vessels. *Wundorfæt* is peculiar to *Beowulf; drinc-* and *maðþum-* occur in *Beowulf* and in prose; *sinc-* is used in *Beowulf* and in *Waldere* I; *ban-* is a metaphor for 'body,' and is widely used in poetry. Of the eleven compounds in other poems, only three (*gold-, Phoenix, Daniel; stan-, Waldere* II; and *husl-, Daniel*) are literal; the remaining eight are kennings, denoting such

various things as 'body' (*eorð-*), 'sun and moon' (*leoht-*), 'moon' (*lyft-*), 'clouds' (*wæg-*), 'Mary's womb' (*hord-*). The simplex, in virtue of its meaning, easily lends itself to metaphorical use. *Hordfæt* is a purely Christian kenning; there are not many of these. The predominantly metaphorical use of these compounds indicates traditional origin.

17. *-floga* compounds: All of these denote 'dragon': the four in *Beowulf* (*guð-, lyft-, uht-, wid-*) are peculiar to that poem. I find only one other, *an-* (*Seafarer*). These look like old, highly specialized, traditional compounds.

18. *-fruma* compounds: Of the six in *Beowulf*, four (*dæd-, hild-, leod-, ord-*) are found in other poems; *land-* and *wig-* are peculiar to *Beowulf*. In the epic, all but *dædfruma* (which is ironically applied to Grendel) denote a prince or war-chief. Most of them are used in this same sense in other poems; but in *Andreas* 75, *dugeða dædfruma* is an appellation for God. *Ordfruma* is most frequently applied to God in religious poetry. All five *-fruma* compounds which appear only in religious poetry are appellations of God: *ead-, lif-, leoht-, þiod-, tir-*. The Beowulfian compounds may all be old and traditional; at least two of those found in religious poems (*lif-, leoht-*) are clearly new formations made by Christian poets.

19. *-fyr* compounds: Of the three Beowulfian compounds (*bæl-, heaðo-, wæl-*), *heaðo-* and *wæl-* appear nowhere else. *Bælfyr* is common; but it keeps its original sense of the funeral fire of cremation only in *Beowulf*. In *Genesis* it means 'sacrificial fire,' the fire which God commanded Abraham to make for the sacrifice of Isaac; in *Juliana* 579 it refers to a fire built to melt a cauldron of lead for the saint's martyrdom. In both *Genesis* 2855 and *Juliana* 580 it is varied by the simplex *ad;* in *Beowulf* 1107–09 *ad* is followed, though not varied, by the simplex *bæl*. This grouping of the two words seems to point to an old formulaic pattern. In *Beowulf* 1119 *wælfyr* is used of the fire of a funeral pyre for men slain in battle; but in line 2582 it refers to the life-destroying fire cast by the dragon; *heaðofyr* has this sense in lines 2522, 2547. Six *-fyr* compounds not in *Beowulf* are found in other poems: *ad-* ('sacrificial fire,' *Exodus*); *æled-* (tautological, *Exodus*); *wælm-* (*Crist*); *heah* (probably two words); *helle-* (*Crist*, possibly two words); *lig-* (tautological, *Exodus*). Of all these, only *bæl-* is certainly traditional; *ad-, æled-, wæl-* may be.

20. *-gást* compounds: The four in *Beowulf* (*ellen-, ellor-, geosceaft-, wæl-*) are peculiar to that poem; all refer to Grendel and his kind. One instance in another poem (*cear-, Guðlac*) is used of the devils that torment the saint; the remaining compounds, all in religious poems, denote either 'angel' or 'God,' 'Christ'; e.g., *ærend-* ('angel,' *Genesis*); *heah-* ('Christ,' *Genesis*); *Wuldor-* (*Genesis*). It is doubtful that *helle gǽst* (*Beowulf, Juliana*) is a compound.

21. *-geat* compounds: The single instance in *Beowulf, bengeat,* is a metaphor; the four in other poems (*burg-, fæsten-, weal-, hord-*) are all quite literal. It therefore seems almost certain that the Beowulfian metaphor—as striking as it is unique—is not traditional, and that the compound *bengeat* is of the poet's own coinage.

22. *-bland, -gebland, -geblond* compounds: In these the base-word denotes a turbulent commingling, usually of water; the compounds are used of the troubled sea. A single Beowulfian instance refers to violent winds (*windblond gelæg,* line 3146). There are three in *Beowulf,* all peculiar to the poem: *sundgeblond, yðgeblond, windblond.* Elsewhere I find *éar-* (*Metra, Crist, Brunanburh*), which means the same, and contains the same image, as *sund-, yð-;* and *ár-* (*Andreas*). Unless *árgeblond* is a scribal error for *éar-,* it is a bad coinage by the author of *Andreas:* 'commingling of oars' or 'turmoil of oars' is a poor, and surely a nontraditional, appellation for 'sea.'

23. *-gewæde* compounds: I find only four in poetry: three (*breost-, eorl-, guð-*) are peculiar to *Beowulf;* and one, the fine *winter-,* is peculiar to *Phoenix. Breost-* denotes 'corselet'; *eorl-, guð-* denote either 'corselet' or 'armor.' The Beowulfian instances look like traditional *kend heiti;* but the fact that none of them appears elsewhere, even in battle-poetry, suggests that they are original with the poet of *Beowulf.* This appears to be confirmed by the fact that the only *-wǽd* compounds which mean 'armor' (*here-, heaðo-*) are also peculiar to *Beowulf.*

24. *-gifa* compounds: The four in *Beowulf* are surely traditional: each occurs in at least two other poems, and the nature of their limiting elements indicates that they were originally appellations for kings or princes. *Beag-* is used in *Beowulf, Elene, Brunanburh, Eadgar,* and *Maldon,* always with the sense 'king' or 'earthly lord'; *sinc-,* in *Beowulf* and *Maldon,* also has this sense; but in *Crist* 460 it is applied to Christ. *Goldgifa* (*Beowulf, Judith, Seafarer*) always means an earthly king or prince; *wilgifa* in *Beowulf* is used of Beowulf as king, but in *Phoenix, Elene, Andreas,* and *Crist* it denotes Christ or God. Of all the *-gifa* compounds not used in *Beowulf,* all but *maðum-* (*Wanderer*) are almost invariably appellations of God or Christ: e.g., *ár-* (*Be manna cræftum*), *blæd-* (*Andreas*); *éad-* (*Andreas, Crist*), *feorh-* (*Guðlac, Crist*), *hyht-* (*Crist, Elene*), *lac-* (*Psalms*), *symbel-* (*Andreas*). In these Christian compounds we see two processes at work: (1) old, inherited *kend heiti,* when their meaning permit, may be transferred directly to religious use; (2) new compounds were formed by religious poets by combining the traditional base-word with limiting words appropriate only, or primarily, to the concept 'God' or 'Christ.' These new compounds afford clear evidence that the vocabulary of Old English poetry is by no means wholly traditional; application of such words as *sincgifa,*

symbelgifa to God, on the other hand, reflect the strong hold which traditional appellations retained over the religious poets themselves. As for *symbelgifa,* the poet of *Andreas* reveals his own awareness of the traditional meaning: to adapt it to use as a term for 'God' he combines it with the genitive *sawla.* It will be noted that *-gifa* compounds for 'Christ,' 'God' are especially frequent in *Crist* and *Andreas.*

25. *-gim* compounds: The single compound in *Beowulf* (*searo-*) is also found in *Metra* and in prose; it and *sinc-* (*Elene*) are literal. Five others are kennings: *god-* (*Elene*), *tungol-* (*Crist*), *wuldor-* (*Riddles*), *wæl-* (*Riddles*), *heafod-* (*Exeter Gnomic Verses, Andreas*). *Godgimmas* is strangely used: *swylce heofonsteorran oððe godgimmas* (*Elene* 1112–13). *Tungol-,* like *god-,* means 'stars'; *wuldor-* denotes 'sun'; the meaning of *wæl-* is obscure; *heafod-* is a kenning for 'eye.'

26. *-gist* compounds: These, both in *Beowulf* and in other poems, are prevailingly ironic. In *Beowulf, gryre-, inwit-, nið-,* and *sele-* are used of uninvited and unwelcome guests—hateful intruders; *gryre-* and *inwit-* are peculiar to *Beowulf.* In *Guðlac, cear-, niðgist* are also ironic; they are used of devils. Of the seven other compounds which appear in other poems, only *wil-* (*Be manna mode*) and *brim-* (*Riddles*) are without irony. Four of the seven appear in the *Riddles,* which might be expected to use irony as one of many mystifying devices; but the widely ironic use of these compounds seems to point to traditional practice. The best of the *-gist* compounds are the Beowulfian *gryre-* and the still better *béod-* (*Andreas* 1087–88: *hungres on wenum, blates beodgæstes*).

27. *-helm* compounds: In these, the base-word has one of two distinct though related meanings: (1) 'helmet' (*grím-, Beowulf, Exodus, Elene; bán-, Finnesburh; guð-, Beowulf* only); (2) 'shelter, covering, concealment' (*niht-, Beowulf, Elene, Andreas, Wanderer, Guðlac; lyft-, Exodus, Cotton Gnomic Verses; heoloð-, Whale; mist-, Juliana; sund-, Riddles; wæter-, Exeter Gnomic Verses; scadu-, Beowulf* only). *Nihthelm toglad,* in *Andreas* 123, is an interesting figure, perhaps involving a deliberate play on the twofold meaning of *helm;* it recalls *guðhelm toglad,* in *Beowulf* 2487. In *Guðlac* 942–943, *Dagas forð scridun, nihthelm genipu* evidently means 'the days passed, the nights *also*'*;* we should expect the second appellation, in this structure, to be a variation of the first, but it obviously is not. *Misthelm* (*Juliana*) is a covering of mist spread by the Devil over men's eyes, to deceive them. *Sundhelm* seems to mean 'covering water'; *wæterhelm* denotes 'ice.'

28. *-hord* compounds: The four in *Beowulf* include two which are quite literal, and which occur nowhere else (*beah-, wyrm-*), and the two traditional kennings *breost-, word-*. Outside *Beowulf* I find only two literal compounds: *gold-* (*Daniel, Psalms*) and *brand-* (*Rhyme Poem*), which

seems to mean 'glowing treasure.' *Goldhord* is also used in *Elene,* and with striking inappropriateness, to denote the Cross, and in *Crist* 787, in an equally inappropriate combination to denote Christ Himself: *astag in middangeard mægna goldhord in fæmnan fæðm, freobearn Godes. Greot-, lic-* are rather infelicitous terms for the body (*Guðlac*); of all the Christian compounds, only *sawlhord,* the 'treasury' enclosing that great treasure, the soul, is a figure for 'body' consonant with traditional poetic practice. *Maðumhord* (*maðumhorda mæst, Exodus* 368), denoting the human and animal freight of the Ark, is a remarkable instance of transference, but is not without justification. Evidently the literal compounds (*beah-, wyrm-, gold-*) are traditional and ancient, even though the first two are not found outside *Beowulf,* and the third is misused by religious poets. The treasure-guarding dragon is certainly old in Germanic poetry: this is attested by *Beowulf* 886 ff.; by the Sigurd legend, and by the famous verses (*Gnomic Cotton*) *dracan sceal on hlæwe, frod, frætwum wlanc.* The two kennings *breost-, wordhord* must have been early-coined figures; the second stands in the opening line of *Widsið.* The transference of *goldhord* to the senses 'Cross,' 'Christ' in *Elene* and *Crist* is violent and shocking.

29. *-hrægl* compounds: The poetic instances seem to be nontraditional, the coinage of individual poets; all but one are peculiar to *Beowulf,* as are the *-gewæde, -wæd* compounds. *Beado-, fyrd-* denote armor; *mere-,* a kenning for 'sail,' is the only really figurative compound known. One, *frum-,* is peculiar to *Genesis:* it denotes the leaves which were the 'first garments' of Adam and Eve. The diversity in the nature of the referents for these several compounds argues against their traditional character; the fact that both *-hrægl* and *-(ge)wæde* compounds are few in number, and that the two base-words do not combine with the same limiting elements, also suggests that the compounds of both are all the creation of individual poets; and indeed each compound of either base-word is peculiar to a single poem.

30. *-hwil* compounds: There are four in *Beowulf* (*dæg-, gescæp-, orleg-, sige-*), none of which appears elsewhere. In other poems the *-hwil* compounds most frequently appear in formulaic patterns, the commonest of which are: (1) *æfter -hwile:* e.g., *æfter gryrehwile* (*Andreas*); *æfter swylthwile* (*Phoenix*); *æfter þrechwile* (*Juliana*); *æfter wræchwile* (*Phoenix*); (2) *-hwile* as object of a verb of suffering, experiencing, enduring: *þrowade earfoðhwile* (*Seafarer*); *gebad langunghwile* (*Dream of Rood*). The first of these two patterns never occurs in *Beowulf;* the second is represented only once (*þæt he dæghwila gedrogen hæfde,* 2726); though there is a rather similar combination in lines 2426–27: *'Fela ic on giogoðe guðræsa genæs, orleghwila . . .'* The fact that all the *-hwil* compounds in *Beowulf* are peculiar to that poem, and that they do not conform to the

patterns observable elsewhere, but occur in a variety of structures, sets them apart from the uses of these compounds in other poems.

31. *-last* compounds: There are not many *substantive* compounds formed with *-last* in poetry; adjective compounds (e.g., *sweart-, urig-*) are quite as numerous. *Beowulf* has four substantive compounds: *feorh-, feðe-, wræc-, fot-*. The first of these is found nowhere else; it is a pregnant word: *feorhlastas bær,* 'he bore his mortal tracks,' means 'he fled dying.' *Feðe-* appears also in *Judith; wræc-* is a common word for that favorite concept of poets, 'exile.' *Fotlast,* surprisingly, occurs only in *Beowulf* and (rarely) in prose. *Wræclast* is certainly ancient and traditional; perhaps *feðelast* is also, in spite of its infrequent occurrence: it is used adverbially, with verbs of going. Only *Beowulf,* however, employs it with strict correctness: to 'go in one's footsteps' is, of course, to go *back* as one had come; but in *Judith* it appears to mean 'go forward': *feðelaste forð onettan*. *Wid-* (*Genesis, Andreas*), 'wide wanderings,' approaches the meaning of *wræclast.*

32. *-leoht* compounds: I find three in *Beowulf,* all peculiar to that poem: *æfen-, fyr-, morgen-;* and one (*heofon-*) peculiar to *Andreas.* The singularity of each of these is astonishing; one would think them part of the vocabulary of common use. All are literal, and probably nontraditional.

33. *-leoþ* compounds: There are four in *Beowulf* (*fyrd-, gryre-, guð-, sorh-;* only *guð-* is peculiar to *Beowulf*). A large number of *-leoþ* compounds appear in other poems; almost invariably they are used as objects of the verbs (*a*)*singan,* (*a*)*galan;* their use is virtually restricted to definite formulaic patterns. It is true that a word meaning 'lay,' 'song,' can hardly be the object of any verb that does not mean 'sing'; nevertheless we must regard such combinations as formulaic, and perhaps originally magical in sense. I find only once a *-leoþ* compound as object of a verb with different meaning: *snelle gemundon weardas wigleoð* (*Exodus* 221). A *-leoþ* compound is used once in the nominative as a variation for a noun which is subject of *wæs ahafen: Forþon wæs in wicum wop up ahafen, atol æfenleoð* (*Exodus* 201); this is also formulaic in appearance, reminding us of *þa wæs æfter wiste wop up ahafen, micel morgensweg* (*Beowulf* 128–129). These compounds lend themselves to emotional or ironic use, according to the sentence-context.

34. *-maðþum* compounds: All of these are literal; I find seven, six peculiar to *Beowulf* (*dryht-, gold-, hord-, ofer-, sinc-, wundur-*); and one (*þeoden-*) peculiar to *Genesis.* This word is not used as base for compounds denoting religious concepts.

35. *-nett* compounds: Of the five in *Beowulf* (*breost-, here-, hring-, inwit-, searo-*), three (*here-, hring-, inwit-*) occur nowhere else; all but *inwit-* denote 'corselet'; the metaphors involve recognition of the netlike appearance of the chain mesh. *Searonet* in *Beowulf* refers, in its limiting element,

to the skill with which the corselet was fashioned: *searonet seowed smiþes orþancum* (*Beowulf* 406); but in *Andreas* this compound is used in the same sense as the Beowulfian *inwitnet,* a 'net of malice,' a cunning snare: '*Hu me elþeodige inwitwrasne, searonet seowað*' (*Andreas* 64). *Fengnet* (literally a net for catching game) is used in a similar figurative sense in *Psalms*. *Fisc-* and *fleohnet* are used quite literally; although the essential quality of the *fleohnet* in *Judith* was that through it 'the chieftain could look upon any who entered, and no man could see him.' *Wælnet* (*Exodus* 202) is a metaphor for a corselet—a much poorer term for a defensive weapon than the Beowulfian *here-, hring-, searo-*. These last, together with *breost-*, seem to me old and traditional.

36. *-ræs* compounds: There are six in *Beowulf* (*guð-, heaðo-, hilde-, hond-, mægen-, wæl-*); only one of these, *guð-*, is found elsewhere in poetry. Most *-ræs* compounds have as first element either a word for 'battle' (*heaðo-, hilde-, guð-, wæl-*) or a word indicating the means or instrument by which death in combat is inflicted: *hond-, Beowulf; gar-, Maldon; sweord-, Fates of the Apostles*. *Mægen-* (*Beowulf*) is almost adjectival: 'a mighty onslaught.' All the foregoing compounds seem to me traditional. *Deaðræs* (*Andreas* 995) is probably of the poet's coinage; in no other *-ræs* compound does the first element denote the result of an onslaught. The word, in *Andreas,* actually means no more than 'sudden death, a swift onslaught of death'; that death is not inflicted in battle, although it is expressed in the imagery of battle: *deaðræs forfeng hæleð heorodreorig*. This is an instance of excessive dominance of conventional modes of expression over a poet's thought; a still more striking instance, actually grotesque in its inappropriateness, may be found in *Genesis* 900 ff. Eve confesses to God that she 'made a hostile onslaught' (*feondræs gefremede*) on the tree which bore the forbidden fruit, 'wrought a feud' with it, and 'pillaged' it.

37. *-rand* compounds: All of these, except the unintelligible *calc-* (*Exeter Gnomic Verses* 143), are metonymies (*pars pro toto*) for 'shield.' There are four in *Beowulf,* three of which (*bord-, hilde-, sid-*) occur nowhere else in poetry; *geolo-* is found in *Beowulf* and in *Elene*. The simplex *rand,* like its compounds, is frequently used as a metonymy for 'shield'; but it is used once literally in *Beowulf: ligyðum forborn bord wið rond* (2672). All the compounds seem to me to be thoroughly traditional *kend heiti*. The variety of meanings expressed in their limiting elements is worth noting: *bord-* denotes the wood of which the shield is made, *hild*(*e*)- the area ('battle') of its use; *sid* and *geolo* are adjectives, the first expressing the breadth of the shield, the second referring to the yellow color of the linden-wood of which it was fabricated. *Bordrand* contains a double metonymy.

38. *-rest* compounds: Of the four in *Beowulf,* three (*flet-, sele-, æfen-*) are quite literal, and are peculiar to *Beowulf;* the fourth, *wæl-,* is a metaphor, and is found also in *Maldon, Guðlac, Genesis,* and *Elene.* The first element in the literal compounds denotes the place where the bed is situated, or the time during which it is occupied: Beowulfian *æfen-* is paralleled by *niht-* in *Andreas. Fold-* (*Crist*) and *land-* (*Andreas*) are metaphors for 'grave'; *bedd-* (*Genesis*) is tautological. Excepting *wæl-,* each of these compounds appears to be restricted to a single poem; they are probably not traditional. *Wæl-,* however, is surely traditional and very old: it occurs in five poems; and we can observe how its meaning fades with time and with use in religious poetry. In *Beowulf* it retains its original meaning, 'a bed of slaughter,' the place where the slain lie dead on the battlefield. The martial context in Maldon preserves this traditional sense. In *Genesis* and *Guðlac* it means simply 'death'; in *Elene* it is applied to the place where the Cross was buried—a flagrant misuse.

39. *-rinc* compounds: The base-word is an old Germanic *heiti* for 'warrior'; all the compounds are certainly traditional commonplaces, inherited from very early poetic practice. There are seven in *Beowulf: beado-, guð-, heaðo-, here-, hilde-, mago-, sæ-; fyrd-* and *gum-* appear in other poems. Each of the nine occurs in two or more poems.

40. *-run* compounds: One would naturally assume that all of these are traditional, both on the ground of the cultural importance of the runes in all Germanic lands, and because almost all the compounds contain a sense of secrecy, mystery, or magic. I am inclined to regard them as traditional and ancient in spite of the fact that each of the known compounds is restricted to a single poem: *beadu-* (*Beowulf*); *hete-* (*Riddles*); *hyge-* (*Elene*); *inwit-* (*Juliana*); *leoðo-* (*Elene*); *searo-* (*Wonders of Creation*); *wæl-* (*Elene*).

41. *-scealc* compounds: Two out of four poetic instances are terms for officers of a royal household: *beor-* (peculiar to *Beowulf*) and *ambeht-* (*Judith, Psalms, Genesis*); the other two are fully converted to religious use: *freoðo-* ('angel,' *Genesis*); *helle-* ('devil,' *Christ and Satan*).

42. *-sceaða* compounds: The eleven compounds in *Beowulf* are all applied to the monstrous creatures slain by the hero—sea-beasts, Grendel and his dam, the dragon; five (*dol-, guð-, hearm-, scyn-, uht-*) are peculiar to *Beowulf.* In religious poetry, all the *-sceaða* compounds are applied to human or demonic foes of God: in *Andreas,* to the heathen; in *Exodus,* to the Egyptians; elsewhere to devils. The somewhat abstract sense of the simplex ('harmer,' hence 'foe') permits wide latitude in the coinage of compounds. The large number, and the wide distribution, of these compounds indicates that the base-word had been used from very early times to form compounds to denote either human or supernatural enemies.

43. *-scua* compounds: These have two senses: (1) 'darkness,' a literal 'shadow'; (2) a ghostly or monstrous being, usually nocturnal. The first sense is the more common. *Andreas* has *dim-*, *heolstor-*, and *hlin-:* the first means simply 'darkness'; the second and third mean 'prison,' as a place of darkness. *Neaht-* (*Wanderer, Seafarer, Guðlac, Genesis, Exodus*) means 'shades of night.' Two compounds have the second sense: (*deorc*) *deaðscua* (*Beowulf;* the referent is the night-ravager Grendel); and (*deor*) *dædscua* (*Crist* I; the referent is Satan). This last may be a scribal error for *deorc deaðscua,* as in *Beowulf* 160 (see *Anglia,* XXXV, p. 255).

44. *-scur* compounds: These are few; the literal compounds (*hægl-*, *Menologium, Andreas; winter-*, *Phoenix*) are surely not traditional; the figurative (*isern-*, *Beowulf; hilde-*, *Guðlac*) just as certainly are; the same metaphor for 'battle' is found in Old Norse skaldic poetry: e.g., *stála skúr, malmá skúr.* In *Guðlac* one of these traditional figures for 'battle,' *hildescur,* shows fading of the sense of the limiting word, and is used in a wholly new sense: 'attacks of sickness.'

45. *-sele* compounds: Seven are peculiar to *Beowulf* (*dryht-*, *gold-*, *guð-*, *heah-*, *hring-*, *hrof-*, *nið-*); five are common to *Beowulf* and to other poems (*beah-*, *beor-*, *eorð-*, *gest-*, and *win-*). The first element in all twelve of the compounds which appear in *Beowulf* expresses one or another characteristic of the hall: its splendor, its hospitality, the good things dispensed in it, etc. All the compounds are literal; even *eorðsele,* which is applied to the dragon's barrow, may properly be called an 'earth-hall,' in view of its columns and arches. One Beowulfian compound, *niðsele,* is used of the subaquean hall of Grendel's dam—a 'hostile hall'; Beowulf refers to Heorot as *guðsele* twice: the first time because he knows he must fight Grendel in the hall, and the second time in his report of the battle to Hygelac. *Hornsele* (*Genesis*) is a gabled hall; *burnsele* (*Ruin*) is a Roman bath; as almost always, in these literal compounds the first element names some characteristic of the hall. The figurative compounds are restricted to religious poetry: *bansele* (*Be Domes Dæge*) is a kenning for 'body'; *will-* (*Phoenix*) is the Phoenix's nest; *deað-* (*Guðlac, Crist*), *wind-* (*Christ and Satan*), *wyrm-* (*Judith*) are appellations for 'hell.' *Dreor-* (*Wife's Lament*) seems to contain not the sense of the noun *dreor,* 'blood,' but the later, faded sense of *dreorig,* 'dreary, dismal.'—The simplex *sele* is most frequently applied, in nonreligious poetry and especially in *Beowulf,* to a royal hall; the Beowulfian compounds are accordingly words of elevated poetic character. In religious poems, however, the simplex may be applied to any structure: it denotes a hermitage in *Guðlac,* a prison in *Andreas,* and (modified by an appropriate adjective) 'hell' in *Christ and Satan: þes windiga sele; þone werigan sele.* In these uses it does not, I think, fade in meaning; it is used ironically.

46. *-smið* compounds: Only two of these retain, in poetic compounds, the literal meaning of the base-word: *wundor-* (peculiar to *Beowulf*), which probably means 'a fabricator of wondrous things' rather than 'a smith of wondrous skill'; and *gold-* (*Metra*). In all other compounds *-smið* has the sense 'causer, instigator': *gryn-*, 'devils' (*Andreas*); *hleahtor-*, 'they that cause laughter' (*Exodus*); *lar-*, 'counselor' (*Elene, Andreas*); *wig-*, 'warriors' (*Crist, Genesis, Be manna mode, Brunanburh*); *wroht-*, 'devils' (*Guðlac, Andreas*). Compounds with figurative meaning are almost wholly restricted to religious poetry.

47. *-spell* compounds: There are fourteen of these in the religious poems; in all of them the base-word means 'speech' (as in *sarspell, Hymns and Prayers* 4, 96) or—much more frequently—'tidings.' In the single Beowulfian compound, *weaspell,* which occurs nowhere else, it does *not* mean 'speech' or 'tidings,' though it is generally so translated; it means a period, an extended time. The context makes this quite clear: ... *se snotera bad, hwæþer him Alwalda æfre wille æfter weaspelle wyrpe gefremman* ('whether the Almighty ever intended to bring about a change for him after a season of woe,' 1313b–15). Here *-spell* is used in precisely the same sense as in the modern colloquialism 'a rainy spell.' This is the only *-spell* compound with this meaning.

48. *-swæþ* (*-swaþu*) compounds: *Wald-* and *swat-* are peculiar to *Beowulf*. The first means 'forest-paths'; the second is a graphic word for the 'bloody tracks' left by the armies of Geats and Svear. *Bil-*, in *Exodus,* seems to mean the 'track' (i.e., the wound) left by a weapon. *Dolh-, wund-,* and *fot-* are used in prose. Both of the Beowulfian compounds occur in combination with *wæs* (*wæron*) *wide gesyne,* which might appear formulaic; but since the most obvious thing about tracks is that they can be seen and followed, I should regard the almost identical preterites as no more than a reflection of the poet's preference; there are not enough of these compounds, nor do those I have found coincide closely enough in meaning, to suggest that they are traditional.

49. *-sweg* compounds: Of the four I have found, two (*benc-, morgen-*) are peculiar to *Beowulf;* in both, the limiting element has adverbial force: 'noise *from* the benches'; 'noise *at* morning.' *Heresweg,* 'noise of a host' (*Ruin*), means the sound of many men rejoicing; *hildesweg* (*Genesis*) is, literally, 'the noise of battle.' The two Beowulfian compounds are richer than these in their connotations and happier in their contexts. After Hrothgar's scop has sung of Finn and Hengest, *Gamen eft astah, beorhtode bencsweg,* 'the noise [of mirth and speech] from the benches grew louder' —a unique use of the verb *beorhtian*. *Morgensweg* (line 129) is the loud Danish lamentation after Grendel's first incursion: when morning revealed the massacre of their comrades, the noise of their grief was great. The com-

pound stresses the tragic contrast between the joy of the day before and the sorrow that came with morning.

50. *-þrym* compounds: In certain of these—quite obviously the oldest—the base-word has the sense of 'valor, strength, might.' There is only one in *Beowulf, higeþrym,* which occurs nowhere else; it means 'valor of spirit.' *Hilde-, ofer-* (in *Andreas* and *Be Domes Dæge,* respectively) mean 'martial force,' 'exceeding power'; both retain the literal senses of the base-word. In religious poetry the sense shifts to something like 'majesty, glory'—most frequently the glory or majesty of God: e.g., *godþrym* (*Crist*); *heah-* (*Guðlac*); *heofon-* (*Andreas*); *wuldor-* (*Andreas*); *mægen-* (*Exodus, Juliana, Crist*). *Cyne-* (common to a number of religious poems) usually means 'royal majesty'; *eðel-* (*Genesis*) seems to mean the glory of a nation.

51. *-wæge* compounds: I find two peculiar to *Beowulf;* in both (*ealo-, lið-*) the base-word means literally a cup or flagon. Two are peculiar to *Guðlac;* both are highly figurative: Eve 'poured for her dear husband a bitter compulsive cup' (*bittor bædeweg*), so that none of the sons of men thereafter might 'avert the wretched drink of the deep cup of death' (*bibugan þone bleatan drync deopan deaðweges . . .*). These two occur in close succession (lines 958, 964). This figure of the cup of death recalls Christ's prayer in the Garden of Gethsemane: "Father, if Thou be willing, remove this cup from me."

52. *-wæstm* compounds: There is only one in *Beowulf* (*here-*); it occurs nowhere else. Klaeber translates it 'martial vigor'; it occurs in Beowulf's vaunting speech (lines 677 ff.) before his fight with Grendel: *'No ic me an herewæsmun hnagran talige guþgeweorca, þonne Grendel hine . . .'* In all other compounds the base-word means, quite literally, 'fruits,' 'vegetation': *eorð-* (*Psalms, Metra*); *fold-* (*Phoenix*); *frum-,* 'first-fruits' (*Psalms*); *lim-* (*Christ and Satan*); *treo-* (*Psalms*). The simplex *wæstm,* however, though it most frequently means 'fruit,' 'vegetation,' may also mean 'growth, physical development,' and hence 'stature, bodily shape'; and it has this sense in *Beowulf* 1352: *on weres wæstmum* means 'in the shape of a man.' In *Beowulf* 677 the metaphorical sense is plain; it appears in no other compound, and we may safely take *herewæstm* as the poet's own coinage.

53. *-wæpen* compounds: I find six in poetry, each one peculiar to a single poem: *Beowulf* has *hilde-* and *sige-; beadu-* and *camp-* occur in *Riddles; here-* in *Psalms; heoru-* in *Judith.* The last shows how completely the original meaning of *heoru* could fade in compounds: *heorowæpnum* (*Judith* 263) seems to mean no more than 'with weapons.' It is, of course, possible that *wæpen*—the more abstract of the two elements of the word—has faded, and that the compound means '(with) swords'; but the fact that *heoru* very seldom retains the meaning 'sword' as limiting word argues against this. Indeed, except as first element in compounds *heoru*

seems almost to have passed out of existence: it occurs as simplex only twice (*Beowulf* 1285 and *Exeter Gnomic Verses* 202), as Klaeber notes in his glossary. It was once an important *ókent heiti,* and was frequently used in Old Norse poetry.—Few and scattered as are the *-wæpen* compounds, those compounds in which *wæpen-* serves as limiting word are almost equally rare in poetry, though they are sufficiently common in prose. This would indicate that *wæpen-, -wæpen* compounds are not traditional; poets evidently preferred more specific terms.

54. *-wela* compounds: None of the four in *Beowulf* (*ær-, hord-, maððum-, burh-*) appears anywhere else; in all these the base-word means 'wealth, riches, treasure.' It has the same sense in a number of compounds used by religious poets (*eorð-, fold-, land-, woruld-*); but these are commonly used disparagingly, to mean the prosperity of this world as against 'treasure in heaven.' Two compounds, *bold-, ead-,* are each used in two distinct senses: (1) worldly wealth (so *bold-* in *Soul to Body; ead-* in *Fates of Men*); (2) heavenly riches, the enjoyments of Paradise (so *bold-* in *Fates of the Apostles* 33; *ead-* in *Guðlac* 1064). A number of compounds are used *only* of the 'possessions' of the blessed in heaven: *blæd-* (*Crist*); *lif-* (*Crist, Fates of the Apostles, Daniel*). One compound, *árwela,* is unique: like *árgeblond* and *áryð,* it is peculiar to *Andreas,* and all three are clearly appellations for the sea. Since 'wealth of oars,' 'commingling of oars,' 'oar-wave' are most inept terms for their referent, we must assume either that the poet of *Andreas* was unhappy in his coinages, or that in all three compounds the first element is a scribal error for *éar-*. Compounds denoting the joys of heaven are obviously the creations of the religious poets. Like other Christian coinages, they are for the most part either new applications of old words or new formations with limiting words chosen to express Christian concepts.

55. *-wine* compounds: There are five in *Beowulf,* without counting the national name *Ingwine;* three of these (*frea-, freo-, guð-*) occur in no other poem. *Gold-* is common to *Beowulf, Elene,* and *Wanderer; mæg-* is common to *Beowulf, Genesis, Exodus,* and *Salomon. Frea-, freo-,* and *gold-* denote 'prince,' 'king'; *mæg-* means 'friendly kinsman, dear kinsman.' *Guð-* (*Beowulf* 1810, 2735) is a kenning for 'sword.' Apart from these I find only *iu-* (*Seafarer*) and *sundor-* (*Fæder larcwidas*), which—unlike *frea-, gold-, freo-, guð-*—are literal terms, not *kend heiti* or kennings. It is interesting that, as against five *-wine* compounds in *Beowulf,* no other poem has more than one. The fact that three of the seven are *heiti* for 'prince' is good evidence that these are old traditional terms; but the kenning *guðwine,* for which there is no parallel elsewhere, seems to me a coinage of the *Beowulf* poet's.

56. *-wrasn* compounds: *Frea-,* which is peculiar to *Beowulf,* refers to

ornamental chains decorating the hero's helmet. I find only two others, both in *Andreas: fetor-,* denoting chains with which a prisoner is bound; and *inwit-,* a metaphor for the malicious snares of foes, with which one is 'bound.' Since both compounds are linked with the adjective *elþeodig,* one might imagine that the combination is formulaic:

> 'Hu me elþeodige inwitwrasne,
> searonet seoðað [seowað ?]...' (63–64a)
>
> '...elþeodigra inwitwrasnum
> bealuwe gebundene...' (946–947a)

But since *inwitwrasn* occurs only in *Andreas,* and the words used in both passages describe a situation specific to the poem, the combination *elþeodig–inwitwrasn* probably merely reflects the poet's individual taste.

57. *-yð* compounds: These are not numerous; *yð* is used much more frequently as limiting element than as base-word in poetic compounds. *Beowulf* has *flod-, lig-, wæter-,* all three peculiar to *Beowulf. Ligyð* is the only compound embodying the figure 'waves of fire'; all others denote, literally, the waves of the sea. *Sæ-* is found in *Runic Poem, salt-* in *Panther* and *Seafarer.* The author of *Andreas* uses the exasperating compound *áryð* (*aryða geblond*), which is even worse than his *arwela, argeblond.* It is difficult to determine whether these compounds are traditional or not; the simplex itself, though more frequently used in poetry than in prose, is not restricted to poetic use.

◇ ◇ ◇

The foregoing study of the compounds formed in Old English poetry on 57 base-words might be challenged on the ground that these constitute only a fraction of the compounds in *Beowulf,* or on the more valid ground that a study founded on the base-words of compounds in another poem—*Genesis,* for example, or *Elene*—might have given a somewhat different impression of the poetic vocabulary. I have, however, examined all the compounds formed, in all extant Old English poems, upon every base-word in *Beowulf;* and I feel that this study is significant for two reasons: first, because the compounds in *Beowulf* are so much more numerous than those in any other poem; and secondly, because *Beowulf,* by its very nature, might be expected to conform more closely to ancient traditional modes of expression than the religious poems. I think the analysis just concluded has yielded certain positive results.

First, it is clear from the examples given above that a great many poetic compounds were created by the authors of religious poems; and that many others, originally without any Christian denotation or connotation, were adopted from the traditional poetic vocabulary and used for—sometimes rather violently adapted to—the expression of Christian concepts. The consequence was a gradual and progressive differentiation of the diction of religious poetry from that of nonreligious—and specifically from that of martial or heroic poetry. There was still a very large vocabulary of words, simplices as well as compounds, available for use by all poets.

It is surprising, as we have seen, how many compounds appear with marked infrequency. A great many of the various compounds formed upon a given base-word occur at most in two or three poems; many are restricted to a single one. Either the total poetic vocabulary was far richer than necessary to meet the need of any poet; or—and this is much more likely—individual poets allowed themselves much freedom in the formation of new compounds. Such new formations—as the foregoing analysis shows—were very often made by mere substitutions of a synonym for one, or for both, of the elements of a more familiar compound. This is to say that, in the expression of concepts, tradition supplied, not the vocabulary, but merely the basic patterns upon which compounds could be acceptably formed.

We find also that, broadly speaking, many of the compounds in *Beowulf* are literal, or embody simple figures; whereas a disproportionately large number of the compounds formed on the same base-words in other poems are figurative, and often embody strained figures; the language of *Beowulf* is richer, and at the same time more temperate, than that of most other poems. Moreover the compounds of *Beowulf* tend to be relatively specific. Over all, the compounds in *Beowulf* are used with more precision, and with more restraint, than those of most other poems. I have shown in chapter i how much more modest, how much less strained, are the kennings in *Beowulf* than many of those in Christian religious poetry.

◇ ◇ ◇

Limiting words: I append lists of limiting words, according to frequency of use:

1) Limiting words which form compounds in *Beowulf,* but in no other poem: *að-, bat-, ben-, drync-, earm-, eoten-, fæt-, fetel-, frea-, gamen-, geosceaft-, gescæp-, gif-, hæft- ('haft'), hreð-, hyð-, hrof-, læn-, lið-, luf-, næs-, nicor-, orc-, seax-, seld-, swat-, swin-, sceadu-, undern-, wald-, winn-, wist-. Fen-* should probably be added to this list: it forms four compounds in *Beowulf* (*-freoðo, -gelad, -hlið, -hop*); the only other compound formed in poetry is the distinctly unpoetic *fenyce,* 'fen-frog,' in *Riddles* 41, 71.

2) Limiting words which form more compounds peculiar to *Beowulf* than compounds peculiar to any other poem: *fyrgen-, gryre-, iren-, lig-, feorh-, morðor-, dryht-, eorð-, land-, uht-, hand-, breost-, æfen-, beag-,*

grund-, gum-, hring-, níð-, beadu-, hild-, guð-, wig-, fyrd-, wæl-, inwit-, lind-, brim-, sæ-, mere-, yð-, sele-, gold-, maððum-, hord-, me(o)do-.

It will be seen that the compounds made with limiting words more productive in *Beowulf* than in other poems are, for the most part, words for concrete things, although there are a few abstracts among them. The concepts expressed in these compounds are, moreover, those which would naturally be much more likely to appear in heroic than in religious poetry—war, battle, varieties of weapon, sea, hall, treasure.

This lends support to Magoun's argument that, if we had other long poems of the heroic character of *Beowulf,* many of the compounds which now appear peculiar to that single poem would be matched. But it is not simply, or primarily, a question of the nature of the theme; there is a much more important matter—that of treatment of the theme. The wealth of compounds in *Beowulf* is largely to be accounted for by the poet's fondness for variation and his taste for projecting vivid images; without these, his vocabulary would have been much smaller in scope and richness.

APPENDIX C

The Limits of Variation

Paetzel's admirable work on variation[1] seems to me to lay somewhat too much stress upon form rather than content, with the consequence that he excludes a number of fine instances which, for me, illustrate excellently the poet's characteristic uses of the figure. For this reason I should like to direct attention here to the points of difference between Paetzel's view and mine, and to give examples of types of variation which he treats rather more summarily than, in my opinion, they deserve.

Paetzel (pp. 189–190) insists that the second member of a substantive variation—the most common type—must stand in the same case as the first, although he admits a number of exceptions. This seems to me too rigorous. Variation involves the repeated expression of the same concept or idea, not in identical terms, but in terms which, while they restate essentially the same concept or proposition, do so in a manner that emphasizes a somewhat different aspect of it. The members of a substantive variation do not often stand in different cases, but occasionally they do: lines 1296–99a of *Beowulf* afford a clear example:

[1] Walther Paetzel, *Die Variationen in der altgermanischen Allitterationspoesie* (*Palaestra*, XLVIII; Berlin, 1913).

Se wæs Hroþgare hæleþa leofost
...
rice randwiga, þone ðe heo on ræste abreat,
blædfæstne beorn.

In purely grammatical terms, *rice randwiga* is nominative, in apposition with *hæleþa leofost;* whereas *blædfæstne beorn* is accusative, in apposition with *þone* (*ðe*), the object of *abreat.* Nevertheless these two combinations of adjective plus noun say essentially the same thing of the same person within the same sentence, in somewhat different terms. To me this is good variation. When the members of a variation possess the same grammatical structure, they constitute a parallelism as well as a variation; but the two figures are not identical. As I have shown in chapter ii, there are variations the members of which do not stand in the same construction.

I have said that one member of a variation may express a concept in general terms, and another may do so more specifically. This is by no means rare; there is an example in lines 39–40:

hildewæpnum ond heaðowædum,
billum ond byrnum ...

Hildewæpnum, a general term for 'offensive weapons,' is varied by *billum; heaðowædum,* 'battle-garments,' refers to defensive weapons, and most often denotes 'corselet'; it is varied by *byrnum.*

Although clauses may stand in variation with substantives (*Gar-Dena þrym–hu ða æþelingas ellen fremedon*), we must recognize many collocations of clause and substantive which are not variations. For example (lines 86–88):

Ða se ellengæst earfoðlice
þrage geþolode, se þe in þystrum bad,
þæt he dogora gehwam dream gehyrde ...

The clause *se þe in þystrum bad* is not a variation of *se ellengæst,* but a restrictive clause: 'that mighty demon who dwelt in darkness'; and *þæt he ... dream gehyrde* is not a variation of *þrage,* but a statement of the cause of Grendel's distress.

Paetzel rightly distinguishes between variation and enumeration (*Aufzählung; op. cit.,* p. 31 ff.): in the verses

. . . . . . se þe moras heold,
fen ond fæsten ...

the three substantives do not stand in variation: the territory inhabited by Grendel contained both moors and fen. In lines 89b–90a, *swutol sang scopes* is not a variation of *hearpan sweg:* the scop's song and its instrumental accompaniment are different things. In lines 112–113 we have a clear case of enumeration rather than variation: *eotenas, ylfe, orcneas, gigantas* are different kinds of *untydras,* for all their common descent from Cain. I doubt that two collocations which Paetzel regards as variations are so in reality: *wop . . . / micel morgensweg* (128b–129a); *lað ond longsum* (134, 192). *Micel morgensweg* seems to me not a restatement of the concept expressed in *wop,* but a description of it: it refers to the sound of the thing rather than to the thing itself. The adjectives *lað* and *longsum* mean two different things: Grendel's persecution was *both* hateful *and* long-enduring. Paetzel regards this combination as one of the exceptions to his rule that words connected by a coördinating conjunction are not members of a variation. In lines 136–137, however, *fæhðe ond fyrene,* taken together, seem to me a variation of *morðbeala mara;* both are objects of *gefremede,* and refer to the same acts. These instances show how difficult it can be to distinguish between true variations and other collocations the individual members of which show closeness of sense-relation.

Nevertheless, identity of meaning—that is, substantial identity, with some, however slight, shift in emphasis—is more essential to variation than is identity of structure. Paetzel does not distinguish with sufficient care between variation and parallelism; yet there is a point at which distinction must be made. In lines 210b–211a:

. . . . . . flota wæs on yðum,
bat under beorge . . .

bat is a variation of *flota;* but *on yðum / . . . under beorge* is not a variation at all, though the two phrases stand in parallel structure; 'on the waves / below the cliff' mean different things. We meet a similar situation in lines 221b–223a:

. . . . . . land gesawon,
brimclifu blican, beorgas steape,
side sænæssas . . .

Here we have parallelism without variation: the poet is enumerating the various features of the Danish coast-line as the Geats raise it in view: 'steep hills' and 'broad promontories' are distinct elements of the landscape.

In my first chapter I mentioned the fondness of the poet of *Beowulf* for grouping together different poetic appellations for a single referent in variations, so that the sum of the members presents a total description or characterization. I gave as one illustration the sequence of terms applied to Hrothgar in Wulfgar's second speech (lines 350–353). Such cases are true variations: each member has the same referent as the others; the several members express it in somewhat varying, and cumulative, terms. Unless each member of the sequence is an appropriate designation for the same referent, we have not a variation, but an enumeration—or, in certain cases, a progression. Very often—as in lines 221–223—the poet enumerates distinct and different details of a general or collective whole, each detail representing its own concept. Such enumerations are not variations, even though they may begin, or end, with a word or phrase which denotes that general whole of which the enumerated details are distinct features. So it is in the instance just cited: the Geats described *land*—sea-cliffs gleaming, steep hills, broad headlands. Again, in lines 333–335a, Wulfgar's address to the Geats enumerates their offensive and defensive weapons:

> 'Hwanon ferigeað ge   fætte scyldas,
> græge syrcan   ond grimhelmas,
> heresceafta heap? ...'

This is an enumeration of different things—shields, corselets, helmets, spears—which stresses, individually, distinct details that, taken together, present the total image of a company of splendidly armored men. This is a favorite device of the poet; but it is not variation; there is unity of effect but complete diversity of detail. Yet an enumeration of this sort may contain variation of its partials, as in the lines closely preceding the last quoted:

> . . . . . .   Guðbyrne scan
> heard, hondlocen,   hringiren scir
> song in searwum,   þa hie to sele furðum
> in hyra gryregeatwum   gangan cwomon.
> Setton sæmeþe   side scyldas,
> rondas regnhearde   wið þæs recedes weal;
> bugon þa to bence,—   byrnan hringdon,
> guðsearo gumena;   garas stodon,
> sæmanna searo,   samod ætgædere,
> æscholt ufan græg ...

Here each of the three concepts involved in the enumeration is expressed in a variation; the various members of each variation stress different aspects of its referent.

I have said that parallelism may subsist without variation: in lines 575b–577 there is a clear instance of this:

> '. . . . . .   No ic on niht gefrægn
> under heofones hwealf   heardran feohtan,
> ne on egstreamum   earmran mannon ...'

Here there is a double parallelism, totally without variation. *Heardran feohtan–earmran mannon* both consist of substantives modified by comparative adjectives, and both are objects of *gefrægn;* but they refer to totally different things. *Under heofones hwealf* means 'anywhere'; *on egstreamum* refers to the specific conditions under which Beowulf was laboring in his adventure with Breca.

The three consecutive statements concerning Hrothgar's state of mind at the conclusion of the Unferth affair might easily be taken for clausal variation; but the only actual variation in these lines is substantival:

> Þa wæs on salum sinces brytta
> gamolfeax ond guðrof; geoce gelyfde
> brego Beorht-Dena; gehyrde on Beowulfe
> folces hyrde fæstrædne geþoht. (607–610)

The three appellations for 'Hrothgar' stand in variation; but the three clauses say different things; their relation is one of cause and effect. Hrothgar was joyous because he now had confidence in effective help; he had that confidence because he had just heard the expression of Beowulf's resolute purpose.

The same or closely similar combinations, having the same referent, may, under one set of circumstances, stand in variation; and under another constitute no variation at all. In lines 672b–673,

> . . . . . . sealde his hyrsted sweord,
> irenna cyst, ombihtþegne . . .

The two terms applied to the sword are not in variation: the second does not repeat the first, but asserts the special virtue of the weapon. The sense is: 'his sword, (which was) the best of blades.' But in lines 801b–803 the circumstances are different:

> . . . . . . þone synscaðan
> ænig ofer eorþan irenna cyst,
> guðbilla nan gretan nolde . . .

Here *ænig irenna cyst–guðbilla nan* are members of a variation, the negation of the first deriving from the verb *nolde*. The terms have substantially identical meaning: 'no best of blades, no one of war-swords.'

One passage (lines 841b–846) which Paetzel does not discuss seems to me to contain a number of borderline cases:

> . . . . . . No his lifgedal
> sarlic þuhte secga ænegum
> þara þe tirleases trode sceawode,
> hu he werigmod on weg þanon,

niða ofercumen, on nicera mere
fæge ond geflymed feorhlastas bær.

Unless we accept as possible elements of a true variation restatements of the same concept or idea in different structural forms, we obliterate the line between variation and parallelism; and we have seen that parallelism may exist without variation. I have cited instances of clauses which vary substantives; these afford sufficient evidence that the members of a variation need not stand within the same clause. Even when two terms stand in identical construction within the same clause, there is no variation unless both say the *same* thing in varying terms. In the passage just quoted, the question is one of identity or nonidentity of meaning, which is the true test of variation. Does the clause *hu he werigmod ... feorhlastas bær* mean the same thing as *tirleases trode?* Both are objects of *sceawode.* Perhaps *werigmod* should be excluded from consideration: it describes Grendel's state of mind, whereas the other terms applied to him set forth his condition. But *hu he ... feorhlastas bær* means 'how he went away mortally wounded'; *tirleases trode* means 'the footprints of the one bereft of glory'; the sense of the two is almost identical: both refer to the bloody tracks of the defeated Grendel as observed by the Danes. Again, *niða ofercumen* and *fæge ond geflymed* are almost identical in meaning: both terms assert Grendel's defeat; the second is more explicit, but the first implies all that the second says explicitly. *Tirleases,* though in a different construction from either of these, is very close in meaning to *niða ofercumen.* I should not claim these as instances of variation; but they are close to it.

These lines are followed by a beautiful double sentence-variation enveloping variation of each sentence-element—substantive, adjective, and verb:

Ðær wæs on blode brim weallende,
atol yða geswing eal gemenged,
haton heolfre, heorodreore weol,
deaðfæge deog ...

Brim–yða geswing is an obvious variation; *weallende–gemenged* is another; but since *weol* repeats the sense of the verbal constructions *wæs ... weallende–(wæs) gemenged,* there is verb-variation also. Another variation is *blode–heolfre–heorodreore.* If we adopt Sievers' emendation of *deog* to *deop* (line 850a), the variation is still richer: *deop* varies *brim–yða geswing* and *deaðfæge* varies *blode weallende–gemenged haton heolfre.* I should agree with Sievers that the emendation brings the passage into closer harmony with Old English stylistic practice (see Paul und Braune's *Beiträge zur Geschichte der deutschen Sprache und Literatur,* IX, p. 138); and it makes better sense.

Two passages containing very similar elements offer an interesting contrast:

1) . . . . þær wæs hearpan sweg,
swutol sang scopes. (89b–90a)

2) Þær wæs sang ond sweg samod ætgædere
fore Healfdenes hildewisan,
gomenwudu greted, gid oft wrecen . . . (1063 ff.)

In the first of these there is no variation: the sound of the harp and the song of the scop are concomitant but different things. But in the second passage there is variation: *gid* varies *sang;* and the sense of *gomenwudu greted* is identical with that of *sweg*—which here, as often, has the sense of 'music.' The members of the twofold variation stand in the order ABBA, which is not unusual.

Paetzel's conviction that the members of a substantive variation must stand in the same case forced him to admit certain exceptions, when identity of referent as between two nouns in different constructions is very obvious. In these exceptional cases, the first member of the variation, as he conceives it, stands in the genitive, the second in nominative or accusative. The genitive may be partitive—as in lines 1425–26a: *Gesawon ða æfter wætere wyrmcynnes fela, sellice sædracan,*—dependent upon a colorless expression of quantity such as *fela* or *wiht;* or it may be possessive, as in lines 2107–08a: *hwilum hildedeor hearpan wynne, gomenwudu grette.* Actually, of course, the first member of these variations is not the genitive alone, but the genitive in combination with the word upon which it depends. *Sædracan* is a variation, not of *wyrmcynnes,* but of *wyrmcynnes fela; gomenwudu* varies *hearpan wynne.* The Geats saw not the entire mass of serpent-kind, but many of them; and it was these that are characterized as *sellice sædracan.* In lines 2107–08, the second element of the compound (*-wudu*) corresponds roughly to the sense of the genitive *hearpan;* the first (*gomen-*) expresses the same thought as the base-word *wynne.*

Sometimes problems of interpretation arise to complicate our consideration of possible variations. This is true of line 850a (*deaðfæge deog*), and of lines 1616b–17a:

. . . . wæs þæt blod to þæs hat,
ættren ellorgæst . . .

Klaeber says of this: "Probably *ættren ellorgǣst* is parallel with *blōd* (logical adjunct and headword forming the terms of variation), though *ættren* could be (and usually is) construed as predicate adjective, parallel with *hāt*..." (his edition, p. 189). Grammatically *ellorgæst* is parallel with *blod;* but I very much doubt that the sentence means 'the blood was so hot, the alien demon so venomous.' I think the expression *þæt blod*...*ættren ellorgæst* stands for *þæt ættrenne blod ellorgæstes:* the sword melted because the blood of the ogress was venomous *and* hot. The structure of *blod–ellorgæst* is that characteristic of variation; if those are right who take *ættren* as predicate adjective, we should have a parallelism; but there is no variation of *meaning* here at all.

I have stressed identity of reference (and closeness of meaning) as the essence of variation; but there are passages in which structural dissimilarity must give us pause, even though similarity of meaning be strong enough to tempt us to recognize a variation, for example, lines 1700–02a:

> 'Þæt, la, mæg secgan se þe soð ond riht
> fremeð on folce, feor eal gemon,
> eald eþelweard...'

The two clauses of which *se þe* is the subject express two different things: (1) the furthering of truth and justice among the people, which is a function of any monarch; and (2) the recollection of all things over a long period of time, which is a quality of advanced age. In uttering these words, Hrothgar has himself in mind: he is both a good ruler and an old man. The adjective-substantive combination *eald eþelweard* gathers these two distinct things together: each of its two words is specifically related in sense to one of the two clauses. *Se þe soð ond riht fremeð on folce* is summed up in the compound *eþelweard;* (*se þe*) *feor eal gemon* in the adjective *eald*. Yet to take *eald eþelweard* as a variation of the total sense of the two clauses seems to me unwarranted: if the point were pressed, we should find ourselves obliged to maintain that the adjective is a variation of one clause, and the substantive which it modifies a variation of the other.

◇ ◇ ◇

All content-words lend themselves to variation; and the figure may assume many forms. The simplest form is the variation of substantive simplices: *flotan–nacan* (lines 294b–295b); *madma–frætwa* (36b–37b); *beagas–sinc* (80b–81a); *guman–weras* (215b–216a). In substantive variations one member may be a compound: *lacum–þeodgestreonum* (43b–44a), *byrne–searonet* (405b–406a); or both members may be compounds: *Gar-Dena–þeodcyninga* (1–2); *healreced–medoærn* (68a–69a). Either member may be expanded, and made more specific, by a genitival modifier: *sorge–wonsceaft wera* (119b–120a), *byrnan–guðsearo gumena* (327b–328a). In these two cases the limiting genitive is not necessary to the sense, nor an essential part of the variation; but in such instances as *heresped–wiges weorðmynd* (64b–65a) or *hearpan wynne–gomenwudu* (2107–08) it is essential to both. In the first of these, the limiting element of the compound (*here-*) corresponds in meaning to the limiting genitive *wiges;* the second element (*-sped*) corresponds to the compound *weorðmynd.* The second instance has already been discussed. Such instances as these appear to be constructed with a conscious appreciation of their rhetorical effect. There are many substantive variations in which each member consists of noun plus genitive: *hearpan wyn–gomen gleobeames* (2262b–63a); *sinces brytta–brego Beorht-Dena–folces hyrde* (607–610). In the last instance each of the three members is a *kent heiti;* all have the same structure; each stands in its own clause.

Adjective variation assumes a number of forms. The variation may consist of adjectives alone: *guðwerigne–aldorleasne* (1586a–87a), *blondenfeaxe–gomele* (1594b–95a). Quite often the second member of an adjective variation is double: *heorogifre–grim ond grædig* (1498a–99a); *gæst yrre cwom–eatol, æfengrom* (2073b–74a). This last example is somewhat doubtful: there is a possibility that it is a progression rather than a true variation.

Adjectival and substantival variation may occur in combination: *geomor sefa–murnende mod* (49b–50a), *beorhte frætwe–guðsearo geatolic* (214b–215a). Some noun-adjective combinations show true variation of substantives with accompanying adjectives which mean *different* things; the adjectives should therefore be excluded from the variation: e.g., *side scyldas–rondas regnhearde* (325b–326a); *swin ealgylden–eofor irenheard* (1111b–12a). The poet's need to attribute different qualities to the same object forces a breach of the variation.

In some cases there is a kind of crossing of noun and adjective variation: e.g., *hringnet beran–brogdne beadusercean* (2754b–55a); *hringnet bæron–locene leoðosyrcan* (1889b–90a). The participles *brogdne, locene,* applied to a coat of mail, have substantially the same meaning as is contained in the second element of the compound *hringnet:* a corselet, like a net, is *brogden.* In such cases it is usually the second substantive which is modified by the adjective. We find the same structure, however, in a larger number of instances in which there is no correspondence in sense between the adjective and the first substantive; the ascription of quality to the referent lies in the adjective alone: *eorðan worhte–wlitebeorhtne wang; Heorot eardode–sincfage sel; secg wisade–lagucræftig mon; guðbyrne–hringiren scir; sænæssas–windige weallas.* In all such cases, the first member of the variation is separated from the second by one or more words, very frequently by the verb.

Prepositional phrases which are adjectival in function may appear in similar position, modifying the second or third member of a substantive variation, but themselves forming no part of the variation: *Men ne cunnon ... selerædende, hæleð under heofenum* (50b–52a). A possible example is lines 579b–580a, in which the phrase probably modifies the second member of a substantive variation, but may be taken as modifying the verb: *Ða mec sæ oþbær, flod æfter faroðe.*

Adverbial variation is common, but has received relatively little attention. Variation of adverb by adverb (*unsofte–earfoðlice,* lines 1655a–57a) is much less frequent than variation of adverb by prepositional phrase or by other adverbial; often one adverbial phrase varies another. Examples of adverb-phrase variation are: *ellor–of earde* (55b–56a); *niþer–under foldan* (1360b–61a); *mid–on gemonge* (1642b–43a). Since nouns are often used adverbially in their oblique cases, they frequently form one member of an adverbial variation: *dreamum–eadiglice* (99b–100a); *eft–niowan stefne* (1787a–89a); *tela–willum* (1820b–21a). Such substantival adverbs may form both members of a variation: *middangeardes–eorþan sceata* (751b–752a). Variation of phrase by phrase may be illustrated by *on sale–on ancre* (302a–303a); *wið Grendel–wið þam aglæcan–wið þyrse* (424b–426a); the real variation here is of course substantival, as in *ofer yðe–ofer brimstreamas* (1909b–1910b). In *ðurh anes cræft–selfes mihtum* (699a–700a) an adverbial phrase is varied by a substantive adverbially used. An adverbial phrase may be varied by an adverbial clause: *on morgentid–þonne dæg lixte* (484b–485b).

There are a few striking adverbial variations of a more complex kind: *feor ond neah–ealne wideferhð–efne swa side swa sæ bebugeð, windgeard, weallas* (1221b–24a). The members here are: linked adverbs, adverbial substantive, adverbial clause. In lines 858–860 opposed adverbs connected by *né* are varied by three adverbial phrases: *suð né norð–be sæm tweonum–ofer eormengrund–under swegles begong.*

Verb-variation is common; there is no need of adding much to Paetzel's account of it. Variation of verbs of speaking is fairly frequent, especially in passages of formal stateliness: *sægde se þe cuðe–cwæð* (90b–92a); *Wealhðeo maþelode, heo fore þæm werede spræc* (1215); *andswarode–word æfter spræc* (340b–341b). Other verbs also appear frequently in variation: *stille bad–seomode on sale* (301b–302a; here the adverbials form part of the variation); *æglæca ehtende wæs–seomode ond syrede* (159b–161a). Infinitives not infrequently appear in variation: *sweorde swebban–aldre beneotan* (679–680a); *to ham faran–wica neosan* (124b–125b).

Verb-variation often forms part of clausal variation:

> Hwearf þa hrædlice þær Hroðgar sæt
> . . .
> eode ellenrof, þæt he for eaxlum gestod
> Deniga frean ... (356–359a)

The two clauses, depending on two varying verbs of motion, themselves say precisely the same thing, although in different constructions; the one is an adverbial clause of place, the other is a result clause. *Sinc ealgode–wælreaf werede* is a clausal variation consisting of substantive variation combined with verb-variation; its members stand in parallel structure. Clausal variation without parallelism is found in *Heo wæs on ofste,–wolde ut þanon* (1292), and in *Ferdon forð þonon feþelastum–foldweg mæton* (1632–33b), and in lines 356–359a.

Progression, like enumeration, may bear a superficial resemblance to variation; their structures are similar. In Wulfgar's first speech to the Geats, two verses after his enumeration of their weapons, he compliments them in three terms, each expressing a different aspect of their appearance or quality, the weightiest and most complimentary term last:

> '. . . . . . Ne seah ic elþeodige
> þus manige men modiglicran.' (336b–337)

The disjunctive structure permits a kind of climax: Wulfgar's meaning is: 'I have never seen a braver company of strangers in such numbers'; but translation masks progression and climax alike. These words are immediately followed by other complimentary lines, which close the speech:

> 'Wen' ic þæt ge for wlenco, nalles for wræcsiðum,
> ac for higeþrymmum Hroðgar sohton.'

Here are balance and antithesis, the substantives employed having similar meanings in the first and third verses; the intrusion of the adversative phrases introduced by *nalles–ac* precludes the expression of more closely identical thought. Wulfgar's first thought is positive: 'Ye have come out of pride'; the second is negative, conceding that the motive of the Geats is not an unworthy one; the third again is positive, and stronger than the other two. The sentence, then, constitutes a progression. Wulfgar's words are courteous to the point of courtliness; their extreme formality is marked by the structure: 'Where do ye come from, men thus splendidly equipped? I have never seen so many valiant strangers in one company. Ye must be men of pride; not exiles, but great-hearted men.'

Such adversative constructions as *ac for higeþrymmum* often round out progressions and variations; but by their very adversative nature they do not lend themselves to use as members of variations. Occasionally a statement introduced by *ac* may come close to variation of a preceding proposition, when—as sometimes happens—*ac* loses its adversative force:

> 'no þy leng leofað laðgeteona
> synnum geswenced, ac hyne sar hafað
> in *n*idgripe nearwe befongen,
> balwon bendum . . .' (974–977a)

The true relation of the clause introduced by *ac* to that preceding is almost causal: 'He will live no longer, for he is mortally wounded.' This is not a variation, but it approaches the variation. Occasionally *né* connects two terms which, saying almost the same thing, almost stand in variation: *næs hio hnah swa þeah, ne to gneað gifa* (1929b–30a).

In chapter i we have examined a number of variations of more than two members. These are not uncommon: e.g., *sawlberendra–niþða bearna–grundbuendra* (1004b–06a); *feo–ealdgestreonum–wundini golde* (1380b–82a); and the vocative instance in lines 1474–76a: *'Geþenc nu, se mæra maga Healfdenes,–snottra fengel, ... –goldwine gumena ...'* All three terms salute the referent in terms of his specific qualities—the familiar sequence of partials; each stresses a different quality, yet each is an appellation for the same person. In these multiple variations the individual members are sometimes arranged in climactic order, as in lines 1380–82a. In one such variation each of three substantives is modified by an adjective: all three nouns have the same meaning, as do two of the adjectives; the last adjective is stronger in its connotation than the other two: *stige nearwe–enge anpaðas–uncuð gelad* (1409b–10).

The possible uses of variation are as numerous as its forms, as we have seen in chapter ii. It is, indeed, a notable instrument of style in the hands of a distinguished poet; it became an instrument of dramatic force and of structural form in the hands of the poet of *Beowulf,* and in his alone.